SANCTIONING

RELIGION?

SANCTIONING

RELIGION?

Politics, Law, and
Faith-Based Public Services

edited by
David K. Ryden
Jeffrey Polet

LYNNE
RIENNER
PUBLISHERS

BOULDER
LONDON

Published in the United States of America in 2005 by
Lynne Rienner Publishers, Inc.
1800 30th Street, Boulder, Colorado 80301
www.rienner.com

and in the United Kingdom by
Lynne Rienner Publishers, Inc.
3 Henrietta Street, Covent Garden, London WC2E 8LU

Library of Congress Cataloging-in-Publication Data
Sanctioning religion? : politics, law, and faith-based public services /
David K. Ryden and Jeffrey Polet, editors.
    p. cm.
  Includes bibliographical references and index.
  ISBN 1-58826-319-3 (hardcover : alk. paper) — ISBN 1-58826-343-6 (pbk. :
alk. paper)
  1. Church and state—United States.   2. Church charities—United States.
3. Federal aid to human services—United States.   I. Ryden, David K.   II.
Polet, Jeffrey, 1962–
KF4865.S26 2005
342.7308'52—dc22

                                                              2004029656

British Cataloguing in Publication Data
A Cataloguing in Publication record for this book
is available from the British Library.

Printed and bound in the United States of America

The paper used in this publication meets the requirements
of the American National Standard for Permanence of
Paper for Printed Library Materials Z39.48-1992.

5   4   3   2   1

Contents

SANCTIONING

RELIGION?

1 Introduction: Faith-Based Initiatives in the Limelight

David K. Ryden and Jeffrey Polet

As George W. Bush ran for president during the summer of 2000, the faith-based initiative was one of the signature ideas of his campaign. Candidate Bush frequently and enthusiastically preached the need to end government discrimination against religious organizations that wished to take an active part in publicly funded social service delivery. The faith-based initiative was a centerpiece of Bush's "compassionate conservatism" agenda. As governor of Texas, he had aggressively and successfully championed integrating faith-based groups into public programs. Moreover, his personal biography included a religious conversion that he credited with straightening out his life, and that gave him a decided air of conviction when he spoke of faith-based social service.

■ The Rise of a Faith-Based Political Movement

At first glance, casual observers might wonder about the reason for the faith-based emphasis. There had been a long and substantial history of governmental collaboration with religious nonprofits in social service provision. Indeed, with the expansion of the modern welfare state in the 1940s and through the Great Society programs of the 1960s, the government found itself increasingly looking to religious organizations to assist it in meeting its obligation to care for the poor.

But the involvement of religious groups in government-sponsored programs was of a particular type and came with certain costs. Those groups that partnered with government were willing to tone down, if not actually remove, the religious content of their programs so as not to offend the dictates of the First Amendment establishment clause. Groups such as Catholic Charities and Lutheran Social Services that were active collaborators with government were *religiously affiliated* groups, with ties to the church, but delivered services via

1

separately established corporate entities. Those entities were essentially nonreligious, having nonreligious governing boards, running on carefully segregated financial accounts, and operating in physical environments where the religious trappings and imagery had been removed.

To some, this arrangement amounted in practice to a form of discrimination against certain types of religious nonprofits, and even against religion itself. It left little room for those agencies that were more intensely and overtly religious, and that relied more openly on religious practice and belief in the services themselves. These types of religious agencies tended to be leery of government, fearing that the acceptance of public funds would force them to compromise the very essence of their religious mission and identity. As a result, some saw the vast social service realm as having been abandoned to secular forces, an objectionable situation for conservatives who already were distrustful of the expansive welfare state. Thus developed the effort to facilitate governmental collaboration with a different kind of religious organization, and to ensure that interaction with the government would not come at the expense of the central religious dimension of the organization.

The political impetus for policy change came with the historic congressional elections of 1994. There had been something of a convergence of conservative scholars and academics, politicians and policymakers, and think tank representatives who advocated with increasing forcefulness for greater direct interaction between the government and religious institutions. That intellectual movement translated into tangible policy results shortly after the Republican takeover of Congress in 1994. The election ushered in a conservative congressional majority that was skeptical of existing welfare state arrangements. Just as important was the increased presence of religious conservatives at all levels of government.

The consequence was the passage of *charitable choice* in 1996, as a part of the historic welfare reform legislation. While the welfare bill itself generated controversy, the charitable choice provision attracted little attention. Not until five years later, when Bush was to shine the presidential spotlight on charitable choice ideas, would it become the subject of debate and disagreement.

Charitable choice did several things. First and foremost, it required that, when the federal government looked to the private sector for welfare assistance, federal officials were to level the playing fields by giving religious organizations the same consideration as any secular nonprofit. Second, charitable choice imposed a series of protections for faith-based groups that were successful in obtaining federal funds, so as to preserve their religious character, identity, and mission. This charitable choice further specified that funded religious groups were obligated to respect the religious liberty of their clients, and that secular alternatives must be made available. Finally, the law stipulated that federal funds could not be directed to support inherently religious practices such as worship or proselytization.

The impact of charitable choice on the delivery of welfare services proved to be modest at best. President Bill Clinton had little choice but to sign the Republican-driven welfare bill into law in 1996. But as chief executive officer in the country, he could exert significant control over the implementation of the law. With respect to charitable choice, this basically meant ignoring it. Absent a determined effort on the part of the executive branch to educate and press state governments to implement charitable choice, most public officials remained in the dark about the requirements of charitable choice, or if they knew about it, had a seriously misguided understanding of it. Studies revealed that only a handful of states made any serious effort to pursue charitable choice. In sum, implementation at the state level was sporadic at best and nonexistent at worst.

■ The Rise and Demise of the Bush Faith-Based Legislative Agenda

When George W. Bush moved into the Oval Office in January 2001, he proved good on his word. One of his early formal acts as president was to establish the White House Office of Faith-Based and Community Initiatives, along with satellite faith-based centers in five federal agencies (Justice, Education, Health and Human Services, Housing and Urban Development, and Labor). Later that spring, faith-based legislation was introduced in the 107th Congress. Originating in the House of Representatives, the central thrust of the faith-based proposal was to expand charitable choice protections for faith-intensive groups seeking public funding. The bill also included a number of other provisions, including tax incentives to encourage charitable giving to religious nonprofits.

Objective observers would have given faith-based legislation a strong chance of passage, in light of the bipartisanship of the 2000 campaign and the previous success in passing charitable choice. Instead, two years later, a highly public and bruising policy debate had left the president's legislative faith-based proposal in shambles.

Were the demise of the Bush legislative efforts the final chapter of the faith-based story, this book might well have not been worth writing. In fact, it was only the beginning. The most important developments with respect to the long-term viability and impact of faith-based policy occurred only after the legislation failed. In December 2002, President Bush announced a new faith-based executive order. The order marked a clear departure in the president's strategy. Unwilling to wait on Congress, the administration simply moved forward on its own to implement faith-friendly contracting rules. In short, the president determined he would do by administrative fiat what he was unable to accomplish legislatively.

The executive order did a number of things. It added faith-based satellites to two additional federal agencies—the Department of Agriculture and the U.S. Agency for International Development—bringing the total number of faith-based centers within federal agencies to seven (it has since been expanded to ten). The order eliminated a number of barriers that had prevented faith-based organizations from partnering with the government, in an effort to create a more favorable environment and set of rules for faith-based groups to pursue government contracts. It directed the satellite offices to thoroughly examine the regulations of their respective departments for existing rules that might serve as obstacles to faith-based contracting. It also earmarked funds for religious applicants, bolstered hiring rights, and instituted greater protections for the religious autonomy and identity of religious recipients of grants. In short, the executive order essentially implemented charitable choice principles through administrative regulation rather than legislation.

The pair of December 2002 executive orders were only the beginning. Since then, the White House has kept up a full court press in its administrative effort to transform the relationship between the federal bureaucracy and the faith-based community. Moreover, it appears that the administration's regulatory strategy is succeeding in ways that charitable choice did not. A report from the White House Office of Faith-Based and Community Initiatives revealed that over $1.1 billion in federal funds in fiscal year 2003 had been paid out to religious nonprofits by the five original departmental agencies with faith-based centers (Cooperman 2004). This figure included substantial increases both in the numbers of faith-based programs funded by the federal government and in the total dollar amounts going to faith-based social service providers. The report also indicated that there were hundreds of first-time grantees. In sum, tangible evidence indicates that the administrative strategy has realized success in advancing the cause of faith-based initiatives. As a result, faith-based partnerships have acquired a significant momentum of their own.

■ Gauging the Long-Term Significance of the Faith-Based Initiative

It appears that the faith-based phenomenon will be with us for the long term. The failure of the Bush legislative initiative has not meant a return to the pre-2000 situation. It is no exaggeration to suggest that the Bush faith-based plan, even in the face of outright failure on the legislative front, nevertheless has succeeded quite dramatically in altering the nature and reality of the relationship between faith-identified service providers and government at the national, state, and local levels. There is now a striking level of activity involving faith-based initiatives, as publicly funded faith-based programs are being explored and advanced on a scale not seen before.

Moreover, the Bush administration arguably has done more than just achieve its original legislative goals through regulatory and executive order. The bigger, longer-term battle is with an ingrained grant-making bureaucratic culture that many see as being antireligion. Concerted efforts by the current administration indeed may have begun to reshape how bureaucratic cultures perceive faith-based organizations as potential partners. These effects enhance the likelihood that, even without supporting legislation, faith-based partnerships will continue beyond the present Bush administration. If a central aim of the Bush plan was to increase the presence of religious groups in the delivery of government social services, the initiative must be judged a legitimate success. As such, faith-based developments bear close watching.

■ The Growing Legal Battle

Most significant for our purposes is a final marker of the faith-based initiative's dramatic forward movement—the marked rise in litigation and judicial activity involving faith-based programs. Faith-based governmental social programs have raised fresh constitutional questions, the answers to which are not necessarily clear. Unsurprisingly, the battle over faith-based initiatives is now moving into the judicial realm, where state-subsidized religious social service programs face a variety of legal and constitutional challenges in lower courts across the country.

It is in the courtrooms where the long-term viability of faith-based partnerships may well ultimately be determined. A flurry of litigation has followed the public attention given the Bush faith-based agenda. A legal landscape that previously was free of lawsuits pre-2000 is now speckled with potentially significant cases and developments. On one hand, advocacy groups and faith-based opponents have turned aggressively to litigation in an effort to stem the tide of greater church-state interaction. On the flip side, religious providers and conservative public interest law firms are litigating issues pertaining to organizational rights the faith-based organizations hope to retain as government contractees. Some of these cases have yielded decisions at the trial level and are now proceeding up the appellate ladder. Others are in the earliest stages of litigation. These lawsuits can be expected to yield precedents that more clearly define both the lines of acceptable religious establishment and the extent of religious exercise rights.

From these legal developments, it is clear that significant dimensions of the underlying church-state dilemma remain unresolved. We now have a dynamic that almost surely guarantees that the legal debate over faith-based initiatives will continue within the context of litigation. Strong political pressure from the White House to promote faith-based action is matched by vigilant faith-based opponents who are challenging and scrutinizing new programs with equal fervor. Consequently, current and future litigation will be instrumental in delineating the constitutional parameters for faith-based programs to come. It is not hyperbole to say that faith-based initiatives could be the most consequential policy idea shaping church-state jurisprudence for years, perhaps even decades, to come. This book is committed to better understanding and enriching that debate.

■ Faith-Based Social Services and the Constitution: Melding Principle and Practice

The idea for this book grew out of the public debate over the Bush faith-based plan, and out of our dissatisfaction with the discussion of the constitutional questions raised. As interested observers, we found the high-pitched public exchanges to be dominated by simplistic, overblown rhetoric that utterly failed to capture or reflect the subtleties and complexities at issue. The most striking aspect of the public debate was just how remote it was from the actual constitutional merits; waged on far too abstract a level, speculation and conjecture quickly predominated over the realities of actual programs.

This book is meant to serve as a corrective. It is premised on the idea that dialectic exists between constitutional theory and practice, a tension that is especially evident in the faith-based policy area. On one hand, faith-based initiatives implicate deep and significant philosophical questions, questions that revolve around the interplay between religion, public policy, and politics, and the constitutional accommodation of that interplay. At the same time, the constitutional rules of church and state play out in very practical ways. In the case of faith-based practice, the devil is very much in the details. Hence the need to focus on tangible examples of faith-based partnerships. The case studies embed the key legal questions in the context of real programs rather than abstractions. Our aim in this book is to place the constitutional issues in the proper theoretical and historical backdrop, then to engage in constitutional analysis grounded in meaningful factual contexts.

The structure of the book reflects this dual emphasis on principle *and* pragmatism, on theory *and* practice. Chapter 2 offers a historical overview of the relationship between religion and politics that is the theoretical framework for the faith-based constitutional analysis. It suggests that the overarching environment within which faith-based policy plays out is a product of four historical developments: the relationship between institutionalized religion and state power; changes in jurisprudence regarding the religion clauses of the Constitution; the culture wars of the twentieth century; and the rise and fall of the modern welfare state. A grasp of these forces is key to understanding the controversies surrounding faith-based programs.

We then move from the big picture to the operation of faith-based policy on the ground, with eight case studies of actual faith-based programs. One important goal of the case studies is to expose the reader to the diversity of the faith-based movement, which also complicates the constitutional questions. Hence the featured cases involve a range of social services, from welfare assistance to prison rehabilitation and general antipoverty programs. They include programs from California to New Jersey and Pennsylvania, from Texas to Michigan, and examine faith-based programs from a statewide level down to congregationally based services. In short, the case studies taken as a whole bring considerable depth and breadth to the discussion.

The authors of the studies come from a variety of disciplinary backgrounds. They share no common predisposition toward faith-based programs, but bring a range of perspectives, some very enthusiastic, others deeply skeptical. The editors themselves differ in their ultimate assessments of faith-based partnerships, their wisdom as policy, and their constitutional soundness. The goal in presenting these case studies, then, is to give the reader a taste of the multiple strands to the faith-based debate, as well as the differing views, perceptions, and opinions on the constitutional status of such programs.

The case studies are divided into three categories. Part One (Chapters 3–5) examines programs that provide special insight in relating faith-based programs to the establishment clause constraints of the First Amendment. Part Two (Chapters 6–7) looks at the other side of the constitutional coin, the impact of public funding on the rights and prerogatives of recipient faith-based organizations. It raises two especially important and controversial issues. One is whether faith-based groups that take public money retain the right to make personnel decisions based on the religion of the employee. The second is whether contracted faith-based groups can be forced to comply with state law that is contrary to their creedal or theological beliefs. The focus of Part Three (Chapters 8–10) is the constitutional challenge in balancing the competing pulls of theoretical and pragmatic forces.

A series of key questions repeatedly surface in the case studies. These common threads and themes run throughout the book:

1. What are the main constitutional themes, lessons, and observations raised by the particular program, and how does it fit within the established law?
2. What are the main issues pertaining to public sector–religious sector interaction, and what does the particular case study reveal about government endorsement of religion (on the establishment side) or governmental interference or burdening of the religious nonprofit (on the free exercise and associational rights side)?

3. What does the case say about First Amendment jurisprudence, applied in the social service context? What is good or bad about it? How can it be improved?
4. How is the constitutional approach to faith-based service delivery a product of principled versus pragmatic considerations? How does the operation of real programs help us understand the relationship between theory and practice, principle and pragmatism?

We attempt to meld the theoretical, historical, and practical considerations into a reasoned and coherent jurisprudential approach. We summarize as accurately as possible the current state of the applicable church-state law, while identifying key open questions that remain. These are the areas upon which the future of faith-based programs may rise or fall, most notably litigation involving the validity of antireligion state constitutional clauses, and the legal proceedings involving hiring and other key rights of publicly funded religious groups. Finally, we suggest ways in which the future of church-state jurisprudence can be enriched and enhanced to better reflect the unique challenges of religion in the public realm. The controversy over funding of faith-based social services offers a window into the ambivalence among Americans regarding the public dimensions of religion. A highly religious people are nevertheless wary of the corruption or co-optation of that religion by the heavy-handedness of the state. That ambivalence is mirrored in church-state constitutional doctrine, which often is premised on a rather thin vision of things religious.

We do not expect to definitively resolve church-state conundrums that have baffled others for decades. But our reflections, informed by the case studies that precede them, can hopefully enlighten and inform this pressing area of the law. Surely the United States will continue to struggle to navigate and negotiate the relationship between religion, politics, and culture, and in that struggle we seek a little more light.

2 Religion, the Constitution, and Charitable Choice

JEFFREY POLET AND DAVID K. RYDEN

In the wake of the terrorist attacks of September 11, 2001, Americans have become even more sensitized to the dangers and difficulties that pertain to the relationship between religious belief and public action. The attacks remain a stunning display of the power of religion to foment social unrest and violence. Likewise, in response to those attacks, President Bush has defended the use of U.S. military power largely through religious language. In his 2003 State of the Union address, Bush evoked an old evangelical hymn in referring to the "power, wonder-working power" of the idealism of the American people, an idealism consonant with the ways of divine providence and a belief in American liberty as "God's gift to humanity." Such rhetoric exacerbates concern about a potential "clash of civilizations" in pitting a religiously enervated but technologically superior West against the highly religious but unmodernized Islamic world.

Even as this drama plays out on the world stage, Americans continue to struggle internally with the proper place of religion in public life. The struggle pits not only religions against one another, but also denominations and sects, as well as those of religious belief against those who profess none. It involves fundamental questions: What is the relationship between private beliefs and public actions? Can a society sustain itself without religious foundations? What is the nature of coercion, and what, if anything, makes it undesirable? Is secularism a faith? What is the public utility of religion? What, exactly, is religion? How do our various commitments relate to one another? In the midst of these larger questions stand a series of more detailed but equally significant questions: What is the proper understanding of the religion clauses of the Constitution? What is the legal status of religiously based organizations? How can desirable social services be most effectively and efficiently delivered to needy citizens?

The debate over the charitable choice provisions of the 1996 welfare reform bill as well as the subsequent development of President Bush's faith-based

9

initiative, we contend, have shed some light on these questions. While the case studies that follow seek to address some of those more detailed questions, we provide here a general framework for understanding charitable choice. The move toward charitable choice programs is best understood as the result of four major developments: the long-standing debates concerning the relationship between the spiritual and the political; changes in jurisprudence regarding the religion clauses of the Constitution; the culture wars of the twentieth century; and the rise and fall of the welfare state.

■ The Relationship Between Institutionalized Religion and State Power

In the West, Christianity has consistently held the proper exercise of religious liberty to be essential to human happiness and public order, and a necessary limit to the power of the state. Though theoretically distinct, these two realms are conflated in reality, potentially generating tremendous social discord. Most significant, the wars of religion that dominated Europe in the sixteenth and seventeenth centuries had the net effect of creating widespread suspicion about whether sectarian religion could operate effectively as a foundation for public order. The most important theorists of this period sought ways to maintain public order that would not evoke the sorts of dissent and passions peculiar to religion, particularly if an organized sect could seize the power of the sword for its own purposes. Though the United States never experienced the widespread religion-based violence of Europe, the European experience impressed itself deeply on the American psyche.

Religion during the founding period had two main characteristics: sectarian diversity within religious unity, and the permeation of religion throughout the public order. [1] Whatever else may be true of religion in the United States, disputes took place largely within the context of Protestant Christianity. When reflecting on these early days, we tend to focus on the disputes and differences to the exclusion of the larger picture. This larger reality was that many Americans were religious, most were Christian, most agreed on basic tenets of the Christian faith, and most were inclined to favor the extension of that faith into the public square. Even if Christianity was not always believed, it was always deferred to, certainly in public declarations. While there were variations in colonial settlements, Americans shared a sense of providential mission, and believed in the divinely ordained nature of the American experiment. The basic impulse of early American religion and settlement was the formation of a Protestant empire, with Puritanism being the operative social and personal ethic.

Two themes that pervaded early church-state relations were religious toleration and a wariness of state power. If they merely had been wary of state power, the colonists could have simply subordinated the state to the church. But since they were religiously diverse, the two powers needed to be separated so one sect could not capture the power of the sword. The protection of religion from the state and one sect from competing sects derived from the widespread belief that the Bible, when properly read, established the "constitution" of both the church and the state. Thus the broad structure of the American order originated not only as a reaction to, but also as an establishment of, the effects of the Protestant Reformation.

During the mid–eighteenth century the Great Awakening introduced both an intensifying degree of denominational competition and mutual accommodation. Stabilizing highly energized religious impulses with their extension into the political sphere became one of the imperatives for religious and civic leaders. The stabilization attempts, however, were constantly thwarted by the sheer diversity of belief, the requirements of survival, and the highly decentralized nature of demographic dispersion on the continent, which fragmented power. Conflict could be avoided by simply moving farther west. The "wilderness" provided Americans with both a cultural mandate and a means to avoid conflict driven by congestion.

These institutional disruptions and church separations paved the way for the political crises of the 1760s and 1770s. In response to the factionalism within the church and the resultant need to justify separationism, a new emphasis emerged that stressed the rights of minorities and individual conscience, while simultaneously developing the nascent national identity. It was preachers more than anyone else who were responsible for leading people through revolution to nationhood. In sum, while religion in America in the seventeenth century was a period of *transplantation,* the eighteenth century was one of *stabilization.*

In time, the rationales for the separation of church and state began to diverge. A comparison of the key metaphor "the wall of separation" as used respectively by Roger Williams and Thomas Jefferson illustrates this shift. Williams founded a new colony committed to freedom of religious expression after his experience with the established church of the Massachusetts Bay Colony. Williams argued that government held no power over the first tablet of the Ten Commandments (dealing with a person's relation to God and form of worship). He felt that government infringement on religious conscience would destroy the citadel of the heart and irrevocably damage true religion and invented the "wall" metaphor to protect the church from the world.

Thinkers more attuned to the Enlightenment, meanwhile, tried to solve religious conflicts by appealing to a core of universally accepted doctrines that emanated from a primordial divine reason, often understood in terms of "Nature" or "Nature's God." This gradual displacement of revelation with reason resulted in the triumph of secular purposes for the guidance of the public realm: the preservation of life, liberty, and property in the interest of ensuring domestic tranquillity. For many liberal thinkers, the secular was legitimate in its own right, while religious ends were reduced to the private sphere of conscience.

There is still widespread disagreement over the role of religion at the Constitutional Convention. John Witte has asserted that the religion clauses of the Constitution are best seen as a compromise struck by four competing groups who found a minimal area of consensus concerning what the Constitution could say about religion. These groups—congregational Puritans, Free Church Evangelicals, Civic Republicans, and Enlightenment thinkers— agreed simply that government should neither proscribe nor prescribe religion. Their primary concern was to protect the liberty of conscience, and restricting the ability of the Federal Congress to make laws respecting an establishment of religion was a means to that end (subordinating the first religion clause to the second).

The alliance between these forces found its most judicious exposition in James Madison. In arguing for the ratification of the Constitution, Madison supported the proposed institutional scheme on the grounds that a representative government tends to moderate the destructive forces of unrestrained liberty. In view of past experiences with human nature, according to Madison, such an arrangement was absolutely necessary to avoid the pitfalls of those regimes that failed to take into account humanity's inherent weaknesses. Isolating the negative effects of human nature meant extending the sphere of government, using factionalism to counter itself. Madison felt that the religious diversity of the people was a far greater guarantee of religious freedom than any institutional arrangement.

The period after the Revolution and Constitutional Convention was marked by an expansion of the power of the church and a weakening of the power of the state. The populist impulses of early-nineteenth-century Christianity mixed religious fervor with a commitment to popular sovereignty, both of which were encouraged by the absence of a dominant religion or a powerful state. These religious expressions were often antinomian, antitraditional, anticlerical (in terms of having a professional and trained clergy), expansive, enthusiastic, resistant to doctrine or restrictions of orthodoxy, disestablishmentarian, anti-intellectual, and profoundly egalitarian. This period of the second Great Awakening lent itself to Jacksonian democracy on the one hand, and scrubbed American society clean of many non-Christian influences on the other.

This combination impressed young Alexis de Tocqueville on his journey through America. Religion, he observed, was the first of all political institutions in America, for while it did not govern directly, the main religious currents in America fit well with the democratic and republican impulses of American politics. Politics and religion in America, de Tocqueville saw, worked harmoniously with one another. The sustenance of American democracy was American religion, and that religion was Christianity. "In the United States there are an infinite variety of ceaselessly changing Christian sects. But Christianity itself is an established and irresistible fact which no one seeks to attack or to defend." In de Tocqueville's estimation, liberal democracy was parasitic on Christianity, while Christianity most fully extended itself into the public sphere in the guise of political liberalism. The problem Americans faced was that their religion and their politics both flowed into the same body of water, one that contained too many dangers for human beings to swim in safely—that was a fixation with equality. De Tocqueville believed that religion was the only reliable check on the extreme dangers of an excessive fixation with equality, but also that American religion was proving unreliable. "In a democracy therefore it is ever the duty of lawgivers and of all educated men to raise up the souls of their fellow citizens and turn their attention toward heaven" (de Tocqueville 1969, 543).

Thus, even though there was a presumption that America was a Protestant nation, there were few theoretical attempts to determine government's role in promoting a Protestant ethos. No compelling reason existed for such reflection, particularly with regard to the actions of the *federal* government. As American society became increasingly pluralistic, the uneasy alliance between Protestant and rationalist thought began to disintegrate. Indeed, Philip Hamburger has argued that the language of "separation" was smuggled into constitutional adjudication as a result of anti-Catholic prejudices that strengthened in the nineteenth and twentieth centuries (2002, 182). On the subject of the separation of church and state, the dominant point of reference was the Catholic Church. Anti-Catholicism may not have been the only consideration, but "for many influential people it was a major concern, one that could elicit their strongest loyalties" (Marsden 1990, 381).

■ The Evolution of Establishment Clause Jurisprudence

Much of the controversy over the establishment clause has centered on education. Essential to any religion is its promulgation, especially among children. The schools provide an intersection for moral, civic, rational, and social development. They stand at the crossroads between family and the state, and represent, more than any other venue, arguments about the future of the nation. In no arena are the consequences of inclusion or exclusion more keenly felt. The ingredients in the brewing church-state controversy were a dominant American Protestantism, an assertive Catholic community, and an emerging system of public education. As the growth of the modern state was spurred by its control of the educational apparatus, its monopoly on education raised important issues of coercion and control.

The Backdrop: Public Education

States and municipalities did not use tax funds to support public education until the 1830s. Previously, the family or church had overseen education. In 1837, Horace Mann founded the first state board of education in New York in the belief that widespread education was a necessary condition for responsible citizenship in a democratic society. Mann sought to place education on a foundation that was both biblical and moral, but void of sectarian dissent.

While public education sought to be nonsectarian, most schools taught some variety of Protestantism, used the King James Bible in the classroom, began and ended each day with prayer, and required a daily profession of faith. This system met with no resistance from a variety of Protestant sects, but troubled the growing Catholic community. In response, Catholic churches began to form their own schools and to seek public funding for their ventures. Especially after the Civil War, the Catholics waged a wide-scale effort to tap the public purse. Although it received no funding for schools, the Catholic Church did manage to get exemptions and funding for its charitable institutions. As Protestant fears grew, Catholic attempts to garner government backing increased, and Congress and state legislatures moved to block the use of public funds by any sectarian organization. The move in Congress was instigated by James G. Blaine, minority leader of the House, who proposed the following amendment to the Constitution:

> No state shall make any law respecting an establishment of religion or prohibiting the free exercise thereof; and no money raised by taxation in any state for the support of public schools, or derived from any public fund therefore, nor any public lands devoted thereto, shall ever be under the control of any religious sect, nor shall any money so raised or lands so devoted be divided between religious sects or denominations. (Morgan 1972, 51)

The amendment breezed through the House with only seven votes against, but could not muster the necessary two-thirds in the Senate. The failure of the Blaine amendment in Congress, however, prompted many states to adopt similar measures. Blaine's anti-Catholicism is well established, and his pillory of the Democrats as the party of "Rum, Romanism, and Rebellion" may have cost him the 1884 presidential election. Nonetheless, Blaine amendments remain an important factor in church-state adjudication.

Although the early twentieth century remained relatively calm on the school issue, the advent of World War II inflamed it. After fighting and dying for their country, Catholics no longer felt like the perennial outsiders in American cultural life. They saw themselves as part of the mainstream, and consequently felt they should enjoy the benefits of American culture and exercise political influence. This newfound Catholic self-confidence made the Protestant "establishment" nervous. A general perception of a "Catholic threat" developed—the United States now had diplomats at the Vatican, Catholics were at the forefront of the anticommunist movement, and within fifteen years one would be elected President. Catholics thus renewed their efforts to gain funding for parochial schools, while people entrenched in power reacted accordingly. This anti-Catholicism found its way onto the Supreme Court as well. Justice Hugo Black's dissent in *Board of Education v. Allen* (1968) pejoratively referred to those of strong religious conviction as imposing their "prejudices and preferences" through a process of "propaganda," the result of which would be "the complete domination and supremacy of their particular brand of religion."

The Courts and the Evolving Establishment Clause

The combination of Catholic growth, Protestant fears, incorporation, and general confusion over establishment clause brought the issue to a head. Catholics had successfully solicited public support for their schools in the area of transportation. The states that agreed to provide transportation for parochial schools, such as New York, did so on the premise that these schools provided a useful public service and should enjoy some public benefits. The New York statute provided state reimbursement for the transportation costs of the parochial student if the school was "remote" or such transportation would be in the student's best interest.

The state of New Jersey had a similar reimbursement system. In November 1946 that program ended in front of the Supreme Court after a taxpayer challenged it as an unconstitutional establishment. *Everson v. Board of Education* (1947) became the first landmark case adjudicating the question of public financing and support of religion.

The Court acknowledged difficulty in drawing a clear line between funds used for the general welfare and those that might aid a religious institution. The establishment clause, Black claimed, meant several things. First, government may not set up a church, nor may any state or the federal government pass laws aiding any or all religions, or preferring one over another. No tax can be levied to support any institution that teaches or practices religion. Finally, the government may not interfere or participate in the activities of religious groups or organizations, *and* vice versa.

Everson may be said to exacerbate the confusion. While the logic of Black's decision would lead to overturning the law, he upheld the statute in question. The Court allowed the law to stand, in part, because it aided the family and not the institution. Justice Robert Jackson, in dissenting, argued that the character of the school and not the needs of the children formed the basis for reimbursement. The statute thus constituted government aid to a religious institution. Jackson interpreted the establishment clause to say that schools as well as government must possess a "strict and lofty neutrality" with regard to religion. "The assumption," Jackson declared, "is that after the individual has been instructed in worldly wisdom he will be better fitted to choose his religion," turning religion into another consumer product related to personal preference. Rutledge's dissent went even further. He asserted that, by definition, religious teaching cannot possibly serve any public purpose since it is inherently a private matter. Any attempt to use a religious justification or motivation for public policy is illegitimate.

Neutrality as a test proved difficult to enforce. The decision in *Abington School District v. Schempp* (1970) reiterated the neutrality test, adding the caveats that legislation must serve a secular purpose and that the primary effect of such legislation must neither promote nor inhibit religion. But William Brennan's concurrence suggested that the doctrine of neutrality already was losing its appeal:

> The fact is that the line which separates the secular from the sectarian in American life is elusive. The difficulty in defining the boundary with precision inheres in a paradox central to our scheme of liberty. While our institutions reflect a firm conviction that we are a religious people, those institutions by solemn constitutional injunction may not officially invoke religion in such a way as to prefer, discriminate against, or oppress, a particular sect or religion.

Brennan placed his finger on the ambiguity underlying discussions of religion and public order. In trying to weave its way through the poles of this paradox, the Court has first seized one horn, then another, sometimes within the same decision.

The Court moved further from the neutrality test in *Walz v. Tax Commission* (1970), in which it ruled that government must demonstrate a "benevolent neutrality" with regard to religion. It held that any institutions that foster mental or moral improvement (ignoring the question of how one might judge such improvement) and that generally help the community should not be taxed. *Walz* added to the emerging establishment test the prohibition against excessive entanglement between government and religion. The Court determined that the amount of supervision necessary in the taxation process would get government too involved in the internal affairs of the church. The neutrality test had pretty much disappeared in *Walz* but would reappear transformed in *Lemon v. Kurtzman* (1971).

The *Lemon* case concerned a Rhode Island statute that gave a 15 percent salary supplement to teachers of secular subjects in nonpublic schools and a Pennsylvania statute that authorized public schools to purchase certain "secular educational services" from nonpublic schools. After acknowledging its own sometimes confused struggles with establishment cases, the Court offered its three-prong test for determining whether a law or program was an unacceptable establishment of religion. To pass constitutional muster, the statute had to serve a secular legislative purpose, had to have a primary effect that neither advanced nor inhibited religion, and could not foster an excessive entanglement between government and religion.

The Court had previously held in *Zorach v. Clauson* (1952) that there could be no absolute separation between church and state. In the *Lemon* case, the Court conceded that there had to be some allowable contact between church and state, but limited itself in determining permissible contact. In the process, the justices jettisoned the "wall" metaphor that had guided church-state relations in the United States for so long. "Judicial caveats against entanglement must recognize that the line of separation, far from being a 'wall,' is a blurred, indistinct, and variable barrier depending on all the circumstances of a particular relationship." In short, the Court declared that it would no longer adhere to a doctrinaire standard for providing guidance in establishment clause cases; rather, the circumstances of each case would be viewed on their own merits, with the Court deciding, apparently from intuition or instinct, if the relationship had gone too far.

While it was clear that all cases would now be tried on the excessive entanglement prong of the test, it turned out that this prong was hardly a test at all. As a result, the Court began to produce anomalous results. In *Tilton v. Richardson* (1971), a law providing secular aid to private colleges was upheld, even though it was virtually the same law struck down in *Lemon*. In *Grand Rapids School District v. Ball* and *Aguilar v. Fenton* (both 1985 decisions), the Court struck down secular remedial learning programs held in private schools even though they provided significant service to the general populace and necessitated little entanglement. Meanwhile, in *Mueller v. Allen* (1983), the Court upheld, on the basis of nonpreferentialist logic, a Minnesota tuition tax-credit program whose effect was almost exclusively to the benefit of sectarian interests.

The state of the law simply had become confused. Justice Sandra Day O'Connor, in her dissent in *Aguilar*, called the Court's decision "tragic," depriving needy students of a meaningful chance in life for "the untenable theory that public schoolteachers . . . are likely to start teaching religion merely because they have crossed the threshold of a parochial school." O'Connor declared the entanglement prong of dubious utility and suggested the Court scrap it altogether.

By the late 1970s, the strict separation of government aid and religious education began to yield to a more permissive, accommodationist view. The Court, in a string of cases, allowed aid in various forms to flow to parochial schools. More significant for charitable choice, the 1988 decision in *Bowen v. Kendrick* allowed government dollars to reach social service agencies, as the Court affirmed a federal statute that included religious service providers as grantees of a program aimed at teen pregnancy.

With this accommodationist turn, the doctrines historically relied upon to preclude public aid to religious schools were likewise diluted. The much-maligned *Lemon* test, while formally retained by the Court, was weakened as a bar to the funding of religious institutions. While the Court still mouthed the language of pervasive sectarianism in excluding religious organizations from public monies, the ground behind the principle was eroding. In *Agostini v. Felton* (1997), the Court closed the door on the era of strict separation, upholding a program that allowed public employees to provide remedial education on site at sectarian schools. In so doing, it abandoned the presumption that public school employees would necessarily be pressured by the pervasively sectarian surroundings of the parochial school into advancing religious ends.

As the principle of strict separation was receding, an alternative constitutional paradigm of neutrality was gaining currency. The cases allowing aid to parochial schools surfaced in a related block of cases that dealt with access to school space and resources for religious organizations.[2] In each of those cases, the Court extended to religious groups the same access to meeting space or institutional resources as enjoyed by nonreligious groups. For the Supreme Court, neutrality of access to government resources increasingly trumped objections that the receipt of funds or use of resources for religious ends violated the establishment clause.

Pervasive Sectarianism and the Introduction of Charitable Choice

The law of church-state separation was still sufficiently ambiguous and hazy, however, to allow dramatically different readings of what it required. That ambiguity explains the dynamic behind the introduction of the charitable choice law in the mid-1990s. The important *Bowen* decision of 1989 embodied those ambiguities. On one hand, the Court permitted the inclusion of religious social service providers in a federally funded statute. The Court upheld the Adolescent Family Life Act, in which Congress explicitly included religious organizations as potential partners in assisting government in addressing the problems of teen pregnancy among unwed mothers. The Court gave further credence to the concept of neutrality; inclusion of religious groups in the program was not mandated. Rather, they were only among the list of private organizations that might qualify for grants. Hence the statute was deemed neutral, on its face, toward religion.

At the same time, the Court continued to adhere to the language of *pervasive sectarianism*. The Rehnquist majority opinion drew the line of permissible funding at those religious organizations that were pervasively sectarian, that is, those organizations so infused with religion that their secular activities could not be separated from their religious ones. Public subsidies were acceptable as long as they applied only to the secular activities of grantee institutions. For pervasively sectarian organizations, the secular activities, by definition, could not be funded without also funding the inseparable religious aspects. To this extent, *Bowen* reinforced the existence of barriers to government aid to explicitly religious social service providers.

Bowen failed to clarify the question of the constitutionality of aid to religious social service providers. On one level, it indicated an accommodationist approach to church-state partnerships, demonstrating the Court's general openness to the inclusion of religious providers in governmental efforts to remedy social problems. The Court allowed grants to go to religious organizations for programs that could easily blur the lines between the religious, moral, and secular sides of the issues of teen pregnancy and sexual activity. But on a more explicit level, *Bowen* continued to limit public aid to overtly religious nonprofits. The pervasive sectarianism limit spelled continued trouble for religiously infused organizations, for which the religious and the secular were inextricably intertwined.

Charitable choice was an attempt to resolve this dichotomy. Religious conservatives found the pervasive sectarian standard unacceptable. Its secularizing pressure on religious agencies that took public funds effectively amounted to a bias against religious service providers and against religion itself, it was argued. The conservatives saw expressively religious nonprofits being driven from participation in public programs. The consequence was to cede the vast social service universe to governmental and secular providers, against which they harbored great skepticism.

The advent of a conservative Republican congressional majority in 1994 and the increased organization and activity of religious conservatives on all levels provided the impetus to address the perceived mistreatment of religious social service providers. With the inclusion of charitable choice in the hotly debated welfare bill of 1996, the conservatives sought to solidify partnerships between the religious sector and government. Charitable choice was an attempt to put pervasive sectarianism to rest as a limit to government funding of religious organizations. It specified that religious groups were to have equal opportunity to vie for government welfare funds, and that they were to retain their religious identity and practices even if funded.

As the 2000 election drew near, this was the outline of the constitutional debate over the coming faith-based initiative. At the heart of it was the question of whether the limitation against aid to pervasively sectarian organizations was still viable. Despite the wishes of its drafters, the 1996 charitable choice bill and its progeny had failed to resolve this question. The bill did, however, continue to weaken *Bowen*'s pervasive sectarianism prohibition. The inconsistencies between charitable choice and the pervasive sectarian limitations of *Bowen* led to a political and legal tug of war over which of these more accurately captured current Supreme Court church-state doctrine. That tug of war had surfaced at the time of the passage of the original charitable choice statute. John Ashcroft, its main sponsor in the Senate, argued that pervasively sectarian groups were now fully eligible on equal terms with wholly secular ones (Ashcroft and Carlson-Thies 1996). In contrast, President Bill Clinton, in signing the original welfare bill into law, interpreted charitable choice as subject to, and to be implemented consistent with, the pervasive sectarian standard.[3]

Among the activities charitable choice explicitly sought to protect were recipient religious groups' freedom to make hiring decisions based on faith requirements and to openly display religious art and imagery. These very same practices previously had been identified by the Court as indicative of a pervasive sectarianism that would *disqualify* an organization from public funding. Proximity to a sponsoring church, the presence of religious art, denominational control, hiring based upon religious criteria, the presence of religious services and activities—all were mentioned in *Bowen* as possible signs of pervasive sectarianism.

In the end, neither the spirit nor the letter of charitable choice—and its protection of the rights of religious nonprofits to fully practice or express their religious beliefs—could be squared with the pervasive sectarianism standard. Charitable choice implied that the secular and religious elements of intensely religious groups not only could not, but also should not, be separated. Indeed, it may be argued that the very attention to the spiritual, as bound up with other aspects of well-being, was essential in the ability of faith-based nonprofits to achieve results. An undercurrent of charitable choice was the tacit faith in the transformative power of religion, and an acknowledgment that religious values might well be shared at some point with a program beneficiary. According to this criticism, charitable choice did more than codify existing First Amendment case law; it permitted funding to go to groups that would be labeled pervasively sectarian under *Bowen*. In so doing, it "pushe[d] the envelope of existing judicial interpretations of the establishment clause" (Ackerman 2000, 34).

Mitchell v. Helms: *Pervasive Sectarianism on Its Death Bed*

The constitutional sands of church-state jurisprudence continued to shift, even in the midst of the 2000 presidential election campaign. Faith-based proponents received an additional boost with *Mitchell v. Helms,* rendered the summer of 2000. In *Mitchell,* the Court upheld federal funding of local educational agencies for library, media, and computer materials, including both public and private religious schools. *Mitchell* was the latest in a string of cases allowing public funds to go to religious schools and presented the strongest evidence yet of the withering of strict aid separation and the rise of formal neutrality. The plurality opinion characterized the pervasive sectarianism standard as "born of bigotry" and called for its abandonment. *Mitchell* showed that at least four members of the Court would be permissive in allowing aid to religious institutions and would almost certainly uphold charitable choice. The *Mitchell* plurality was unable to win a decisive fifth vote, thus giving a glimmer of hope to separationist opponents of faith-based initiatives. Justice O'Connor's more cautious concurring opinion in *Mitchell* refused to accept neutrality as the sole governing principle of aid to religious organizations. Even after *Mitchell*, five justices would still scrutinize public funding of religious organizations by a standard more demanding than simple neutrality. According to O'Connor, "No aid to religious mission remains the governing understanding of the establishment clause as applied to public benefits inuring to religious schools."

Most facets of President Bush's faith-based initiative introduced in 2001 were noncontroversial constitutionally. Tax incentive proposals to encourage giving to religious service providers generated little constitutional fuss, as did offers of technical assistance for religious groups. The crux of the constitutional debate centered on several relatively simple questions, the answers to which would prove far more complicated. Could government financially aid religious social service organizations? What was the nature of those organizations that would qualify for aid? What conditions or restrictions would accompany the aid?

The substance of that debate occurred at the intersection of the contradictions between charitable choice and the pervasively sectarian standard noted above. *Mitchell*, while bolstering the arguments of charitable choice proponents, did not definitively foreclose the arguments of the opponents. While the plurality opinion hoped to bury the pervasive sectarian limitation, Justice O'Connor's hedging left the door ajar. But with the principle of neutrality gaining currency and separationist doctrine in decline, faith-based opponents were relegated to waging a rear guard action. At issue was how much separation remained in the evolving realm of the establishment clause.

Separationists read *Mitchell v. Helms* as maintaining the pervasive sectarianism restriction, albeit narrowly. Rabbi David Saperstein, director of the Religious Action Center of Reform Judaism, gave voice to the separationist position in his testimony on House Resolution 7 before the House Constitution subcommittee. He asserted that the "constitutional prohibition against direct government funding of sectarian organizations" survived *Mitchell v. Helms*.[4] In opposing the House version of the faith-based initiative, Saperstein stressed the special concerns associated with the flow of government funds flowing to pervasively religious organizations (U.S. House Committee on the Judiciary 2001, 6–7). Even if the doctrine of pervasive sectarianism as a constitutional barrier were to fall, the policy concerns behind it still would deny public funds to religious entities (Saperstein 2003; Luchenitser 2002).

In contrast, promoters of an accomodationist standard approved of government aid for religious activities and organizations, provided it be applied evenhandedly and without favoring a particular faith or denomination. Any standard that would bar intensely religious groups from public contracting offended basic notions of fairness. As long as a clear secular purpose was being advanced, the extent of a group's religiosity was immaterial to its qualifications to address a problem and receive public funds. Neutrality permitted incidental benefits to the religious side of the funded organizations as long as the secular ends were met. Unsurprisingly, those in this camp argued in the wake of *Mitchell* that the "doctrine [of pervasive sectarianism] has now lost all relevance" (Institute for Public Affairs Public Policy Library 2001).

Indirect Aid After Zelman

At least one facet of this debate was foreclosed with the much anticipated school voucher decision in *Zelman v. Simmons-Harris* (2002). Charitable choice had contemplated a variety of mechanisms through which faith-based organizations could partake of government funding, including direct aid (via grants and contracts) and indirect aid (through vouchers or coupons).

Zelman resolved one of the longest-running and most controversial of establishment clause questions: whether the government could constitutionally provide vouchers that would be used for private school tuition. Given the parallels between school vouchers and the use of similar modes of indirect payment for social welfare programs, the Supreme Court's vote in *Zelman* to uphold the constitutionality of the Cleveland voucher program was a big victory for the backers of faith-based social services.

The Court upheld the voucher scholarship program by a narrow 5–4 vote, the majority opinion resting squarely upon the principle of neutrality. As long as the voucher program was neutral as to religion, the Court said, it was not an establishment of religion. The program was neutral on its face, providing no incentive or encouragement to use vouchers at religious rather than secular schools. Aid went to religious schools only as the result of the independent decisions of individual parents, thus avoiding the danger of government endorsement of or support for religion. Assistance was available "to a broad class of citizens who, in turn, direct[ed] government aid to religious schools wholly as a result of their own genuine and independent private choice." Even though most of the tuition aid ended up with religious schools, parental choice insulated the voucher program from carrying government's endorsement or approval.

The specific implications of *Zelman* for voucher-based social service delivery programs were clear. If vouchers were okay for schools, then "you can surely have vouchers for adults who need substance abuse treatment and want to get that treatment from a religious program" (Goodstein 2001). Even voucher opponents conceded that broad constitutional objections to indirect aid would fail in the wake of *Zelman*. Charles Haynes of the antivoucher Freedom Forum First Amendment Center foresaw that "voucher arrangements for government grants to religious groups for social services are now certainly going to be seen as not only possible, but constitutional" (Goodstein 2001). Constitutional scholars agreed that, "as applied to social service programs, the voucher device would permit government to finance beneficiaries who choose to obtain services at faith-based providers, so long as secular providers were among the available choices." After *Zelman,* vouchers are "the constitutionally safest game in town" for advancing faith-based initiatives (Lupu and Tuttle 2003, 4).

Zelman virtually ensures that voucher-oriented programs will be at the center of attempts to bring religious providers into the sphere of social service provision. If the state wishes to preserve the overt religious dimensions of the provider, vouchers will be the preferred funding mechanism. For program administrators who want to avoid constitutional challenges while allowing faith-based organizations greater latitude to adhere to their religious mission, vouchers are the likely vehicles of choice.[5] There may still be constitutional challenges, but those will be limited to questions of implementation.

■ The Impact of Culture Wars on Church-State Jurisprudence

A third developmental factor shaping the law of church and state is the rise of culture wars in the United States and their impact on the Court. The term "culture war" has a long and troubled history. In the U.S. context, it developed because of a breakdown in social harmony, especially between religious believers and social life and public institutions. James Davidson Hunter, in his book *Culture Wars* (1991), has identified five major fronts in the battleground between the camps he labels "orthodox" and "progressive": education, the family, the media (including art), law, and electoral politics. At stake is a competition to "define social reality," and to control the major cultural institutions. For conservative Christians, such control and definition were largely a given throughout U.S. history. Several developments contributed to religiously orthodox citizens morphing into social outsiders: the cultural revolution of the 1960s, the liberal legal revolution of the Courts of Earl Warren and Warren Burger, the expansion of government authority over the socialization and transmission of culture, and the breakdown of a comprehensive and agreed upon public philosophy. This culture war was triggered by the codification of certain values into law, most notably in the banning of public school prayer in *Engel v. Vitale* (1962) and in the constitutionalizing of abortion rights in *Roe v. Wade* (1973). At stake in a culture war is control over the symbols of meaning from which citizens' adherence to the culture is drawn, and it remains peaceful so long as no one gains an advantage.

While much of the discussion about culture wars rests at the surface, it points to a much deeper crisis. At stake is Friedrich Nietzsche's question of whether a society that has experienced the "death of God" can sustain itself on something other than raw power and bureaucratic regulation. This secularism, Kathleen Sullivan has argued, is the desired result of the social contract embodied in the religion clauses, where religions and sects agree to the formation of a secular state to protect themselves from each other. According to Sullivan, religions have no right to object to the secular state, but have an unlimited right to exit (1992, 198). That is, if one does not like the secular schools, he or she can withdraw and attend another, though without the expectation of funding from public sources.

This approach, however, codifies the idea that, in the culture wars, one side has the force of law and the state on its side, leaving the other side increasingly frustrated and alienated. On one side are those who seek a pluralism, where believers maintain the right to express themselves on an equal basis with "secularists." On the other side are people such as Richard Rorty (2003), who contends that the only way to realize a peaceful and humane society is for those who hold to religious beliefs to abandon them in favor of his secularism. Rorty characterizes religion as inevitably "hateful" and "invidious," only masking people's "sadistic impulses." Small wonder why those of faith feel themselves on the defensive.

Alan Wolfe, in *The Transformation of American Religion,* has taken a less exclusivist tack. Wolfe has attempted to negotiate the culture wars by convincing his secular friends that evangelical Christianity is a toothless tiger, so thoroughly co-opted by the secular culture as to be virtually indistinguishable from it. "The time has come," he writes, "for you to stop using the faithful as targets to promote an understanding of religion's role in public life that discriminates against those who make belief central to the way they live" (2003, 4). Wolfe believes that religion is no longer demanding or powerful enough to do what conservative Christians require of it. For that reason it is a weak enough enemy in the culture wars that secular objections are unnecessarily extreme.

One wonders whether Wolfe fully grasps what Christianity specifically and religion in general are really about. Drawing attention to his own lack of faith, he investigates religion in such a way as to ensure that he will not discover a vibrant one in the United States. This obliviousness to the significance of religion to its adherents, as well as the confidence in the secular state to provide meaning and obedience independent of any religion, reflects in many ways the Court's approach in establishment clause cases. Profound and important questions remain as to the ultimate outcome of such an experiment and whether this approach can continue effectively to care for and sustain the citizenry. This trivialization of religion, whether done for secular or religious reasons, could have severe consequences. Indeed, the fear of such consequences is what drives the proponents of charitable choice and the recent faith-based social services initiative.

One possible casualty of such trivialization is the potential of a crisis of legitimacy and legitimation. Even the sense of purpose that rang in the civil theology of John Kennedy's inaugural address has virtually disappeared. The push toward cleansing the public square of overtly religious symbols and reference has meant the growing need for a new source for legitimizing the public moral judgments that all governments must inevitably make. Hence Brennan's dissent in *Lynch v. Donnelly* (1984), in which he concluded that allowing a city to display any religious symbol had a primary effect of placing the "government's imprimatur of approval on the particular religious beliefs exemplified by the (symbol)." Brennan found the widespread use of religious symbols perplexing, but stated that "such practices as the designation of 'In God We Trust' as our national motto, or the references to God contained in the Pledge of Allegiance can best be understood as a form of 'ceremonial deism,' protected from establishment clause scrutiny chiefly because they have lost through rote repetition any significantly religious content." In other words, only that religion that has ceased to mean anything can be tolerated in the public square. But U.S. history reveals a much more robust role for religion in the formation and sustenance of democratic institutions:

> The special relevance of religion to the legitimation of democratic societies lies on the fact that legitimation, in an ideal sense, must play a dual function if a democratic society is to be strong and enduring. On the one hand, legitimation means tacit acceptance of the nation and its policies by citizens and other relevant actors, as well as a degree of loyalty to, or conviction about, the nation's methods and goals. On the other hand, legitimation involves an articulation of transcendent purposes of ideals in relation to which the nation can be judged. In the first sense, legitimation quiets dissents that might become socially disruptive; in the second sense, it might invoke questions that help correct society's course and ensure its violability over the long run. In democratic societies both of these functions rest more on the persuasiveness of legitimating beliefs, including religious convictions, than they do on the powers of coercion. (Wuthnow 1988, 242–243)

In the absence of religious legitimation, some value other than moral law, tradition, or religious authority must act by default as this source. Science and technology are likely candidates to fill this role. This was evident in *Epperson v. Arkansas* (1968), in which the Court invalidated a state statute forbidding public school teachers from teaching the theory of evolution. As several of the case studies that follow illustrate, the requirement for an alternative source of legitimacy and authority is frequently what creates disagreement in whether regulatory demands can or should be made upon charitable organizations.

The Court has appointed itself the guardian of the peace in the United States. The possibility of religious strife remains for the Court the sine qua non of its jurisprudence. Justice O'Connor, particularly in her formation of the endorsement test, has noted that it ought to be the province of the Court to ensure that negative feelings are not generated by any government action. This fear of civil strife informs much of her jurisprudence, and is especially

prominent in her *Casey* abortion decision. Michael McConnell has argued
that O'Connor and others have laden the excessive entanglement prong of the
Lemon test with their fears of political divisiveness (1992, 130). Justice Black
evidenced this mind-set in *Board of Education v. Allen* (1968): "The First
Amendment's prohibition against governmental establishment of religion was
written on the assumption that state aid to religion and religious schools generates discord, disharmony, hatred, and strife among our people, and that any
government that supplies such aids is, to that extent, a tyranny."

The Court's focus on these concerns creates two major problems. First,
they remove any negotiation of differences from the political realm and its
representative institutions. Instead, they locate it where there is little accountability or sensitivity to the concerns of the various actors. *Casey,* for example,
is a display of this democratic bypass. Second, they predicate all decision-
making upon a concern for the potential feelings of various players in the
public square. Besides the obvious problem of subjectivity, such a rule can
provide no guidance for legislation.

As it pertains to religion, judicial supremacy in adjudicating these disputes is problematic not only because of its antidemocratic impulse, but also
because the justices have shown so little sensitivity to religious motivations.
Stephen Carter (1993) has eloquently demonstrated the way the Court has
consistently trivialized religious concerns, and Michael McConnell has publicly wondered whether the clumsiness of the Court's rulings is attributable to
a lack of experience with or comprehension of things religious. This perhaps
is why O'Connor's endorsement test has proven so inadequate. Any decision
for one thing will necessarily be a decision against something else, the result
of which will be to have the effect of making some people feel excluded.

The privatizing of religion suggests the exclusion of the deepest concerns
of a majority of Americans, and is likely to create a latent sense of hostility
over the disharmony between one's public life and one's private one. This focus on the "feelings" of various parties in the public sphere has extended not
only to the *effects* of legislation or rulings, but also to its *causes,* as in the
Romer and *Lawrence* cases, in which the ruling hinged on whether the motives of one set of litigants might be "invidious" or derived from hatred. Constitutional legitimacy is derived solely from a consideration of whether those
motives are impure. If they are, they will necessarily create bad feelings and
disrupt the public peace.

When religion and politics are too radically separated from one another,
there is a significant danger that the law loses both legitimacy and efficiency
(Berman 2000). Not only might people begin to wonder why they ought to obey
(the problem of legitimacy), but the law may well lack the requisite levels of
trust that compel compliance without resort to physical coercion. A political
system that relies purely on the threat of violence to maintain order is a tenuous

one indeed. It develops into an arid public arena bereft of meaning and a sense of shared purposes, a coercive legalism that operates as a type of secular ideology. In trivializing religion, the Court runs the risk of having people idealize constitutional principles for their own sake, not because of their capacity to generate an understanding of the human good. Under such circumstances, it may only be a matter of time before people come to recognize these idols as essentially hollow, and consequently reject them. This is the deeper significance underlying the so-called culture wars, motivating in good part the Court's understanding of itself as the keeper of the peace. But any good theory of law arguably must do more than simply attempt to maintain peace among warring factions (Berman 2000). In any event, the culture wars have manifested themselves in the intense rhetorical and policy battles over how best to deliver social services given expansive welfare programs delivered by a largely secular state.

■ The Rise and Fall of the Modern Welfare State

The poor will always be with us, and therefore so will the need to alleviate poverty. Social welfare may be handled by a variety of public and private means, but it tends to require increasing government action as societies grow larger and more complex. Indeed, state-sponsored social welfare developed in part because of material changes brought about by industrialization, in part because of changes in theology, and in part because of changes in consciousness that were part and parcel of the social changes. Industrialization produced wealth, but also attendant dislocations. With the emergence of industrial capitalism have come corresponding population increases, longer life expectancies, lower infant mortality rates, and greater social ambulation, all of which increase the number of poor persons and strain society's ability to care for them.

U.S. history has witnessed a variety of approaches to caring for the poor. In colonial America, the stress was on personal charity and generosity, the seamlessness of the fit between social life, religion, and governance, and the sharp moral distinctions between poverty (inability to sustain oneself because of profound hardship) and pauperism (need due to indolence). The distinction rested on theological assumptions about human nature and its general tendency toward vice and deception. These theological suspicions, however, were balanced by Gospel-based imperatives to care for the poor and live charitable lives. This balance required that anyone engaged in acts of charity had to be acquainted personally with the recipient of his or her charity so that discretion could be properly exercised. Puritan theology, with its emphasis on election, stressed the discriminatory nature of divine love and extrapolated from that to embrace a similarly discriminatory approach to human charity.

Changes in modes of charitable activity mirrored, in many ways, changes in the philosophical and religious social substructure. The combination of philosophical materialism, industrialism, and the quieting of American religion after the second Great Awakening led to debates over the nature and origin of poverty. The answers to that debate had serious consequences for policy. If poverty is systemic, then the source of poverty is external rather than internal, and the person in need cannot be blamed for his or her condition. What is required is not personal reform, but rather widespread systemic economic or political reform. Conversely, if poverty is viewed as one form of the natural state of human beings, and wealth can be explained only through a combination of personal industry and divine favor, then poverty is best handled either through familial love and discipline or by local organizations that personalize charity and stress individual reform.

One of the great forces for change in American charity was the development of the social gospel movement. It emerged, in part, out of Protestant liberalism and its engagement with the three great intellectual challenges of the latter half of the nineteenth century: Darwinism, the Enlightenment, and biblical criticism. Rather than ignoring these challenges, liberals embraced them and reconfigured theology in an attempt to adapt Christianity to them. To this end they emphasized immanence over transcendence, reason over faith, moral education over religious cultivation of habit, altruism over charity, and progressivism over conservatism; they were more impressed by the relativity of knowledge than claims to universal truths. Liberals no longer believed in the total depravity of human beings, instead emphasizing the infinite human capacity for self-amelioration and perfectibility. Rather than await the Kingdom of God, liberals believed in bringing the Kingdom of God to earth through human effort.

Impressed by the theological achievements of liberalism, social gospel theorists were also taken with the emergent social sciences. If science in the nineteenth century demonstrated that human beings could control nature, the infant social sciences of the twentieth century promised the possibility that human beings could control human nature.

Social gospel thinkers such as Josiah Strong and Walter Rauschenbusch explicitly rejected Puritan understandings of sin, charity, and divine election. They were universalists on the question of salvation, and by extension believed that human charity ought to be equally unconditional and universal. The God of love and the new dispensation were emphasized over the God of justice or holiness. Government was believed to be the agent of God, and since sin and personal behavior were not relevant, they stressed systemic reform over personal contact. The earlier emphasis on bonding and affiliation was replaced by a confidence in government programs, not only to ameliorate poverty, but also to eliminate it. Poverty was socially caused and could be socially eliminated. Without this evolution in theology and social thinking, the programs of the New Deal and the Great Society would not have been possible.

The George W. Bush plan could not have occurred without another round of major changes in thinking about welfare service delivery. The development of the Great Society programs and the attacks on them commenced by Ronald Reagan demonstrated changing conceptions of social welfare. The Reagan revolution in social welfare, codified into law by the welfare reform bill signed by Bill Clinton, was predicated upon two beliefs. First, the federal government had arrogated to itself too much authority in the delivery of services—thus requiring a "new federalism" that would return much of the responsibility to the states and local governments. Second, there was a growing conviction that the experiment of Great Society–type welfare programs had been a failure. The latter contention was made most forcefully by Charles Murray in his paradigm-shifting book *Losing Ground* (1994). Murray argued that Great Society programs that had spent billions of dollars on poverty relief not only had not solved the problem, but also had exacerbated it. They were successful only in creating welfare dependency, the perpetuation of underclass hopelessness, and the entrenchment of bureaucratic interest and power.

In *The Tragedy of American Compassion* (1992), Marvin Olasky aimed another broadside at the Great Society programs. In particular, Olasky found blame in the uncoupling of poverty from shame and the diminishment of the importance of personal connections and self-transformation. The result, he contended, was a dehumanizing government behemoth that was unresponsive to particulars. Olasky emphasized the need for personal not social change, arguing that welfare reform could only happen if it included spiritual reform. We must be compassionate to each other, he argued, because we are all equally dependent on the compassion of a judging God. In short, there can be no sound social policy without a sound theology underpinning it.

Olasky's book more than just signaled the declining legitimacy of the Great Society and the welfare state. It proved to be instrumental in shaping Bush's thinking on faith and social policy. Olasky became a personal adviser to Bush, drafting Bush's platform of "compassionate conservatism," which included the use of faith-based organizations for the delivery of welfare services. The religious nature of these programs, for both Olasky and Bush, was manifestly *not* beside the point. It was precisely because these organizations were religious, and thus capable of moving individuals toward the sort of personal reform that alone could remove them from poverty and destitution, that made faith-based agencies desirable partners for government monies. Given Bush's own battle with alcohol and the spiritual renewal that freed him of that demon, he could not help but be impressed with an analysis that stressed that social problems were actually spiritual problems demanding spiritual solutions.

■ **The Bush Faith-Based Plan**

De Tocqueville observed that the strength of American social life was its healthy middle, the "platoons of democracy" that composed civil society and provided a buffer between individual citizens and their government. These "mediating institutions" not only provided avenues of participation for citizens in their government and society, but also directed the flow of government authority downward, providing an essential check against tyranny and guaranteeing greater efficiency and accountability. These cells of civil society not only made people feel connected so as to be drawn out of their egoism, but also limited the massive growth and regulatory reach of government.[6] Twentieth-century liberalism emphasized individual autonomy and government action, slighting this healthy middle. Contemporary communitarian and conservative critics have argued for the revitalization of voluntary associations, which they claim can only occur if space is cleared by the scaling back of the presence and programs of government.

The Bush faith-based initiative was intended to level the playing field for religious organizations to occupy that space. To accomplish this, government regulations had to be simplified to make it easier for congregations and other religious organizations to apply for funds. Those regulations also had to be amended to remove government discrimination against religious organizations in its determination of who is to receive public support. "The goal," Stanley Carlson-Thies has written, "was not to privilege churches and church-based charities, but rather to eliminate federal obstacles that have uniquely hobbled them" (Carlson-Thies and Skillen 1996, 58).

The initiative enjoyed broad support from the public. A plurality of Americans believed that religious organizations would be more effective than any other type of organization in the delivery of antipoverty services. Americans who approved of these organizations believed that recipients of aid should have freedom of choice in how it is delivered. But they also believed that religion was a rich source of compassion *and* had a capacity to change people, both of which made them desirable partners for government (Pew Survey 2001). A Hartford Institute study discovered that "the largest proportion of congregational energy goes into providing relief for people in need, but nearly as much is directed at the education and self-improvement of others who may be less immediately needy" (http:hirr.nartsem.edu/index.html).

Few people would reject the proposition that religion produces desirable social benefits, both direct and indirect, although this is not to gainsay the political danger religion brings to the public realm. Congregations and faith-based organizations contribute to the secular well-being of society. The question with respect to the exchange between government and these institutions is not about "whether" but rather about "how much." The answer to this question is in large part determined by reflection on two sets of considerations.

One set concerns matters of fairness and the protection of rights, and the other deals with the scope and effectiveness of programs. On the latter point, there simply are insufficient data to reach solid conclusions, and judgment has largely been reserved. Consequently, the argument has centered on those questions involving fairness and the protection of rights.

This was the shoal upon which the Bush legislative agenda foundered. The attempt to pass legislation in Congress failed for a variety of reasons. The plan provoked intense opposition from its enemies, but lacked a national coalition of interests and groups who would fight for its passage with equal fervor. A highly publicized story over White House negotiations with the Salvation Army brought to a head the central controversy over religious groups' hiring rights. Events beyond the president's control, most notably the terrorist attacks of September 11, 2001, drew the priorities and energies of the administration away from faith-based work. The defection of Jim Jeffords from the Republican Party threw control of the Senate to the Democrats. For these and other reasons, the White House was left with the strategic path of pursing its faith-based goals via executive action. It did so aggressively.

■ Conclusion

As the Bush administration took the reins of the executive branch in 2001, the picture on the constitutional prospects for the faith-based initiative was mixed. From one perspective, the outlook appeared highly favorable for the plan's backers. Both in the broader sweep of establishment clause interpretation and in more recent developments, the law was moving steadily in an accommodationist direction. The Bush plan to solicit involvement of faith-based providers in publicly funded social service programs appeared on solid footing at least on the legal, if not the political, terrain.

Yet significant doubts remained. Charitable choice legislation allowed for practices that were by no means clear under the existing establishment clause case law. Specific practices allowed under the statute—permitting a grant-receiving organization to hire based on religion, the open display of religious art and imagery in the workplace, preservation of the organization's religious expression and practice—all had been mentioned in earlier cases as possible signs of a pervasively sectarian organization. For many evangelical organizations, the sharing of faith—proselytization—is an essential component of their religious practice.

The underlying spirit of charitable choice also seemed at odds with the notion of nonestablishment. Subsidizing religious social welfare groups implies that religion itself may be shared or transmitted at some point in service delivery. The belief that religious groups have a special capacity to address problems effectively presumes they be free to share the tenets of their particular belief

(Ryden 2003). "The intent of charitable choice [appears to be] that the religious entities receiving direct public aid be able to employ their faiths in carrying out the subsidized programs; and to the extent they do so, a constitutional question seems to exist even under the Court's revised interpretation of the establishment clause" (Ackerman 2000, 32).

The struggles and conflicts outlined in this chapter are not merely abstract musings or theoretical conundrums. Rather, they have practical impli cations for how religion in its various forms fares in American law and culture. By pushing the envelope of existing judicial interpretations of the establishment clause, "charitable choice programs [remain] vulnerable to the possibility of litigation" (Ackerman 2000, 33). Indeed, as we will see, such litigation now is in full flower. While the outcome of challenges to the legality of collaborations between faith-based organizations and government is yet to come, one thing can be counted on: the legal battle over faith-based social services is likely to be one more contentious chapter in the long history of the American experiment in balancing religion and politics.

■ Notes

1. This background is based on a variety of sources. The interested reader is referred first and foremost to Sydney Ahlstrom's magisterial *A Religious History of the American People* (New Haven: Yale University Press, 1972). Also please see generally, Winthrop Hudson, *Religion in America*, 4th ed. (New York: Macmillan, 1987); Patricia Bonomi, *Under the Cope of Heaven: Religion, Society, and Politics in Colonial America* (New York: Oxford University Press, 2003); Mark Noll, *A History of Christianity in the United States and Canada* (Grand Rapids: Eerdmans, 1992); Mark Noll, *Religion and American Politics: From the Colonial Period to the 1980's* (New York: Oxford University Press, 1990); Martin Marty, *Pilgrims in Their Own Land: 500 Years of Religion in America* (New York: Penguin Books, 1984); Edwin Gaustad, *A Religious History of the American People* (New York: Harper Collins, 1990); Nathan Hatch, *The Democratization of American Christianity* (New Haven: Yale University Press, 1989); and Donald Mathews *Religion in the Old South* (Chicago: University of Chicago Press, 1977).

2. *Widmar v. Vincent*, 454 U.S. 263 (1981); *Board of Education v. Mergens*, 496 U.S. 226 (1990); *Zobrest v. Catalina Foothills School District*, 509 U.S. 1 (1993); *Lamb's Chapel v. Center Moriches Union Free School District*, 508 U.S. 384 (1993); *Rosenberger v. Rector of the University of Virginia*, 515 U.S. 819 (1995).

3. The president maintained that stance as he signed later charitable choice provisions into law, explicitly construing them as "forbidding the funding of pervasively sectarian organizations." Even after *Mitchell v. Helms* came down in the summer of 2000, Clinton commented, upon his signing into law the Children's Health Act in October 2000, that government funding would be limited under the act's charitable choice language to those groups willing and able to "separate their religious activities from their substance abuse treatment and prevention activities" (*Weekly Compilation of Presidential Documents*, statement on signing the Children's Health Act, October 23, 2000, 2504).

4. An article in *Liberty* magazine embraced this position as well, arguing that, *Mitchell* notwithstanding, "if a religious institution cannot segregate its religious from its secular activities, then government aid to that institution is therefore unconstitutional" (http://www.libertymagazine.org/article/articleview/240/1/31).

5. President Bush wasted no time in adopting this strategy, calling in his 2003 State of the Union address for $600 million in voucher-based drug treatment funding.

6. De Tocqueville spent a great deal of time in *Democracy in America* speculating about such a possibility. The two greatest dangers of democratic government, de Tocqueville believed, were closely related: the tendency toward egoism in place of a vigorous and outward-looking individualism, and the formation of a large regulatory state. When de Tocqueville speculated on what tyranny would look like in a democracy, he saw the formation of a large governing apparatus that would envelop all human affairs and concerns with petty and complicated rules and regulations. Citizens would accept this because in the end their egoistic materialism would win out over the burdens and responsibilities of the life of the spirit. America would become "a flock of timid and hardworking animals with government as its shepherd" (1989, 692). This dystopic possibility would both be made possible by and legitimated by Protestant theology, which emphasized the loneliness and isolation of the ego in the face of its Creator. De Tocqueville thought that Catholicism, with its complicated systems of mediation, would in the long run be better for the health of a democracy.

The emphasis on mediating institutions was taken up by modern conservative theorists such as Peter Berger and Richard John Neuhaus in their book *To Empower People* (1996), which was read by President Bush and provided an intellectual framework for charitable choice programs. The book distinguished between minimalist and maximalist understandings of the interaction between government and religious organizations. The former allowed for a proliferation of religious groups in the delivery of services. The latter contemplated actual sponsorship of such programs by the state. But in each case, there is a great deal of accommodation. De Tocqueville's ruminations on civil society have experienced a renaissance among contemporary communitarian thinkers, who have exercised substantial influence in government circles. Indeed, these two strains found agreement in the 2000 election, as both Bush and Gore argued for the expansion of charitable choice options. Nor should it be forgotten that the 1996 bill was passed by a Republican Congress and signed into law by a Democratic president.

PART 1

Constraints of the Establishment Clause

The opening of the Bill of Rights states that "Congress shall make no law respecting an establishment of religion." The phrasing of the First Amendment has created no small amount of confusion and dispute about the nature and extent of government interaction with religious entities. It is generally agreed that government may not *prescribe* religious belief (that is, force people to believe certain tenets of faith), but neither may it *proscribe* it (disallow certain beliefs, though it may place limits on certain expressions of faith—sacrificing infants, for example). Our political leaders are not de facto ecclesiastical leaders as well. Clearly there is some sort of separation of our political institutions from our religious ones—almost certainly to the benefit of both. The American experiment in disestablishment falls somewhere between the extremes of a state-controlled church and a church-controlled state. Within these extremes, however, important questions remain as to what the First Amendment will allow by way of government financial support for religiously affiliated social service provision.

Since the passage of charitable choice, there has been a distinct shift in the government's funding of religious entities, a shift that has serious and potentially far-reaching implications for the understanding and application of the establishment clause. The purpose of the chapters in Part One is to explore the primary facets of these developments through an examination of select faith-based programs.

In Chapter 3, Sheila Kennedy analyzes the recent trend toward government support of faith-based policies in the context of corrections and criminal rehabilitation. This development tests the boundaries of the establishment clause in new ways, since it entails government funding of "transformative" programs where religion is at the center of the treatment. Kennedy is skeptical of the legality of such programs, suggesting that it is especially important that faith-based programs rely on more than religion, but be expected to implement professionally accepted practices and standards as well. In Chapter 4, David Ryden parses a faith-based welfare-to-work mentoring program in southwestern Michigan. Ryden finds serious constitutional flaws in the program, notwithstanding its apparent success. He concludes that it is essential that programs be carefully crafted to include structural/procedural safeguards for religious liberties, even when the program is not transformative or intensely religious on its face. In Chapter 5, Heidi Unruh and Jill Sinha offer a favorable assessment of a congregationally centered antipoverty program in Philadelphia. They conclude that a healthy dose of common sense and flexibility on the part of both the religious entity and its public counterpart go far toward ameliorating the twin dangers of religious establishment and compromising the religious mission of the funded church.

These case studies certainly do not exhaust the full range of establishment clause issues raised by faith-based initiatives. But they do touch on a host of important factors that impact the church-state debate. The following are some of the more significant questions to keep in mind while reading these chapters:

How does the type of social service being delivered affect the constitutional footing of the program? The case studies explore the use of religious organizations in providing correctional, mentoring, and antipoverty services. But government collaborations with faith-based providers can now be found with virtually any social service imaginable, from health care and housing for low-income families to reducing domestic violence and helping at-risk youth. The use of the establishment clause analysis is likely to differ depending on the nature of the services. Among the relevant actors—the government agency, the service deliverer, and the beneficiaries—different groups will see different "constitutional values."

What is the role of religion or faith in the services? A related question is simply whether the religious aspects of the program are tangential or central to the primary thrust of the services. Is religion ancillary? Or is the program religious at its core? More recently, public funds have flowed to programs that openly embrace religious activities, such as the InnerChange program, which is the subject of lawsuits in Iowa, or faith-based prisons, the first of which was opened in Florida. Other examples abound. President George W. Bush, in his 2003 State of the Union address, announced his intention to ask Congress for $600 million for a faith-based voucher plan to aid in the treatment of drug addicts, alcoholics, and other substance abusers. Judges sitting on the bench in Chattanooga, Tennessee, have implemented Project Transformation, which offers nonviolent drug offenders, in lieu of prison, the option of faith-based treatment consisting of thrice-weekly sessions with a Christian counselor. In programs such as these, faith is at the heart of the treatment, and public funds aiding such efforts heighten the fear of impermissible religious establishment.

What type of religious organization is the recipient of public funds? Is it separately incorporated? Does it have some measure of independence from an umbrella church or denomination, along the lines of Catholic Charities or the Jewish Board of Family and Children's Services? Or is the faith-based program one in which the government funds a congregation or religiously infused entity directly? Is the grant/contract recipient an umbrella or intermediary organization, one that provides a buffer between the provision of services and the oversight of the government?

What are the structural details and workings of the funding for the program? When analyzing faith-based programs for constitutionality, the weathered cliché about the "devil in the details" has never been more apt. Has the program been implemented with one eye unflinchingly on the preservation of constitutional values? What is the funding mechanism through which the state furnishes financial aid? Does it use indirect payment methods through vouchers or coupons, or is it through the direct payment of a grant or contract? If the latter, is there careful accounting that ensures public funds are used to pay only secular and not religious aspects of the program? Does the program provide for beneficiary choice by making available a menu of providers? Are clients able to avoid religious activities? Does the faith-based provider give clear notice to beneficiaries of the religious character of the program? Are professional standards and thorough oversight provisions in place, to gauge efficacy of the program but also to ensure compliance with constitutional boundaries? Passing constitutional muster under the First Amendment will depend in no small part on the minutia, that is, on the attention paid to the practices and workings of the program.

What are the crucial definitions and labels that infuse the church-state debate, and what assumptions or issues are bound up in the ambiguity and confusion in those terms? Definitions matter a great deal to the constitutional analysis. Yet the key terms are plagued with a striking degree of imprecision. This in turn detracts from a clear and comprehensible establishment clause doctrine. What qualifies as *establishment*? Or to use the alternative preferred by Justice Sandra Day O'Connor, when does government support cross over into unacceptable *endorsement*? What does it mean to prefer a standard of governmental *neutrality* toward religious nonprofits? When does a government policy toward a faith-based policy or organization represent in practical terms either hostility or bias in favor of a particular faith or religion? Against or in favor of secularism? Answers to these questions certainly are likely to prove problematic and challenging. Yet answers are necessary to determine whether a faith-based collaboration between a religious entity and the state is either constitutionally acceptable or taboo.

These are just some of the unresolved questions facing courts as they seek to clarify the church-state parameters of faith-based social services. While the authors in Part One make no pretense of definitively resolving the debate, the featured case studies make a significant contribution by providing us with the factual context of actual practices necessary to shape and inform the decision-making process.

Religion, Rehabilitation, and the Criminal Justice System

SHEILA KENNEDY

Although government partnerships with religious organizations and their af-filiates have been a feature of the social service landscape for decades, chari-table choice legislation has raised hackles on both the left and right. Civil lib-ertarians object to provisions that, for the first time, would allow employment discrimination with public funds, and worry that the legislation is part of a new assault on the separation of church and state. Activists of the religious right demand assurances that funds will not flow to disfavored groups like the Nation of Islam or the Scientologists. African American pastors in urban ar-eas—arguably the main beneficiaries of the initiative—are concerned that "government shekels" will be accompanied by "government shackles," that the costs and regulatory burdens involved in collaborations with government will divert resources from client services and will mute their prophetic voice. Caught in the middle are public managers, who must make the legislation work in the face of significant administrative challenges.

Those administrative challenges can be grouped into three major areas: outreach and contracting procedures, contract administration, and evaluation. In each of these categories, political realities and constitutional constraints will significantly complicate the manager's job. While the administrative challenges are significant for all government programs, however, the evange-listic nature of many faith-based criminal justice programs implicates the constitutional issues in ways that other programs may not.

■ Background

Federal and state government units have provided services through nonprofit and religious organizations since the inception of government social welfare programs, although the media characterization of charitable choice and President George W. Bush's faith-based initiative as "new" or even "revolutionary" has tended to obscure that history (U.S. Senate Judiciary Committee 2001). In a 1969 study of findings from a 1965 survey of 406 sectarian agencies in twenty-one states, Bernard J. Coughlin reported that 70 percent of them were involved in some type of purchase of service contract with the government (Coughlin 1965). A 1982 study by F. Ellen Netting, focusing on government funding of Protestant social service agencies in one midwestern city, found that some agencies received between 60 and 80 percent of their support from the government, and that approximately half of their combined budgets were government financed (Netting 1982). In 1994, government funding accounted for 65 percent of the nearly $2 *billion* annual budget of Catholic Charities, and 75 percent of the revenues of the Jewish Board of Family and Children's Services (Monsma 1996; Brown and McKeown 1997).

The rhetoric used by congressional supporters of charitable choice suggested that "faith-based," a new term now being applied to religious providers, was intended to have a specialized meaning. But neither the legislation nor representatives of the White House Office of Faith-Based and Community Initiatives defined what "faith-based" was to mean for purposes of charitable choice initiatives, or explained how these organizations differ from the religious entities that have been partnering with government for decades. Many of the religious providers with the longest histories of social welfare provision are faith-based in the most literal sense—that is, the provision of essentially secular social services is motivated by their religious beliefs. Feeding and clothing the poor, tending to the sick, and housing the aged are approached by such organizations as religious duties, rather than as opportunities for proselytizing or transforming the individuals served, and their services do not differ significantly from those provided by secular providers. Charitable choice is generally understood to be an attempt to reach out to religious providers that have not historically partnered with government agencies, and whose programs include more specifically religious content.[1]

Given this history and background, it would have been helpful had Congress addressed several important questions: What does "faith-based" mean for purposes of these charitable choice initiatives? How do the faith-based organizations targeted by charitable choice legislation differ from those with a long history of governmental contractual relationships? What are the barriers to their participation in social service delivery, and to what extent are those barriers constitutionally mandatory? What is the availability and interest, and what are the capacities, of these organizations? Few of these questions, however, found their way into the congressional debates about charitable choice (Kennedy 2001), and none were addressed by the legislation. The resulting ambiguities have created substantial public management issues, issues that are particularly acute where the services involve drug treatment and prisoner rehabilitation.

Charitable choice legislation was explicitly predicated on the assumption that faith-based organizations—particularly those we might describe as faith-*infused* organizations with an overtly religious content to their service delivery—are more effective and efficient at providing assistance than the secular and religiously affiliated nonprofits that have been delivering the bulk of tax-supported social welfare programs on government's behalf.[2] These claims have been made most frequently in the area of drug treatment, where Teen Challenge, for example, claims a success rate of 85 percent (Goodstein 2001). Such a success rate would indeed be impressive—even remarkable; however, independent researchers point out that the success rate calculation is based upon the number of clients completing the program. If the calculation is adjusted to include those who start the program but do not finish, the rate drops to 25 percent (Goodstein 2001). Furthermore, different drug programs define "success" differently, making meaningful comparisons very difficult. In fact, there are no independent, empirical data available either to support or to rebut a presumption that drug treatment providers who make religion central to their service approach, or faith-based organizations in general, are more effective than secular providers.

For the past three years, I have been Principal Investigator on an Indiana University—Purdue University at Indianapolis project to study and evaluate charitable choice implementation in three states—Massachusetts, North Carolina, and Indiana. At this writing, final research findings have not been issued; however, the observations that follow are based upon portions of that research.

■ Outreach and Contracting Procedures

Charitable choice was intended to make government contracts more "user friendly" to faith-based organizations that had not previously partnered with the public sector, so as to encourage their entry into social service partnerships (DiIulio 2001). This meant that the first task for public managers was to inventory their current procurement processes in order to identify and remove existing barriers to their entry. Public managers were then to develop criteria for identifying, and mechanisms for reaching out to, new faith-based partners.

Not surprisingly, the identification of barriers disadvantaging faith-based organizations has elicited different responses in different states. Massachusetts significantly revamped its procurement processes in 1995, with the express purpose of making the government contracting process more accessible and transparent to all potential bidders. Massachusetts officials believe the revamped process does not contain barriers to faith-based participation; furthermore, the state points to its long history of contracting with Catholic, Lutheran, and Jewish agencies (Jensen 2001). While Massachusetts received an "F" from the Center for Public Justice on its recent "report card" rating the states on implementation of charitable choice (Charitable Choice Compliance 2000), state officials took the position that the legislation was intended to "level the playing field," and Massachusetts' field was already level.

North Carolina has approached implementation primarily through an existing effort: the Communities of Faith Initiative of the North Carolina Rural Economic Development Center. Launched in the early 1990s, the program worked across denominational and racial lines to address the needs of rural inhabitants of North Carolina, particularly those living in or near poverty. The most numerous and powerful institutions in rural North Carolina were the churches; accordingly, it was through an alliance of those churches that the center proposed to deliver services. Subsequent to the enactment of charitable choice, the center has held two conferences, and has entered into a contract with the North Carolina Division of Social Services to initiate a church-based pilot program to support rural families as they move from welfare to work. "Faith demonstration awards" were made to five faith-based projects, most of which serve more than one county but none of which are statewide in scope. Communities of Faith also does training for faith-based organizations; in 2000, organizations from forty-two North Carolina counties attended its "Faith with Works" seminars.

Indiana has been ambitious in implementing charitable choice. The state established an initiative called FaithWorks, designed to reach out to faith-based organizations that had not previously contracted with the state, and to assist them with capacity building and technical assistance. FaithWorks' short-term goal is to give such organizations the tools, access, and information needed to become competitive with traditional providers. Its long-term goal is the creation of networks and links that will allow the faith community to sustain an effective presence in the area of social service delivery. As part of an overall outreach effort to the faith community, six informal meetings were held around the state in February 2000. Invitations were sent to houses of worship and nonprofit service providers affiliated with religious organizations, although any interested organization was welcome to send representatives. Approximately 1,000 people attended. During the year, 400 organizations received technical assistance, either through state-paid consultants or by attending state-sponsored workshops. Workshops addressed descriptions of the charitable choice legislation, state procurement procedures, the contracting process, effective proposal development, requirements for the Temporary Assistance for Needy Families program, and fiscal management and accountability.

"Affirmative action" outreach programs aimed at publicizing the goal of a level playing field, such as Indiana's FaithWorks or North Carolina's Communities of Faith Initiative, are one method of achieving participation by faith-based organizations. Complete revamping of the procurement process, similar to the Massachusetts effort, is another. Both approaches require that states confront a threshold issue, however: establishing appropriate criteria for bidders.

Supporters of charitable choice have criticized states' insistence that responsive bidders have professional credentials and meet professional norms. In an article for *Commentary,* written just before he became director of the Corporation for Community Service, Leslie Lenkowsky argued for "elimination of arbitrary rules that allow, for example, the use of professional therapy but not pastoral counseling" (2001, 23). If an agency is putting together a request for proposals for counseling services, and requires that successful bidders employ licensed social workers or certified drug counselors, has the state discriminated against faith-based organizations offering unlicensed "pastoral counseling"? Lenkowsky clearly believes it has, although other religious spokespersons disagree. Addressing the House Committee on Government Reform's Subcommittee on Criminal Justice, Drug Policy, and Human Resources, Reverend Horace R. Smith, president and chief executive officer of Group Ministries Baltimore, testified:

> In its present state, the proposed initiative seems to allow funds to be distributed to community and faith-based organizations basically because they meet the criteria that they are either community or faith-based. The criteria for distribution of funds needs to go beyond that narrow stipulation. There should be some form of standardization these organizations are held to. There's a danger that those we seek to service won't receive the level of help they actually need because there presently is not any standard of care within the faith-based community. (U.S. House Committee on Government Reform 2001)

Reverend Smith strongly endorsed certification requirements, calling himself "a strong advocate for accreditation."

States are accountable for the quality of the services they provide, and have a legal obligation to evaluate the ability of bidders to provide services at an appropriate level. If the bidder offers "pastoral counseling" in lieu of professional certification, how is the probable efficacy of that counseling—and thus the responsiveness of the bidder—to be assessed? If the state appears to relax or discard professional standards when the bidder is a faith-based organization, secular nonprofits and current state contractors may justifiably object that an unconstitutional preference is being shown to religious organizations in violation of the establishment clause. In his recent testimony on faith-based solutions before the Senate Committee on the Judiciary, John L. Avery of the Association for Addiction Professionals (NAADAC) focused upon precisely that issue: "NAADAC's concern is not with who provides care, but rather by what clinical standards that care is provided. We are committed to the application of science-based best practices, perhaps as most succinctly stated in the National Institute of Drug Abuse (NIDA) publication,

'Principles of Drug Addiction Treatment, a Research-Based Guide'" (U.S. Senate Judiciary Committee 2001). Avery emphasized that, for his organization, the "salient issue is the clinical competency of the treatment provider" and concern for consumer protection and public safety. If faith-based organizations believe insistence on evidence of "clinical competency" is discriminatory, and the NAADAC believes that failure to require such evidence is malpractice, it is no wonder that many public administrators feel caught in an untenable situation.

States have also taken different approaches to the issue of who qualifies as a faith-based organization. Massachusetts, as indicated, considers all religiously affiliated providers essentially fungible, both with other sectarian organizations and with secular providers. All are officially considered equal and evaluated solely with respect to the responsiveness of their bid. If lack of prior experience or absence of credentialed personnel operates to disadvantage some bidders, that is unfortunate but irrelevant. In Indiana, the state "counts" as faith-based organizations only those participating in its Manpower Placement and Comprehensive Training program. This welfare reform demonstration project includes cash assistance and employment services programs for needy and eligible families with dependent children, and is funded with funds from the Temporary Assistance to Needy Families program.[3] This approach has allowed the state to sidestep the more difficult constitutional issues involved in drug treatment and prison contracts by concentrating its outreach in less problematic areas.

In his recent testimony before the Senate Committee on the Judiciary, constitutional law professor Douglas Laycock raised a different outreach issue. Laycock noted that "choosing someone to deliver social services is more complex than picking the low bidder on a pencil contract. How do you keep thousands of government employees—federal, state, and local—from discriminating on religious grounds when they award grants and contracts?" (U.S. Senate Judiciary Committee 2001). The validity of this concern is underscored by statements issued by Pat Robertson and others, warning the administration against contracts with the Nation of Islam or the Scientologists. Laycock endorsed a "reporting requirement" that would require "explanation" of any obvious over- or underrepresentation of religious providers. Whatever the merits of such a requirement, it would be yet another bureaucratic task requiring at least some level of resource allocation. Whether such a mechanism would minimize claims of bias is an open question. As Richard Foltin of the American Jewish Committee has noted:

> It seems almost inevitable that, whatever claims may be made that contracts
> will be allocated on the basis of merit, in any given community the religious
> groups most likely to receive funds will be those associated with "main-

stream" faiths. And, even if the contracts are allocated on a totally objective basis, there is likely to be sharp distrust and suspicion that this is not the case. (American Jewish Committee 1990)

■ Contract Monitoring

Early experience in Indiana suggests that monitoring faith-based organizations new to the contracting regime requires considerably more resources and more "hands-on" help than is needed with more experienced providers. This can be expected to diminish as such providers become more sophisticated about government's expectations.

More troubling is the significant constitutional issue involved in monitoring. The free exercise clause protects religious organizations against unwarranted intrusion, a concept that is subject to interpretation. Even if audit and accountability measures are perfectly appropriate constitutionally, elected officials have expressed concerns that, should state agencies find the compliance of faith-based organizations inadequate, charges of bias will be leveled and may well resonate politically. To the extent charitable choice focuses upon inner-city churches, race will inevitably become a part of the political equation, a prospect that concerns even strong supporters of charitable choice and vigorous outreach efforts.[4] If government oversight is not to be viewed as racially or religiously discriminatory, great care will need to be exercised to eliminate unintended disparities in the monitoring process. Oversight methodology and criteria will need to be well conceived and clearly communicated to faith-based contractors before the fact.

State agencies are constitutionally required to ensure that government funds go only to support secular activities. Consistent with that requirement, the original charitable choice legislation prohibits use of tax dollars for proselytizing and bars providers from conditioning services on participation in religious activities. Public managers are responsible for compliance with those restrictions; however, states have limited managerial resources with which to monitor programmatic content for constitutional compliance. Middle managers hired to administer service contracts cannot be expected to recognize any but the most egregious First Amendment violations. Moreover, they have limited time to devote to such issues. If a violation is alleged and proven, however, the state can be held liable. As the Welfare Information Network frames the issue in a section of its website devoted to discussion of frequently asked questions:

> State or local jurisdictions should consider these terms ["faith-based organization" and "proselytization"] when working on contracting arrangements

that are covered by Section 104 of the federal welfare reform law, P.L. 104-193, also known as the "charitable choice" provisions. Contracting with funds under the Temporary Assistance to Needy Families Program is covered by Section 104. The law does not offer definitions of "religious organization" and "proselytization," and although some states may have defined these terms in case law related to schooling or other issues, they are not familiar to many contract officers.

Given the lack of precedents, states and local jurisdictions generally have avoided legally binding definitions in their contracts, especially as to what constitutes proselytization. Instead, dialogue and "gut instinct" are guiding the implementation of the ban on proselytization when contracting with federal funds. This approach could include: ensuring that organizations bidding on a contract know in advance about the prohibition on using the contract funds for proselytization; talking with the contracting organization about the state or local agency's expectations, and the consequences of any problems reported with proselytization; and ensuring that participants are aware of the ban and what steps they can take if they feel uncomfortable receiving services from a religious provider. For example, Section 104 provides welfare recipients the right to seek alternative providers. Religious organizations have certain rights under Section 104 as well. (www.financeprojectinfo.org/win/, accessed January 20, 2005)

As Reverend Eliezar Valentin-Caston of the United Methodist Church warned in his testimony to the Senate Committee on the Judiciary: "As long as government attempts to separate what is religious from secular in entities like churches, synagogues, mosques, etc. it risks becoming excessively entangled with religion, thus advancing it or hindering religion, both clear violations of the establishment clause" (U.S. Senate Judiciary Committee 2001).

Finally, there is the requirement that secular alternatives be provided for welfare recipients who do not want a faith-based provider. Public managers will need to identify such alternatives and fund them. This should not present a problem in urban areas. But it can be a challenge in more rural states, rural areas of states, or in very homogeneous communities where alternative providers may not be convenient or even available.[5] A related problem arises when a client who has been assigned to a faith-based organization becomes uncomfortable with the religious context of the programming and requests a change of provider. The state must have procedures to allocate or recapture payment and find a replacement provider in such circumstances.

■ Evaluation

State agencies should evaluate the efficacy of all service providers, secular or religious. Such evaluation was problematic well before the passage of charitable choice; in all three of the states under study, the social welfare system is so radically decentralized and uncoordinated as to make sound evaluation of programs virtually impossible. In addition, welfare populations are notoriously difficult to track: poor people move frequently, often do not have telephones, and are frequently unresponsive to or intimidated by survey forms and other formal inquiries. The lack of credible data is one reason that welfare policies generally elicit such strong disagreements among scholars and policymakers.

Public managers must measure programmatic success—once defined—without intruding upon the constitutional prerogatives of the religious organization. This can be especially difficult when the faith-based organization has chosen not to form a 501(c)(3) affiliate (a separately incorporated, affiliated nonprofit organization meeting the requirements of Section 501[c][3] of the Internal Revenue Code). Monitoring and evaluation of fiscal performance will require review of books and records, since program costs may not have been segregated from other financial information. Even if there is a separate 501(c)(3), some inquiry into the finances of the religious organization may be necessary if, for example, a church or synagogue is providing substantial in-kind support. Any analysis of the cost of providing services will include the value of volunteer time, use of church equipment and facilities, and similar accommodations. Valuing those accommodations may require more review than the faith-based organization feels is constitutionally appropriate.

■ Rehabilitation or Redemption: The Constitutional Dimension

The discussion thus far has addressed issues applicable to faith-based social service contracts generally. When the programs being provided are faith-*infused* drug treatment and prison counseling, however, there is an almost insurmountable constitutional barrier to direct government funding. The nature of the dilemma is illustrated by the testimony of numerous advocates of religious interventions: they are very clear in their belief that the only way to help teenagers on drugs, or prisoners, is through religious conversion. A recent statement from Jack Cowley, national director of operations for the InnerChange Prison Fellowship Ministry, is illustrative: "We believe that crime is a result of sin, therefore, a relationship with Christ can keep one from a life of crime" (Pyeatt 2001). Unlike social services such as job training and placement, day care, or medical assistance, faith-infused drug and prison programs use explicitly religious doctrines as their programs. It is not accidental that so many prison programs are called "ministries."

Programs such as InnerChange, Teen Challenge, or House of Hope are centered on religious belief; acceptance of Jesus, the importance of biblical precepts, and personal morality *are* the program. Such programs might be called "faith-infused." Prison Fellowship Ministries, one of the most prominent of the prison programs, describes itself as "Christ-based." Its vision is "that God's kingdom will be manifested as the redemptive grace and peace of Jesus Christ are experienced by those impacted by crime." According to the organization's website, crime is fundamentally a moral and spiritual problem that requires a moral and spiritual solution. "Offenders do not simply need rehabilitation; they require regeneration of a sinful heart" (www.pfm.org, accessed January 20, 2005).

As Mark Earley concluded in an interview on the InnerChange Freedom Initiative with the O'Reilly Factor:

> What we need in the correctional system in America is an opportunity for hearts to be transformed, not simply for people to get some skills. What we provide in this program is not only a skill, but a transformed heart through the power of the Gospel. (Earley 2003)

Drug and prison programs such as InnerChange have religious conversion as their primary purpose. Other programs encompassed by the charitable choice initiatives may create environments within which constitutional violations are more likely to occur, but the programs can be conducted in a constitutionally appropriate fashion; funding for programs in the mold of Teen Challenge and Prison Fellowship's InnerChange, however, is clearly funding *for* religion and—under decades of First Amendment jurisprudence—constitutionally prohibited.

In 1947, Justice Hugo Black summarized the meaning of the First Amendment's religion clauses in an eloquent paragraph that has been cited in numerous religious liberty cases:

> The Establishment Clause means at least this: Neither a state nor the Federal Government can set up a church. Neither can pass laws which aid one religion, aid all religions, or prefer one religion over another. Neither can force nor influence a person to go to or to remain away from church against his will or force him to profess a belief or disbelief in any religion. No person can be punished for entertaining or professing religious beliefs or disbeliefs, for church attendance or non-attendance. No tax in any amount, large or small, can be levied to support any religious activities or institutions, whatever they may be called, or whatever form they may adopt to teach or practice religion. (*Everson v. Board of Education* 1947)

The mere fact that tax dollars are paid to a religious organization, of course, is not equivalent to funding religion. Government may constitutionally purchase services, including social services, from sectarian sources, or enter into other partnerships that involve the transfer of tax dollars to such entities so long as the funds do not support inherently religious activities. The relative lack of concern over government's historical support for religious social services is at least partly because the secular nature of those services is readily apparent. Hospitals and nursing homes are providing medical care; day care facilities are supervising children; job placement counselors have secular counterparts engaged in providing similar, if not identical, programs. While economists remind us that dollars are fungible, it is relatively simple to calculate the cost of nursing services or child care and to subsidize only that (secular program) cost.

In the parochial school context, over which there has been much more debate and litigation, programs that have passed constitutional muster have historically been those involving an identifiably secular benefit available to all citizens—immunization, speech and hearing testing, transportation— where exclusion of children attending religious schools was deemed to burden the free exercise rights of parents opting for religious education. When public aid has been disallowed, the Supreme Court has pointed to the "pervasively sectarian" nature of the religious school, and the impossibility of ensuring that only secular program elements benefit from the expenditure of public funds. Pervasively sectarian organizations are defined by the courts as those in which the religious elements are so fundamentally interwoven into every aspect of programming that it would be impossible to separate them for purposes of ensuring that support goes only to the secular portions. Despite recent cases that have arguably relaxed the historical wall of separation between church and state, *direct* government aid to pervasively sectarian organizations remains unconstitutional.

In *Agostini v. Felton* (1997), the Court (quoting from *Witters v. Washington Department of Services for the Blind* [1986]) explained that any public money earmarked for secular purposes that ultimately goes to pervasively religious institutions must do so "only as a result of the genuinely independent and private choices of individuals." Many constitutional commentators believe that a voucher program for social services allowing recipients to choose between religious and secular providers would be constitutional. If public dollars have been allocated for a secular purpose (drug treatment or offender rehabilitation, for example) and if there is a "genuinely independent and private" choice of service provider, then there is no constitutionally persuasive reason to prevent an elderly person seeking nursing home care from spending his or her benefits in a nursing home run by his or her religious denomination, or to prevent a drug-dependent teen from choosing to enroll at Teen Challenge. As the Court struggles for neutrality in its application of the religion clauses, as it searches for a formulation that neither burdens nor benefits religious practice and belief, the exercise of intervening independent choice sufficient to insulate government from a charge of endorsement would seem to be the fairest way to achieve evenhandedness. Many constitutional scholars thus believe that a voucher program would be legally and practically preferable to direct contractual relationships between faith-based organizations and government agencies. Such an approach could allow religiously infused drug treatment programs to participate; however, as a pending challenge to InnerChange in Iowa demonstrates, it would not solve the practical and constitutional dilemmas posed by prison ministries.

The complaint in the Iowa lawsuit, *Americans United for Separation of Church and State v. Prison Ministries* (2003), challenges the constitutionality of Prison Fellowship, saying the InnerChange Freedom Initiative is a "pervasively religious" prerelease program operating within a state facility. Inmates who participate are housed in a separate unit and immersed in "24-hour per day Christ-centered Bible-based programming" and

> during nearly all their waking hours, [they] are subjected to intensive, evangelical, Biblically-based instruction from a Christian fundamentalist standpoint. In rooms whose walls are lined with scripture, the inmates study the Bible, memorize Bible verses, and pray. In Prison Fellowship's own words, the "major purpose of the program" is "transformation" to be "brought about by depending on Christ."

A substantial portion of the InnerChange program's budget comes from state revenues, including a settlement of state tobacco litigation as well as profits generated for the state through charges for telephone calls placed by inmates and often paid for by their family members, friends, and attorneys. As the complaint recites: "State moneys that were obtained from persons who do not subscribe to the religious teachings of the InnerChange program and from a fund that was created to generally benefit the public health have thus been used and allocated to pay for pervasively religious, evangelical, fundamentalist Christian instruction."

The complaint further alleges that the InnerChange program only accepts those who subscribe to or are actively willing to cooperate in a program of fundamentalist, evangelical Christianity. It cites the program's own literature to demonstrate that successful completion requires adoption of very specific religious behaviors and principles. "The State's sponsorship and financing of the InnerChange program thus discriminates against inmates who do not subscribe to the particular form of Christianity taught by InnerChange."

In addition, the complaint charges that inmates who participate in the InnerChange program receive numerous privileges denied to nonparticipating inmates:

> InnerChange participants live in an "honor unit" where they are given keys to their own cells and access to private bathrooms, while non-participating inmates live in a "lock-up unit" where correctional officers have sole control over locks to cell doors and where the toilet stools are located in the middle

of cells. InnerChange participants receive a broad range of other benefits denied to non-participating inmates, such as additional visits with family members, free telephone calls to family members, access to computers and word-processing equipment, and access to big-screen televisions. The operation of the InnerChange program therefore gives inmates incentives to subject themselves to religious indoctrination.

The final allegation of the complaint raises the issue that has been most politically salient: religious discrimination in employment. "Prison Fellowship and InnerChange have a publicly announced policy of employing only Christians as staff members and allowing only Christians to serve as volunteers. . . . State funds are used to pay portions of the salaries of InnerChange employees. The State is thereby financing religious discrimination in employment."

It remains to be seen if the description of the program as outlined in the complaint can be proven at trial. No doubt, religiously infused prison programs can be devised that do not grant captive populations incentives for religious conversion or use tax dollars to fund religious personnel or activities. However, the nature of a prison makes it extremely difficult to devise a genuinely voluntary program or to offer inmates meaningful secular alternatives. The ultimate disposition of *Americans United* should outline the limits of permissible ministry activities within prison walls.

■ Conclusion

Religious organizations are doing wonderful things. Indeed, it is impossible to overstate the extent of the contribution being made to this nation by people and organizations of faith. Recognition of that fact does not, however, impel an uncritical embrace of charitable choice, as many of those same religious organizations have cautioned.

The question is not about whether these organizations are doing good work. They are. Nor is it about whether government should partner with them. It does and it always has. The real questions are about when and how the partnering should occur, with which organizations, and under what circumstances. Answering these questions adequately will require us to revisit some foundational issues that have gotten lost along the increasingly politicized way. At a minimum, it will require making distinctions among faith organizations—distinctions that are critical to constitutional analysis. Religious organizations are not interchangeable, and their programs range over a continuum that spans from virtually secular to faith-influenced to faith-infused. If public managers are to make informed choices, and citizens are to receive services that are constitutionally and therapeutically appropriate, those distinctions must be appreciated.

■ Notes

1. This has led some scholars to suggest that charitable choice is not about inclusion of religious providers, but is instead about shifting a fixed pool of government funds from some religious providers to others.

2. The majority of human services are now provided by nonprofits for whom government funds have become the principal source of revenue (Salamon 1995; Stone, Griffin, and Hager 2001).

3. This approach to categorization has generated anomalies. Horizon House, for example, is a homeless shelter created and supported by a group of churches and other nonprofits. Its executive director is an ordained minister. Indiana does not consider Horizon House to be "faith-based" for programmatic purposes; however, the Career Resource Center, a for-profit corporation that participates in the Manpower Placement and Comprehensive Training program, is classified as a faith-based organization, and self-identifies as faith-based.

4. It is instructive that I have encountered this issue on several occasions, but always "off the record." It is a persistent background concern that no one wants to acknowledge publicly.

5. As Douglas Laycock noted in his testimony, "We have not succeeded in guaranteeing even one provider for all people who need these services. How can we plausibly guarantee a choice of providers?" (U.S. Senate Judiciary Committee 2001).

When Does Mentoring Become Proselytizing?

David K. Ryden

The best way—perhaps the only way—fundamentally to change the tragic reality of long-term welfare dependency is for our society, including policy makers, to realize that spiritual transformation must be a central component of the fight against poverty. . . . Unless policies take into account the importance of the inward transformation of belief and character, nothing else will work properly. . . . What is needed is a holistic approach based on a new model of partnership between religious organizations, government, and other institutions in society. (Sider and Rolland 1996, 463)

President George W. Bush did not let the lack of legislative success deter him from aggressively pursuing his faith-based agenda during his first term. Even as The Charity, Aid, Recovery, and Empowerment Act (CARE) languished in the Senate, Bush through executive order established faith-based centers in five key federal departments (Justice, Education, Housing and Urban Development, Labor, and Health and Human Services). Through these five departments, the White House Office of Faith-Based and Community Initiatives (WHOFBCI) awarded more than $1.1 billion in competitive grants to faith-based organizations in fiscal year 2003 (Cooperman 2004). Faith-based centers were subsequently created in the department of Agriculture and the U.S. Agency for International Development.

A main focus of the federal grant programs was on intermediary organizations that help connect federal programs to smaller neighborhood nonprofits that otherwise probably would not partner with the government. The Compassion Capital Fund (CCF) paid out $24.7 million in its first year (2002) to twenty-one such intermediaries to solicit grassroots involvement in programs for at-risk youth, welfare-to-work, and substance abuse rehabilitation. By early 2004 the total paid out of the CCF to intermediary organizations was estimated at $65 million (Page 2004).

One strand of the faith-based focus on intermediary organizations was a Labor Department grant program in the area of job training and employment. In 2002 the department initiated a federal grant program to faith- and community-based intermediaries. These grants were specifically intended to employ umbrella associations to link the unemployed to the government-operated One-Stop Career Centers at the heart of the public work force investment system.

The Labor Department grants were renewed for 2003; $5.6 million in additional funds also was awarded to ten new groups (Farris 2004). Among those was Good Samaritan Ministries (GSM), a social services organization that supports a network of approximately eighty Christian churches of various denominational affiliations in the southwestern corner of Michigan. GSM's clearinghouse provides people with short-term needs with referrals to churches that can meet those needs. The services include emergency food, clothing, housing, transportation, day care, home repairs, and more. The GSM Neighborhood Alliance equips churches to meet longer-term needs of the community as well. Last and certainly not least, the organization has been active in partnering with state and local county officials on welfare and job training issues.[1]

GSM received a $500,000 Labor Department grant to work with the local work force development board to expand and improve available employment services. GSM's approach naturally grew out of its philosophy of relational ministry, to deliver services in the context of a caring and supportive network of personal relationships. GSM's dual commitment was to provide outreach opportunities for every church member in the area, while placing every one of its clients in a ministry relationship with a volunteer church or individual. The grant proposal reflected this philosophy, with an emphasis on placement counseling, personal coaching and mentoring, financial counseling, language and basic life skills instruction, and graduate equivalency diploma (GED) classes.

GSM proposed to recruit new grassroots partners for the work force board's career service network by issuing $250,000 in subgrants to smaller local groups. This too was a natural fit for GSM as an intermediary organization. Among its stated purposes was that of "mobiliz[ing] churches toward community ministry." GSM describes itself as the "bridge" that connects government poverty programs with churches and other faith-based organizations that can help administer those programs. As an intermediary, GSM provides administrative assistance for grassroots ministries as they interact with the public sector. It helps churches with the "politics" of community ministry, shepherding them through the bureaucratic processes and offering congregational coaching, mentor training, and volunteer development. On October 8, 2003, GSM announced fourteen new subgrants totaling $250,000. The recipient organizations were almost all faith-based entities, enlisted to provide pre- and postplacement training, GED training, English language instruction, employment mentoring, financial counseling, and immigration assistance.

The grant was the largest ever received by GSM, but it was not the first. Indeed, GSM has had substantial interaction with public officials, particularly at the local and county levels. In the mid-1990s, GSM partnered with state and local government offices in a pioneering faith-based welfare-to-work effort called Project Zero (PZ). That project received considerable national notoriety for its success in moving welfare families into the work force. A central component of the program was the reliance on local churches and their parishioners for mentoring and counseling of welfare clients, of which GSM was one.

GSM's role in Project Zero deserves a close look, especially given GSM's success in securing new funds through the current faith-based initiative. It demonstrates the perils and potentialities of church-state unions, and offers a useful framework for confronting perplexing First Amendment questions. The earlier government-sponsored faith-based program is a welcome frame of reference—for current GSM-governmental collaboration and for other organizations partnering with government in an environment more attuned to potential constitutional infractions, as well as for those hoping to clarify the constitutional dos and don'ts of faith-based programs.

The PZ experience suggests a two-part constitutional analysis of faith-based partnerships. In the case of GSM, the constitutional problems were mostly of a *structural* nature, and easily remedied by careful attention to the details of implementation. Other problems—those that are *substantive*—are more problematic because they entail the utilitarian application of religion for advancement of secular goals. This is less of a problem for welfare-to-work programs than for programs of a transformative nature, where religion is at the core of the services. Moreover, these substantive concerns implicate the religious dimension that some say is at the heart of the success of faith-based programs in realizing government's secular objectives. The problems of PZ were primarily structural. Looking at GSM some years later, it appears to have learned from its earlier experiences. The learning curve of GSM indicated that faith-based agencies can mature into sophisticated and savvy entities able to hold their own in a partnership with the state, and able to assist others in that endeavor as well.

■ Good Samaritan and Project Zero—Ottawa County Style

Well before the national faith-based movement surfaced in 1996, isolated states had recognized the role of faith-based nonprofits in social service delivery. As early as 1981, Michigan had explicitly acknowledged a role for faith-based organizations in its antipoverty efforts (Davis 2004, 2). In the 1990s, Michigan aggressively pursued welfare policy innovation under Republican governor John Engler, implementing tough welfare reform built around themes of strengthened families, personal responsibility, self-sufficiency, and community involvement.

The Initial Launching of the Project Zero Pilot

As charitable choice legislation materialized on the federal level, Michigan was renewing its welfare to work efforts. This included Project Zero, a pilot program instituted by Michigan's Family Independence Agency (FIA) in six counties across the state. The stated goal of the program was to reduce to zero the number of Aid to Families with Dependent Children (AFDC) households within each pilot site who were without earned income. Within a year, the program had yielded impressive results. As the pilot neared the end of its first year in the spring of 1997, state officials announced that in Ottawa County, a sleepy, conservative pocket nestled in the southwestern corner of Michigan, the stated goal had been accomplished, and every single AFDC family had realized some earned income. Those results earned Ottawa County widespread exposure, as the *Wall Street Journal* (1997), *USA Today* (1997), the *Washington Post* (1997), and other national media outlets trumpeted its success.

Project Zero's Community and Faith-Based Emphasis

Project Zero anticipated the Bush faith-based policy's dual emphases on faith and community in delivery of social services. At each pilot site, FIA staff were encouraged to identify the most pressing barriers to employment in their region and to devise solutions to fit that specific population. In particular, they were urged to stress the inclusion of community resources for support. Those counties initially selected for PZ—in Detroit, the Upper Peninsula, southwestern Michigan—were distinct. Among the initial PZ sites, a host of differences—in culture, economy, politics, and ethnic and demographic makeup—suggested that the causes and effects of welfare might also differ. Thus PZ adopted versatile and flexible strategies to address the needs of the welfare clientele, and how best to move them into the work force in their communities.

But PZ went beyond merely enlisting community resources and support; it also included an explicit faith-based element that dovetailed with charitable choice. Michigan welfare policy acknowledged faith-based organizations and sought to recruit them as active partners. The FIA admitted that "many of the problems identified as barriers to self-sufficiency are beyond the ability of the FIA to resolve alone" and noted the "need to be more creative in [its] approach to resolving these issues by reaching out to the community and their faith-based organizations for help." It identified a variety of social ills that compelled the involvement of faith-based organizations—teen pregnancy, divorce and domestic violence, child and day care, and welfare. The FIA resolved to work closely with faith-based groups "to identify appropriate and supportive roles they can play in helping their community residents become self-sufficient" ("Michigan's Block Grant Proposals" 1996).

The Contractual Arrangement Between Ottawa County FIA and Good Samaritan

This faith-based emphasis was evident in the first Project Zero plans, as three of the six initial sites focused their community support efforts on private, faith-based organizations. In Ottawa County, it took the form of a $100,000 contract to GSM to recruit and train volunteers from local churches to serve as mentors for those on welfare. GSM was based in Holland, a city of some 35,000 residents and located at the southern end of the county. Of special interest to the county was GSM's relational ministry, through which it enlisted and trained teams of parishioners from local churches to furnish struggling families with budget and financial advice, emotional and spiritual support, and more.

Ottawa County previously had worked with GSM, having referred clients to it for assistance. That prior working relationship led FIA director Loren Snippe to directly solicit GSM's involvement in the PZ pilot. Project Zero was not opened to bids or a grant application process. Rather, an exclusive contract was extended to GSM to establish a mentoring program for the county. Under the contract, GSM recruited and trained volunteers from local churches to mentor welfare clients on any and all obstacles they might face in obtaining and keeping a job. The training included such topics as housing, financial management, transportation, child care, house and car repairs, employment referrals, résumé and interview preparation, and grooming. Mentoring was not required of welfare recipients, but was voluntary. PZ families were given the option of participating in the GSM mentoring program. No alternatives were provided. Those who took part expressed a denominational preference, for which GSM would find a match. Participants were under no obligation to attend worship or structured religious activities.

Encountering Problems: GSM's Relational Ministry in Practice

Close scrutiny of GSM revealed significant church-state problems. The organization's mentor training and promotional materials and the comments of then-director Bill Raymond revealed a distinctive Christian message at its core. GSM openly acknowledged strategies that encompassed a sharing of faith that almost certainly ran afoul of charitable choice and established church-state limits. GSM's printed material persuasively argued for the freedom of faith-based organizations to operate in the realm of social service. But it should have raised red flags for the county. According to GSM:

> The church is not just an extension of the social service system and true change will not occur if all that happens is that the church is co-opted in the service of the state. . . . The church can extend what social services does, but the effectiveness of the church is directly tied to its ability to speak to spiritual realities and the role God plays in an individual's life. The good news is more than good casework. (GSM 1997, sec. 4, p. 14)

This philosophy clearly played out in GSM's relational mentoring approach, which had as its intended ultimate conclusion a spiritual objective. By GSM's own admission, its strategies were evangelical in nature, to equip Christian mentors and volunteers "to model the life and Lordship of Christ and *to present the Good News of Christ in word* and deed ministry to the community" (GSM 1997, sec. 1, p. 3, emphasis added). GSM's involvement in PZ was "a way for church members to . . . share the good news of Jesus Christ with welfare families." Mentoring was to be "holistic—concern[ing] physical, emotional, [and] *spiritual well-being*" (GSM 1997, sec. 3, p. 1, emphasis added). Spiritual support was an essential means of helping and servicing the client.

The informational materials did suggest that religious counseling would happen only when "requested and appropriate." But the dominant message contradicted this limitation. The building of an ongoing relationship between mentor and client was to culminate in "an enfolding of the family into the friendship circle of the church or people in the church" (GSM 1997, sec. 4, p. 23). Mentors were "free to share their faith and deal with spiritual issues" in a spirit of friendship. Indeed, the object of relational ministry was to build "an honest, caring relationship that allows for the communication of the claims of Christ in both word and deed" (GSM 1997, sec. 5, p. 24). Mentoring was meant to lead to "opportunit[ies] for church members to share their faith in word and deed ministry" (GSM 1997, sec. 4, p. 2). It was to nurture a level of trust and familiarity between mentor and client over time, to allow for the open and explicit sharing of faith.

Project Zero as implemented in Ottawa County in 1997 presented a serious conflict with church-state constraints and charitable choice. Indeed, GSM's practices paralleled contradictions in the charitable choice statute. On one hand, charitable choice is careful to specify that no government funds are to be spent for sectarian worship, instruction, or proselytization (U.S. Congress 1996). The Ottawa County–GSM contract echoed that language, banning proselytization. On the other hand, charitable choice protects religious organizations participating in governmentally sponsored programs from being forced to alter, mute, or eliminate the practice or expression of religious belief (U.S. Congress 1996). Likewise, GSM appeared unrestrained by acceptance in fully practicing and expressing its religious purpose. Its printed materials exhorted governmental agencies to let faith-based participants pursue their "spiritual/ministry perspective and motivation" (GSM 1997, sec. 4, p. 14).

The spirit underlying charitable choice likewise suggests an intrinsic tension. Even while it is careful to prohibit the use of funds for religious dissemination, its empowering of religious groups in social welfare programs is founded on a tacit acknowledgment of the transforming power of religion. Yet the attributes of religious organizations to remedy behavioral dysfunction do not warrant greater involvement in social service delivery unless at some point, in some way, the underlying religious belief or message is shared with the program beneficiary. Contrary to its specific language, then, charitable choice presumes a degree of witnessing of faith.

GSM's mentoring program embodied this tension. It implied that recipients of mentoring could only truly turn their lives around once they were instructed in spiritual and religious truths. The secular benefits of productivity and work were to be achieved only when accompanied by spiritual transformation. Unsurprisingly, then, the PZ materials of GSM clearly contemplated a place for the sharing of faith between mentor and client:

- Mentors earned "the right to be heard" and engage in "friendship evangelism."
- The mentoring relationship was described as "social outreach and evangelism."
- GSM explicitly warned that "social services need to understand that faith conversations will take place between church volunteers and welfare families."
- Volunteer mentors were expressly encouraged to "spiritually engage people and share their hope in Christ." (GSM 1997, sec. 4, p. 9)

The director of GSM at the time, Bill Raymond, described it this way:

> We do not want to force people into any kind of church attendance, religious observance, Bible study against their will. But . . . families on welfare are fully capable of making informed choices based on the leading of God in their lives. As they develop a relationship with individuals from a local church, it is quite conceivable that they will choose to get involved in some type of religious activity. They are free to do that. We also take it maybe a step further and say "the church volunteers are free to live out their faith with word and deed, and not only demonstrate it by actions, but verbally talk about it with families without violating the separation of church and state." (Raymond 1998)

Whether practices such as those advocated by GSM would be found to violate charitable choice ultimately will depend upon judicial determinations of what constitutes proselytization. But the dictionary definition of *proselytization* indicates an effort to "induce someone to convert to one's faith" (*Webster's*

1996). GSM made no apologies for training its mentors to do precisely this. The goal of its relational ministry, to share the Gospel, would appear to rise to the level of proselytization.

■ The Constitutionality of Project Zero: When Policy and the Constitution Collide

Fundamental differences of opinion persist as to the correct interpretation of the First Amendment. The perceived constitutional viability of faith-based programs will depend much on how strictly or loosely one reads the establishment clause and the degree of separation it imposes. Yet even under a generous reading of the clause, Ottawa County's implementation of PZ was afflicted with clear constitutional defects, and would unlikely have survived a test in court.

Balancing Policy Effectiveness with Constitutional Demands

A brief look at the tripartite *Lemon* test that traditionally provides the general constitutional framework for establishment queries reveals the difficulties.[2] The first prong, the presence of a legitimate secular purpose, is easily satisfied, given the goal of moving welfare recipients to work. The constitutional failings arise at the intersection between the second and third prongs, and the tension that lies therein. Those criteria simultaneously require that the primary effect of the state action neither advance nor inhibit religion *and* that the program not foster excessive entanglement between government and religion. PZ illustrates the difficulty of satisfying one without breaching the other. Ottawa County took pains to avoid excessive entanglement with GSM, keeping its regulatory oversight to a minimum. Given their working familiarity with GSM, county officials were comfortable adopting this posture. But that hands-off approach gave unfettered freedom to GSM and its mentors to mix the spiritual and the secular, to the point where it imperiled the middle prong of the *Lemon* test.

Project Zero illustrates the competing pulls of policy and constitutional considerations. Often it is precisely what enhances the policy effectiveness of a given program that creates the legal problems. That which makes church-state partnerships attractive as a legitimate policy mechanism is their constitutional Achilles heel. Religious nonprofits are appealing precisely because of their creativity in using alternative means of program delivery to fit local communities and individual clients. Yet the constitutional constraints in the form of government regulation dampen the autonomy and innovation responsible for success of religiously affiliated and other nonprofit organizations.

Bill Raymond, the director of GSM, claimed the Ottawa County program worked so well because the county kept its governmental hands off GSM's operations and strategies. Both the county and the state gave GSM leeway to best determine the paths to pursue its policy objectives, with minimal regulatory and oversight burden. According to Raymond, these governmental burdens are what strip a religious organization of its unique ability to effectively offer life-transforming services. The county's deference to GSM was attributable to a long-established working relationship and a level of trust in the organization to achieve successful outcomes. But the hands-off nature of the relationship was problematic from a constitutional point of view. Ottawa County's aversion to micromanaging GSM raised serious theoretical and practical legal questions.

The county's inattentiveness allowed GSM and its mentoring churches to permit the overt sharing of faith. The ambiguities in charitable choice and establishment clause doctrine questions demanded closer governmental supervision until charitable choice was defined and clarified. It remains to be seen whether this can be accomplished without compromising the unique effectiveness of faith-based programs.

Religious Advancement

Holding PZ up to the light of *Lemon* suggests constitutional weaknesses from a variety of perspectives. The establishment clause does not allow public funds for the *advancement of religion.* Yet this is precisely what GSM's mentors were urged to do. A strong likelihood existed that PZ funds would in fact result in the advancement of religion by the state. GSM's expectation was that the religious convictions of its mentors would be interwoven with the secular job-related mentoring. The organizational philosophy evinced a perceptible promotion of religious conversion via a program subsidized by the government. PZ, as interpreted and implemented by GSM, presented a distinct possibility that religion would be advanced, directly or indirectly, through the use of government funds.[3] The result was a serious problem under the establishment clause.

Denominational Favoritism

A second weakness with PZ was *the absence of denominational neutrality and evenhandedness,* as a result of the exclusivity of the relationship between Ottawa County and GSM. One aspect of the establishment clause is clear: the government cannot favor one religion, denomination, or faith over another. Yet this is precisely what Ottawa County did. Based on the its familiarity with GSM's programs linking families to church support teams, Ottawa County approached GSM to solicit its formal participation in PZ. The process was exclusionary. There was no bidding or solicitation of applications from other organizations. Its sole focus was on GSM. The consequence, whether or not intentional, was a policy skewed in favor a particular religious entity.

GSM is an explicitly Christian organization. While it is ecumenical and works with a range of denominations within the Christian community, it did not include Jewish, Muslim, or other faiths. Given the decidedly Christian cast to the network of churches working with GSM, it might well convey a message of governmental preference for the Christian faith over others, especially since alternatives were not offered.

Favoring the Religious over the Secular

Likewise, PZ ran afoul of the constitutional requirement of *evenhandedness between the secular and the religious*. In short, it favored religion over nonreligion in sponsored services. By its very terms, the contract between GSM and the FIA was skewed in favor of religious organizations. The services were specifically designated to occur within the context of faith. GSM was contractually obligated to match clients with providers of "faith-based mentoring services," to specifically "recruit faith-based organizations to assume responsibility for family support services for referred FIA clients" (GSM 1997, sec. 4, p. 1). Consequently, GSM limited its recruitment for mentors to Christian churches in the area. The absence of any secular organizations indicated a preference for the religious over the secular and was an unacceptable establishment of religion.

The Absence of Choice

Charitable choice specifies that beneficiaries who object to the provision of services from a religious organization need not be denied the services. The government must make available a comparable secular alternative for those recipients who want to avoid the religious context for services. Those who desire mentoring ought not to have to choose between mentoring from religious sources or none at all. The element of choice is central to the protection of the religious liberty of program beneficiaries, though it no doubt imposes heavier burdens in resources required. Neutrality requires the option of a secular equivalent to faith-based providers of authorized services.

In contrast to Ottawa County's failure to furnish an alternative secular provider to GSM, neighboring Kent County, which was added to the expanded Project Zero program the following year, took specific measures to remedy these inequities. Kent County, which includes Michigan's second largest city, Grand Rapids, erected a mentoring program that resembled Ottawa County's in many ways. But while predominantly religious in orientation, the program was constructed to include diverse faiths and several that were not explicitly faith-based. The mentoring was coordinated through the Grand Rapids Area Center for Ecumenism (GRACE), a faith-based umbrella organization. In addition to mainline Protestant denominations, Catholic parishes, the Christian Reformed faith, and fundamentalist churches, there were ministerial associations specifically aimed at African American and Hispanic minorities, a Jewish temple, and organizations without a specific faith identity. GRACE went much further to ensure a menu of faith orientations, including non-Christian mentoring options.

Project Zero and the Neutrality and Endorsement Standards

The *Lemon* test has received its share of criticism, while weathering countless efforts to cast it aside. But PZ would not likely have survived scrutiny under alternative theories of establishment clause doctrine. Under the neutrality approach favored by several justices (*Mitchell v. Helms* 2000), the state could enact policies whereby benefits go toward religious activities, provided governmental assistance is dispensed on a neutral basis and offered equally to all religious groups as well as to religious and nonreligious groups. Others have posited a similar rule of "positive neutrality" that would permit religious organizations to receive public funds provided similar or parallel programs of alternative religious and secular natures are also publicly supported (Monsma 1996, 44, 178). The Ottawa County PZ program as structured and implemented would have failed this proposed neutrality test. The county's solicitation of GSM and the exclusive contract do not approximate "equal access" to participation in the mentoring program, either for non-Christian religious organizations or for secular associations.

For similar reasons, the Ottawa County mentoring arrangement would have encountered trouble under Justice Sandra Day O'Connor's "endorsement" test (*Lynch v. Donelly* 1984). An exclusive contracting arrangement between the county and GSM connotes an endorsement of that organization's religious identity. When the contract dictates that the nonprofit only recruit churches and Christians to serve as mentors, it smacks of governmental endorsement of Christianity over other faiths and over the nonreligious.

■ That Was Then, This Is Now: Lessons from the Good Samaritan Experience

The Ottawa County Project Zero program was never legally challenged. Nor were there complaints from participants that religion was being forced on them by well-intentioned but misguided mentors. So why engage in a post hoc judgment about a relatively insignificant welfare assistance program some five years after the fact?

GSM has aggressively, and successfully, pursued bigger and better avenues of public funding under the Bush faith-based initiative. Another $500,000 Compassion Capital Fund grant was awarded for 2004–2005. In June 2004, GSM received another federal grant of $128,000, this time from the Corporation for National and Community Service to fund an AmeriCorps after-school mentoring program (Robbins 2004). Finally, GSM has been identified by the federal government as one of a handful of intermediary organizations nationwide on the cutting edge of faith-based service delivery. As a result, it is being held up by the federal faith-based office as a model partner.

It is crucial, therefore, that past practices inform present circumstances, for GSM *and* its public partner, as well as for others considering faith-based partnerships. Broader lessons can be gleaned from GSM's experiences, past and present, to better ensure that ventures between faith-based organizations and government are undertaken on solid constitutional footing.

The Structure/Substance Dichotomy

Project Zero may well have failed a legal challenge if it had faced one. The focus on evangelism in the mentor training, the emotional vulnerability of those receiving services, the exclusivity of the relationship between Ottawa County and GSM—all of these combined to suggest significant constitutional defects in the county version of PZ.

In thinking about how to remedy the constitutional problems in PZ, it is helpful to identify two distinct sets of constitutional issues, those pertaining to *structural* weaknesses, and those regarding *substantive* concerns. The structural category included organizational aspects of the program that undermined principles such as neutrality, equal access, and evenhandedness. The partnership lacked an objective bidding process. The mentoring was exclusively run through GSM without offering any alternatives.

These structural flaws are relatively easy to remedy. They simply require that procedural protections be built into a program to ensure fidelity to constitutional values. Values of equal access and nonendorsement are answered by crafting a grant process that includes a variety of grantees, from different faith traditions and from none at all. The religious liberties of program enrollees are protected by ensuring that programs offer an array of choices through a menu of providers from whom to choose. Clear opt-out provisions advance free exercise and avoid establishment concerns by allowing one to avoid religious aspects of the program. In short, constitutional concerns of the structural sort can be alleviated through careful attention to detail as the program is implemented.

The substantive concerns are more problematic. They refer to those elements of a program that have a distinctive religious dimension, where religion itself is a substantive component of the services being provided. GSM's involvement in PZ presented substantive concerns, though the religious component did not necessarily dominate the program. There were important pieces to the mentoring that had nothing to do with religion (counseling on family finances, job training, help with preparing for an interview, transportation). But the mentoring process had an undeniable religious twist to it, with its emphasis on religious witness.

Substantive concerns are more difficult to remedy, since they implicate the paradox that remains at the center of charitable choice and establishment clause doctrine. Does the Constitution allow public funding of a secular purpose through religious organizations employing means that also incidentally advance, promote, or involve religion? For GSM, it was the religious dimension that was to ensure the long-term effectiveness of its mentoring and other relationally based services. Welfare dependency was to be broken only through "the inward transformation of belief and character" (Sider and Rolland 1996, 463). For GSM and other faith-identified service providers, it is not an option to remove the religious facet for constitutional reasons. From their vantage point, effective administration of welfare programs necessitates a spiritual component. The sharing of religion is not just allowed; it is an imperative.

The crafters of PZ implicitly acknowledged religion as an important step toward realization of the secular objectives of welfare policy. The advancement of religion was ancillary to the advancement of the work objectives of the plan. The critical question is whether the inevitable extension of religion is constitutionally objectionable, given the success in achieving the secular purpose of reduced welfare dependency. Can the philosophy behind the undertaking to bring religious groups into the public policy arena be reconciled with the long-standing constitutional prohibition against the advancement or promotion of religion by government?

One reply is that as long as the requisite structural safeguards are in place, the substantive facets of the program ought not to matter constitutionally. Some argue that the substantive religious cast to a publicly funded program should not be objectionable as long as participants are notified of its religious nature, have secular alternatives, and are free to opt out of those religious activities. Others contend that publicly funded programs must have the obligatory structural procedures in place *and* be free of religious substance.

Intermediaries: Constitutional Bane or Blessing?

The GSM experience raises important constitutional questions related to the role of intermediary faith-based organizations. Intermediaries were a central focus of the Compassion Capital Fund as means of getting funds into the hands of smaller, grassroots nonprofits that are at the front line of serving the needy.

Those neighborhood-based groups often are unable realistically to obtain federal funds due to technical barriers—lack of staff, insufficient grant-writing expertise, inadequate organizational infrastructure. Intermediaries assist those grassroots organizations with the grant writing and technical assistance needed to secure and administer a federal grant.

But intermediaries present challenges for ensuring accountability and supervision of faith based partners of government. The delegation of welfare services to the private sector always poses something of a dilemma for the requirements of responsible, democratically accountable governance. It weakens formal channels of accountability, putting greater stress on the reliability of those processes through which oversight and supervision can be maintained. This challenge is amplified with faith-based privatization, since it includes the additional requirement of compliance with church-state strictures. In PZ, the contracting organization was intermediary between the state and the actual mentors. This made it more difficult to oversee the extent to which mentors might be proselytizing or evangelizing clients. The absence of complaints could be evidence of poor reporting or inadequate oversight or proof that no evangelizing was taking place.

On this issue, GSM now exhibits a much greater sensitivity to the church-state complications. Much of this is the tone set by the top of the organization. To former GSM director Bill Raymond, the intermediate structure of GSM was precisely what ensured that the GSM/PZ approach passed constitutional muster. Raymond argued that this buffer between public funds and ultimate service provision insulated the church and state from each other. Hence "state funding [does not] contaminate the church and what the church is free to engage in or not engage in. [And] the churches do not benefit directly; they don't have any direct reimbursement or direct funding through state money" (Raymond 1998). The implicit message is that GSM need not concern itself with what its mentors were doing to evangelize those in the PZ program.

Current director Janet DeYoung articulates a different organizational stance. GSM cannot proselytize, evangelize, or force faith on anyone when public funds are involved, and its training and interaction with faith-based actors reflects that. Religion is viewed more as a motivational force; the faith factor produces volunteers, who grow in their faith through their service to those in need. Mentors can share their faith naturally, when circumstances allow, but GSM plays no part in promoting that.

GSM also has grown more sophisticated in gauging the success of its publicly funded programs. PZ was trumpeted as a resounding success, but when pressed, DeYoung admitted that there was no way of determining long-term success, since there was no tracking of those who went through the PZ mentoring. In contrast, GSM recently contracted with the social science research center at the local college to conduct an empirical evaluation of its clients. It monitors them at various intervals to determine the extent to which mentoring has had a positive long-term impact on client functioning.

Multilevel Constitutional Analysis of Contracting Practices

Finally, GSM's involvement in publicly funded programs then and now illustrates how meeting constitutional standards is dependent upon practical details of implementation, such as governmental contracting practices. For example, the exclusivity of the original Ottawa County–GSM arrangement carried a message of governmental endorsement of a particular group and the religious faith associated with it. In contrast, the current Labor Department grants were awarded via a contract application process. They did not show a governmental preference for religion over secularism, since the GSM grant was only one of a number of awards that went to organizations of all stripes and colors, both religious and secular.

However, the government's contracting practices can be scrutinized constitutionally on multiple levels. The original PZ program was wanting on a micro level, as administered by a particular Michigan county. Questions also exist regarding GSM's use of the funds as an intermediary. It has passed on $250,000 in fourteen subgrants pursuant to a formal application process. Arguably, the government is constitutionally responsible for these contracting practices. Since those grants have gone almost exclusively to religious community organizations, some might argue that this represents a form of vicarious endorsement of religion by the government.

The other question pertains to the balance between religious and secular providers. The recipients of Labor Department grants are a diverse collection of religious and nonreligious entities, though the religious ones are predominantly Christian. The number of total grantees is perhaps too small to amount to an endorsement of Christianity over other religions. A better example might be Health and Human Services (HHS), which as of early 2004 had paid out $65 million from the Compassion Capital Fund to intermediaries. Again, there was balance between religious and nonreligious groups, but no non-Christian religious groups were among the thirty-two HHS grants nationwide (Page 2004). Several Jewish groups did receive grants, but only indirectly through intermediaries.

Does this violate the principle of nonendorsement? Does the grant making of HHS to intermediaries represent an establishment, not of religion over nonreligion, but of Christianity over Islam, Judaism, or other faiths? And does nonestablishment require proportional fairness in different faiths and denominations receiving funds? The constitutionality of the faith-based policy may depend on answers to these questions.

■ Conclusion

The partnerships between Good Samaritan Ministries and government are helpful reminders that, as faith-based initiatives move forward, inspiring and creative policy ideas must be accompanied by careful attention to the mundane details of implementation. Those on both sides of the contracting equation must heed the need for structural safeguards to ensure sound constitutional footing. Meanwhile, important questions remain as to what substantive religious social services ought not to be advanced with public funds. The establishment clause boundaries of permissible faith-based programs will become clear, but likely not without the passage of time and significant judicial activity.

■ Notes

1. The descriptive information on GSM is taken primarily from its website, http://www.goodsamministries.com. I also interviewed current executive director Janet DeYoung on May 14, 2004, and her predecessor, Bill Raymond, in 1998.

2. The three-part test from *Lemon v. Kurtzman* (1971) required that government funds (1) be intended for a legitimate secular purpose, (2) have a primary effect which neither advances nor inhibits religion, and (3) not result in an excessive entanglement between religion and government.

3. GSM's participation in PZ illuminates some of the problems with church-state doctrine, especially the "pervasive sectarianism" standard for permissible public funding of religious institutions. The Ottawa County–GSM contract had a legitimate secular purpose of moving people into the work force. But that secular purpose was bound up in a religious purpose of testifying to the Gospel of Jesus Christ. GSM's relational ministry was premised on the belief that people will not escape dependency unless and until they experience a spiritual transformation. GSM viewed its responsibility to address both facets in a holistic fashion. For GSM, conveying spiritual truths and values was essential to the secular goals of responsibility and self-sufficiency. Religious and nonreligious strategies and practices were intertwined, equal parts of the character and mission of GSM. Good Samaritan Ministries arguably fit the description of a "pervasively sectarian" organization disqualified from securing public money.

5 A Church-Based Welfare-to-Work Partnership

HEIDI ROLLAND UNRUH AND
JILL WITMER SINHA

The history of Cookman United Methodist Church is a common one among urban churches of the mid–twentieth century. Cookman, built to serve an Anglo working-class population, thrived in the booming postwar industrial economy. The church's impressive architecture, ornate woodwork, and soaring ceiling exuded the confidence and upward aspirations of its members. All that changed in the 1960s and 1970s. Like so many others, Cookman's neighborhood was devastated by "white flight," loss of industry, crack cocaine and heroin, increasing violence, redlining, and decaying city infrastructure. The congregation dwindled to a handful of Anglo church members who commuted for Sunday worship, driving through predominantly poor, African American neighborhoods. The rest of the week, the large stone edifice stood empty, with its doors locked. One Sunday in the 1970s, a black activist group stormed into the service and chained themselves to the altar, refusing to leave until the church opened itself to the community. That was the original congregation's last service.

After several years, the church reopened with eight attendees from the neighborhood, as an energetic young pastor slowly began rebuilding a congregation. In 1992, Reverend Donna Jones became the church's first African American (and first woman) pastor. Since then, Cookman has developed a reputation as a church that serves the community through such ministries as after-school nutrition programs, community dinners, and an informal counseling program.

In 1997, Reverend Jones and others grew increasingly concerned about the impact of welfare reform and felt compelled to respond. They discovered that welfare reform made it easier for government to work with congregations and faith-based nonprofits to provide services to families on public assistance. Several members of Cookman attended a conference in Harrisburg sponsored by the Pennsylvania Department of Public Welfare. Reverend Jones became active in meetings sponsored by the Metropolitan Christian Council of Philadelphia to organize churches' response to welfare reform. One option was through a funding program launched by the state welfare department called Community Solutions.

Cookman Church sought the help of faith-based nonprofit consultants. Reverend Jones and a small team of supporters—including several former welfare recipients—developed a proposal to train and place thirty hard-to-employ welfare recipients over a three-year period. The state shocked the church by awarding it a $150,000 contract. Cookman's overtly faith-based approach was a plus, setting it apart from other religiously affiliated applicants. Sherri Heller, deputy secretary of the Pennsylvania Department of Public Welfare, explained the state's shift in openness to faith-based service providers:

> What does it really take for a young single mother to get up at 6:00 in the morning and put a toddler in a snow suit and stand at the bus, and go to an entry-level job? The answer is they have to be inspired by something, by someone. For some people, it's a vision of a better future; for some people, it's caring about their children's future; for some people, it's faith in God. (*Lehrer News Hour* 1999)

■ Program Description

Cookman's state-funded program, Transitional Journey Ministry (TJM), was initially designed for welfare recipients facing multiple barriers to employment who had not found work in their first attempt. The Community Solutions contract ran from 1998 to 2000, with state funds supplemented by small denominational and foundation grants. This chapter focuses on the first three years of TJM's experience with state funding.

TJM included job preparation services (such as teaching participants how to dress for a job interview or use public transportation), job placement and retention support services, graduate equivalency diploma (GED) preparation, computer training, life skills education, and a confidence-building self-esteem class. Participants also had access to a church-sponsored food and clothing pantry. All program activities took place on church property.

Explicitly religious activities were an integral part of the program, including daily morning devotionals, group prayer times, weekly worship services, and a spiritual development class that explained Christian teachings and invited clients to make a faith commitment. The program also tried to match graduates with volunteer mentors from various churches. The state required that these spiritual components be privately funded and voluntary. Clients signed waivers stating that they were aware of its Christ-centered nature and of their right to opt out of religious activities. Even in its secular program components, however, TJM maintained a clearly religious atmosphere. The self-esteem class, for example, used a book that refers to God and faith in a general sense (but that was not specifically Christian), and the teacher allowed students to initiate and lead the group in prayer (though she herself did not introduce prayer).

The informal, relational dimensions of TJM were as important as its formal program components in addressing the emotional and spiritual needs of clients. The handbook indicated the program's relational approach: "If you have any special needs or problems and you need prayer, . . . [i]f you need someone to talk to or you just need a hug, we are here and we want to help you." Clients would often contact staff for support outside program hours. As staff developed relationships with clients, they would sometimes give spontaneous spiritual counseling or offer to pray with clients. Most TJM staff were Christians, though not all attended Cookman United Methodist.

TJM was candid with prospective clients about its religious motivations and identity. A TJM brochure introduced the ministry as "a Christ-centered job development program." The program, however, did not discriminate against clients based on their faith, but rather sought to create an atmosphere open to all faith traditions. TJM initially attracted most of its students through recruiting fairs at which TJM represented itself as a Christian program. The first year, most clients selected the program out of necessity—it was close by, they needed the computer training, or it was the only program that would take them. In subsequent years, more clients said they chose the program because of its religious orientation.

Because the church had no prior experience with welfare-to-work programs or government contracting—and because the state had no prior experience in collaborating with a church—the learning curve was steep. The church and the state began with differing interpretations of charitable choice and expectations for the relationship. Along the way, the state demanded significant changes in the program, which led the church to reconsider the value of working with the state. However, TJM negotiated a set of program operations satisfactory to the state while allowing the program to maintain its faith-centered approach. TJM's story thus offers an illuminating case study of the promise and perils of charitable choice.

Administrative Issues

TJM experienced significant administrative challenges to implementation of the state contract, relating to funding, facilities, case management documentation, and incorporation status. These challenges arose primarily from its small size, inadequate resource base, inexperience, and lack of preparedness. While these concerns do not raise constitutional questions, they point out how practical and philosophical issues are intertwined at the grassroots level.

The first challenge related to TJM's contract as requiring "outcome-based" as opposed to "fee-for-service" payments. Under outcome-based contracts, service providers are paid after they fulfill the goals or deliver the expected results of the contract. This created a cash-flow crisis for the program, which had little additional funding or reserves. As a result, some staff went for months without a proper salary. The church had to ration payments to staff as personal emergencies arose. Only the extraordinary commitment and faith of the staff kept them working diligently without pay. Reverend Jones describes how they got by initially, "surviving on prayer and faith."[1] She now advises other faith-based programs not to apply for state funds without substantial reserves to cover start-up costs.

TJM's financial struggles were compounded when state payments were late. When planning the budget, TJM drew on a compensation time line suggested by state officials. But things did not go as planned. Jones explains, "We were inexperienced and naive and believed them, and planned on that pay schedule. Unfortunately, since [the state] is a bureaucracy, it ended up being a longer amount of time. That created significant challenges for us."

Problems with the facilities—overcrowded classrooms, shortages of computers and supplies, excessive heat, poor restroom facilities—also were a major source of client complaints about the program. Initially, the church was not required to make renovations for the program. It was understood that churches did not have to meet the same building standards as professional for-profit or nonprofit organizations. But after inspections, a state supervisor deemed the church classrooms unacceptable and decreed that the program furnish new carpeting. Already behind budget, TJM did not have the money for this expense. Eventually some program money was used for carpet, furniture, and desks, a change appreciated by the clients.

A third administrative challenge was paperwork. Initially, staff failed to document case management correctly, leading to financial penalties. What TJM considered case management would frequently transpire through informal contacts with clients. Spontaneous conversations, phone calls, home and hospital visits, and other unscheduled meetings were regular features of TJM-client interactions, but were not documented. To get credit for case management, staff had to set up a detailed filing system. Though they did adapt, staff complained that onerous paperwork requirements decreased both the actual interaction with clients and the quality of their relationships. Reverend Jones struggled to maintain the church's distinct identity while meeting the state's regulatory expectations, insisting, "We're not a bureaucracy. We're a church."

Finally, TJM wrestled with incorporation. Several of the twenty-three agencies in Philadelphia that received funding under Community Solutions were faith-based, but Cookman was the only church. Its decision to administer the contract as a church rather than separately incorporate was both practical and principled. At the time, the church simply lacked the time to apply for

501(c)(3) status (as a separately incorporated, affiliated nonprofit organization meeting the requirements of Section 501[c][3] of the Internal Revenue Code). Also, as TJM's fiscal officer explained, "When the proposal was written we wanted to make a statement. We wanted to let them know that the church still cares and is very much involved." Once the program was in place, TJM pursued incorporation, hoping to bring several outreach ministries together under one administrative umbrella called Neighborhood Joy Ministries. Midway through the process, however, the application met bureaucratic delays and was withdrawn. Ultimately, TJM hoped to send a message to the congregation and the community that meeting the needs of struggling people is the business of the church.

Programmatic Issues

Despite the state's desire to include faith-based programs in its service provision network, there was disagreement at first over what "faith-based" meant, and little guiding precedent. As described below, some policies were developed through trial and error.

Expenditures on religious elements. One early source of confusion was whether Bibles could be purchased as a class text using state funds. Staff believed that TJM, as an overtly faith-based program with devotions and worship as part of its curriculum, could purchase Bibles for students. They assumed that, since the Bibles were going to be used for the nonsectarian purposes of GED preparation and not just for religious instruction, there was no conflict. However, the program's state monitor informed them that no government money could be expended for Bibles. Fortunately for TJM, a private contributor stepped forward to cover the cost of the Bibles.

The prohibition against expenditures of public funds for religion did not, in TJM's case, restrict the religious dimensions of staff job descriptions. State funds could not be used to compensate staff time spent on explicitly religious activities. Because TJM's contract was performance based, staff reimbursement was based on secular activities aimed at achieving student performance standards. Some staff who provided secular program services took part in the optional religious activities, but were not paid direct compensation for this time. Thus TJM's math and English teacher taught the faith development class and helped at the church's after-school program (neither of which was funded by the state). This arrangement might well skirt some constitutional concerns; staff's capacity to conduct religious activities with clients certainly benefited *indirectly* from public funding even though they were not paid directly for these activities. Moreover, staff still had *informal* religious interactions with clients on secular program time, though religious and secular components were formally segregated. Cookman's pastor, to avoid church-state entanglements, accepted no state funds and worked with the program solely in a volunteer capacity.

Religious program component. Reverend Jones initially interpreted charitable choice to allow TJM to integrate religious components as it saw fit as long as it was overt and upfront in its religious orientation. TJM assumed that clients exercised their choice in their selection of a faith-based program. As one staff member noted: "People have a choice to come here or not, and therefore whoever comes can be in a religious class. We have free rein to offer it." While TJM did not require clients to attend religious programming, the option of nonparticipation was not highlighted unless someone specifically requested it.

In response to a complaint that the program was too religious, the state program monitor, Bryon Noon, required TJM to explicitly state that participation in religious activities was not required. Clients were entitled to know that they might choose to attend TJM but not partake in the faith-based components. Additionally, TJM had to provide "equal and separate training" for those who chose not to participate in religious activities. Previously, clients who objected to participating in a religious activity had been allowed to leave early. TJM now had to plan alternative secular activities.

The TJM handbook was modified to comply with this policy, informing clients of the spiritual components in more detail and in bold letters:

- Please note that the spiritual component of this program is NOT MANDATORY. You do not have to participate in prayer, Sisters of Faith or the Friday Service.
- If you choose not to participate, another spiritual or non-spiritual activity will be provided.
- You are not permitted to leave the program early or come in late due to spiritual activities.

Clients entering the program signed waivers affirming their awareness of its Christ-centered nature and their right to substitute other educational activities for the religious components. This disclaimer was reviewed verbally during the orientation. While most participated in religious activities, some did avail themselves of this right. A Muslim client, for example, opted for computer training in place of spiritual development class. She had chosen TJM specifically because it was faith-based and staff gave her space to say the prayers required by her faith. She commented, "I come here and get the benefits without compromising myself. They respect me and I respect them" (quoted in John-Hall 1999, 607). No further complaints were received.

Termination policies. A significant conflict arose over the state's policy of terminating clients who miss ten days of the program, regardless of the reason. TJM staff objected to the strict termination policy, complaining that it was unrealistic given the stressful and chaotic conditions of clients' lives.

Knowing that termination could result in the sanctioning of welfare benefits, TJM preferred to implement the attendance requirement more flexibly, taking into account special situations such as abuse, child care failure, and illness. The state threatened to cancel the contract for TJM's failing to report absenteeism or drop noncompliant clients. In response, TJM revised the handbook to stress the mandatory termination policies and implemented stricter attendance documentation. Enforcing the state's policy changed the nature of the relationship with clients, placing staff more in the role of disciplinarians.

Nevertheless, TJM staff were reluctant to turn their backs on clients. Dropping clients without regard to their circumstances violated the message of Christlike love that TJM was trying to communicate through the program. In certain cases, TJM arrived at a compromise: it would follow the termination rule, but then immediately reenroll the client. Though this adversely affected TJM's outcomes and subsequently cost the program thousands of dollars in outcome-based payments, TJM was willing to absorb it to maintain a caring atmosphere informed by Christian values.

Welfare philosophy. Some of the tensions between TJM and the state reflected underlying differences in their approaches to welfare reform. In the church's view, the state's rigid work-first strategy limited the effectiveness of the program and compromised the dignity of clients. "The state is some abstract entity that looks at people as numbers," said TJM staffer Mae Slater. "The church should not." The staff of TJM entered the arena of welfare reform because they were concerned that the law could hurt vulnerable women; their experience with the welfare department did not convert them to the state's approach. An article in the *Philadelphia Inquirer* describes their critique of the state's welfare policies:

> The biggest drawback, Ms. Jones says, has been the state's unwillingness to let Cookman run the program in a way that she believes is most beneficial to the trainees. Cookman wants people to have at least three months of life-skills classes before they begin job-hunting; the state mandates that they seek jobs right away. The result, the pastor believes, is that people are placed in jobs they can't maintain because they aren't ready for them. "It has been a challenge because if they are offered a job right away, they have to take it," she says. "It's difficult, because most people coming to us aren't coming from the faith community, so you want to have that opportunity to offer the life skills, like parenting, self-esteem, job-readiness, to develop a relationship with God and spirituality. The way it is now, we don't have time to." (John-Hall 1999, 607)

To call attention to the new five-year benefit limit, state officials wanted TJM to put up posters with clocks and reminders in big red letters about the looming cutoff date for welfare benefits. TJM refused. In its assessment, women were not ignorant about the cutoffs, just angry. Likewise, Reverend

Jones expressed similar anger at "the inflexibility, the callous way that people are treated." She viewed the cutoffs as likely to cause a sense of failure and fatalism among clients.

Reverend Jones was convinced that the Pennsylvania welfare department's stance toward the needs of welfare recipients and the goal of self-sufficiency was unrealistic. She and TJM staff have been outspoken critics of the welfare system. Opponents of charitable choice worried that the receipt of state funds would muzzle the political views of faith-based agencies. But Cookman's status on the front lines of charitable choice in fact gave it more opportunity to weigh in on welfare reform and a more respected voice. The state neither penalized Cookman for its advocacy nor changed its policies. For the state, impartial and inflexible rules are a key to managing dozens of contracts with a range of private agencies. The state firmly believes that its work-first philosophy, while not perfect, will pay off for beneficiaries in the long run. TJM need not agree with the state's approach to welfare, but it must play by the state's rules to receive its money. Cookman accepted these conditions while maintaining a wary relationship with the government. As Reverend Jones insisted: "We don't work for the state."

■ Assessing the Role of the "Faith Factor"

TJM's track record, though not universally successful, compared favorably with other state-funded welfare-to-work programs, consistently improving over the term of the program. A thorough look at how the faith dimension of TJM contributed to its effectiveness would require more empirical analysis. Yet two factors appear significant. One is the emphasis on spiritual transformation for people in crisis. The other is the role of faith in staff motivation and interactions with clients. Faith of staff shaped the deeply relational nature of the program, cited as a strength by both clients and state evaluations. Client perceptions of the program revealed a generally positive view of the faith factor as a resource in helping them move toward self-sufficiency.

Spiritual Transformation

TJM demonstrates that a government-funded program can emphasize spiritual transformation as a means of realizing social objectives. Without violating the establishment clause, TJM as a faith-based program was uniquely equipped to supplement government welfare with "Christian principles and Christian values of hope, of personhood, because the government sometimes loses sight of persons, whereas [in] the church, our whole focus and mission is on the soul, is on the person." Clients' transition from welfare could be advanced both by job skills and spiritual resources. Said Reverend Jones:

> The Sisters of Faith curriculum that we use is trying to build that inner
> strength, so that when the stressors come, people have some tools that they
> can use to manage the stress—whether it is prayer, or reading, or meditation,
> or just going in the living room and screaming out to God . . . it's that cur-
> riculum that is going to sustain them when the kid is sick, the boss is calling,
> they have to work overtime, and they have to take the third shift. (*Lehrer
> News Hour* 1999)

Program monitor Bryon Noon concurs: "I think churches are in touch with
their population on a different level than those who are just in a training program. The spiritual connection may help the clients get past some of the other
barriers."

TJM's philosophy linked spirituality with personal empowerment. Its
spiritual vision, according to TJM staff, promoted self-sufficiency by impart-
ing moral direction, self-confidence, and hope for the future. The handbook
cover quoted a Bible passage: "I can do all things through Christ which
strengthens me" (Philippians 4:3). A passage in the handbook highlighted the
program's religious orientation: "We want you healed in your Spirit, mind
and body. We want you self confident and self-assured. We want you totally
prepared for, and able to participate in the world of work. We know with
God's help and your determination, you will succeed." Yet never did TJM
claim that *only* through faith in Christ could clients achieve self-sufficiency.
The program's success stories included clients who converted to Christian
faith and those with no interest in the spiritual message. Staff expected spiritual transformation to enhance program outcomes, but it was not required for
clients to benefit from the program's therapeutic and educational services.

TJM staff also differentiated between encouraging clients to make spiritual commitments and recruiting them to membership at Cookman. Some
clients did join the church. But Reverend Jones was concerned that the charitable choice prohibition on state funds for "sectarian worship, instruction, or
proselytization" prevented TJM from specifically promoting Cookman.
Hence she took pains to avoid the impression that her church was using government money to build its membership.

Staff

Bryon Noon, the program's state monitor, believed that TJM staff brought a
distinct set of strengths to the program:

> They've been helping people realize there's consequences to all your deci-
> sions and all your choices. . . . They're also bringing a lot of life experience
> relating to the ladies in one fashion or another. And I just think there's a lot
> of true caring going on—I think it's just a very supportive atmosphere. . . .
> They want to know how best to serve their clients and I think that's the
> strength of the program.

These attributes are certainly not limited to Christians. But the staff qualities of empathetic availability, dedication to client welfare, and a message of moral responsibility were unquestionably related to their religious convictions.

The faith of staff was also critical in sustaining a sense of ownership and purpose while adapting to the state's requirements. As one staff member stated, "I don't look at it as a job. I look at it as a ministry." Even as compliance with state regulations resulted in a loss of flexibility and affected the nature of staff-client relationships, the fundamental mission of the program remained. Staff held to their independent faith-based identity and resisted viewing themselves merely as an arm of the state.

Staff's religious commitments also served as a key program asset in motivating their willingness to work hard for little pay. Their shared faith inspired mutual support through a trying first year. Although the program did not make religious faith a criterion for employment, almost all the staff were Christians. Reverend Jones remarked, only partially in jest, that this was because only people who believed in the program's mission would be willing to put up with their job for long.

■ Client Perceptions of the Faith Factor

Overall, clients indicated that the staff's spirituality and the religious character of the program positively impacted their experience in the program. Spirituality was the facet that students most frequently identified as beneficial; it was cited as the most important factor in a third of the client evaluations. Clients remarked that at other agencies, they encountered angry or demoralizing attitudes. At TJM, clients reported that they felt respected and loved, and that staff conveyed a sense of compassion.

Clients also perceived that the spiritual nature of the program contributed to their confidence in their ability to realize personal goals. One program graduate wrote about the value of the religious dimension in her evaluation:

> I had a strong feeling that I would achieve a lot [at TJM]. What brings this feeling to me is the way that [we] start the day off with prayer. Remember without the Lord you won't get far. God is a good God, that's why I know if we have a positive attitude with school and the Lord we would get our GED, diploma, computer training, and learn how to be around people and remain friendly.

Another client reflected, "Learning about God helps you . . . it motivates you toward your education. I felt like if I like had God in my life before, it would have helped me more toward my education. It leaves you more at peace." Aside from the complaint that triggered the introduction of opt-out waivers for spiritual activities, no other client complained about the spiritual dimension of the program. Other aspects, however, did draw criticism. The program's 1998 annual report noted a decline in student morale "due to crowded class conditions, changes in staff, and poor physical environment" (TJM 1998). Positive perceptions of the faith-based aspects of the program were not sufficient to meet client expectations for program outcomes or to mitigate other shortcomings.

■ **Lessons from Transitional Journey Ministry**

TJM's welfare-to-work program illuminates the enormous potential and challenges of church-state collaborations. It is a matter of both practical concern and public policy that the issues surrounding charitable choice look different in actual operation than on the debate floor. This case study highlights lessons for the struggle over the interpretation, implementation, and possible expansion of charitable choice.

First, faith-based and community initiatives involve two distinct but related challenges: directing public funds to faith-based organizations *and* including grassroots agencies in government partnerships. Not all faith-based organizations are community-based; not all grassroots organizations are religious. In TJM's case, the two intersect. TJM shares with other publicly funded community groups concerns over building financial and administrative capacity, adjusting to bureaucratic demands and delays, negotiating for flexibility implementation, and raising principled objections to state welfare-to-work strategies. Policy deliberations should approach these faith-neutral issues differently than they approach matters that involve intrinsically religious questions. Yet even these regulatory issues can have religious implications. This was evident in TJM's conflict with the state over mandatory termination of absentee clients. TJM had to accept that it would not be regulated differently from other agencies simply because it was faith-based.

Another lesson is the central importance of staff who share in the religious mission of the organization. Their religious motivations helped sustain TJM staff through difficult times; these motivations also played a vital role in preserving the program's autonomous identity as an extension of the church rather than an arm of the government. Staff's faith commitments contributed to the caring, positive atmosphere perceived by clients. In programs that work intensively with needy populations, staff must be considered as more than the sum of their qualifications. TJM's identity and effectiveness rested on relational dimensions that transcended its programmatic components. Moreover, other ministries of the church drew on TJM staff for volunteer support. For organizations with finite resources, the ability to use staff in multiple roles, some of them explicitly religious, may be critical. These observations lend support to allowing faith-based organizations to retain their right to consider religion as a factor in employment decisions.

The religiosity of TJM staff was a product of self-selection rather than employment policy. Initially, the program had to scramble to find qualified people without the luxury of screening based on religion. While Reverend Jones doubts that many avowed atheists would want to work in the TJM environment, she intended that the program be welcoming to staff regardless of their faith. Two people who were not Christians who joined the staff did not object to the program's spiritual elements because they were voluntary. But *forcing* TJM to hire someone who rejected the program's core religious beliefs and mission would undoubtedly undermine the program.

Third, despite initial disagreements and misunderstandings, church and state were able to reach common understanding about the regulation of religious components. Using public funds for explicitly religious items or activities is prohibited, even when such purchases serve an ostensibly secular purpose. Clients are entitled to informed choice about participation in spiritual components. TJM's recruiter explained the importance of informing prospective clients about the program's religious environment:

> We are a Christ-centered job development program. We talk about being holistic and why we feel we need to be holistic in our approach to what we're doing. . . . I definitely let [prospective clients] know ahead of time what it is and who we are, because we want them to know. They have to make a choice of which program they want to go to. So we want them to know what they're coming to.

Bryon Noon clarified the state's position regarding making religious activities optional:

> If someone chooses not to use a Bible, then Cookman has to then use Huckleberry Finn or something else . . . or do the same type of work, just not with the Bible. If there's something specific in their program that they're offering, they have to provide that to someone who chooses not to participate in the faith-based component. . . . Even though it says Cookman United Methodist Church, [clients] can still choose to go there, but not choose to partake in the faith-based component.

For TJM, the First Amendment entitles clients to choice at two points: in the selection of programs based on full disclosure of their religious nature, and in their participation in specific religious activities of the program they have selected. If religion is built into program activities, clients who object to the religious dimension must be provided activities of equal educational or therapeutic value so that the goals of the program can still be realized. While spiritual transformation may be encouraged as a way of enhancing clients' ability to succeed, clients should be able to obtain the promised service without adopting the program's religious beliefs and practices. Moreover, the religious components must be privately funded, and offered in such a way that they do not carry a governmental imprimatur. Within this framework, faith-based organizations are free to express their religious identity by operating the program in a religious environment, by articulating the spiritual basis for their program, by engaging in informal religious discussions with willing clients, and by offering optional activities designed to provide clients with spiritual nurture and instruction. This strategy balances constitutional considerations with the potential of the spiritual dimension.

TJM's approach is consistent with the guidelines for faith-based organizations issued by the White House Office of Faith-Based and Community Initiatives, which state:

> A faith-based organization should take steps to ensure that its inherently religious activities, such as religious worship, instruction, or proselytization, are separate—in time or location—from the government-funded services that it offers. . . . [They] may not require program participants to attend or take part in any religious activities. Although you may invite participants to join in your organization's religious services or events, you should be careful to reassure them that they can receive government-funded help even if they do not participate in these activities, and their decision will have no bearing on the services they receive. (WHOFBCI 2003)

TJM's case, however, sheds light on the difficulty of interpreting the clause "sectarian worship, instruction, or proselytization" as phrased in charitable choice. Does "sectarian" refer to religious persuasion within a particular faith tradition, such as United Methodist? Or does it refer more broadly to any religious reference, requiring organizations to avoid religious speech altogether? TJM understood it to distinguish between optional program components that teach or express Christian faith and that are privately funded, and secular aspects of the program conducted in a religious atmosphere, which may be publicly funded and mandatory. TJM also distinguished between activities that are exclusively Christian and those that are spiritual in a more general sense. The self-esteem class, for example, used a book that was theistic but not specifically Christian. Staff encouraged clients to join *a* church, but not *their* church. Reverend Jones said she hoped that Muslim clients would become more devout Muslims through the program.

TJM thus avoided both a religiously saturated program and a religiously sanitized one. While this interpretation worked well for TJM, it illustrates the difficulty of allowing general religious speech while avoiding specific sectarian instruction or proselytization. The establishment clause was not intended to neuter all manifestations of religion in agencies that receive government funding. But the prohibition certainly precludes at least the promotion of a specific church affiliation or conversion experience. Somewhere in between, the balance between agencies' right to religious expression and government's prohibition against establishment of religion awaits fine-tuning.

Finally, all parties involved in a partnership—state welfare departments, faith-based organizations, and the people they serve—benefit from clear communication about their respective rights and responsibilities. For TJM, the early misunderstandings involving case management, payment schedules, and church-state issues might have been prevented had welfare department staff and TJM staff discussed their expectations in more detail. This is particularly important for faith-based organizations that are new to collaboration with government, as was Cookman.

■ Conclusion

Despite good intentions, building a church-state relationship can be an awkward process. Early in Transitional Journey Ministry's contract with the state, Reverend Jones discouraged other churches from following in Cookman's steps, asserting, "The State is not ready to partner with churches." TJM staff criticized the state bureaucracy and questioned its strategies. Likewise, welfare officials sometimes questioned whether TJM was capable of living up to its end of the deal. Both sides slowly learned to cooperate with the other.

Today, Reverend Jones supports faith-based initiatives under the protective structure of charitable choice. Were it not for the freedom allowed by charitable choice for TJM to create a program consistent with the congregation's beliefs, and using Christian staff, Reverend Jones doubts it would have been worth it. "Before, I never considered federal money because I felt it meant we couldn't maintain our religious integrity," she explains. "The gospel is liberating, and we're dealing with people who need to experience that freedom and hope" (John-Hall 1999, 607). The state's willingness to respect and value TJM's religious autonomy was critical to the success of the collaboration. So too was TJM's willingness to comply with charitable choice provisions protecting clients' religious freedom and to adapt to the state's bureaucratic demands. The positive relationship that TJM developed with its state program officers was also an important asset in navigating the tensions.

TJM's experience also suggests that the religious dimensions of the charitable choice issue are intertwined with more pragmatic variables. TJM strengths—accessibility to inner-city clients, a relational connection with the population being served, a staff dedicated to "ministry" over salary, an atmosphere that prioritizes people over bureaucracy—also led to struggles to develop financial and organizational capacity. As a small congregation of modest means, Cookman lacked the internal resources to support ministry on the scale of TJM. Its financial dependence on the government intensified the pressures of working out the church-state issues. If the government values the unique assets that inner-city faith-based institutions like Cookman bring, it must be prepared to respond to their unique capacity needs.

Programs like TJM demonstrate that potential exists for blending state-funded social services with church-based spiritual and emotional support, and that it can be done without compromising the church's religious identity or clients' First Amendment rights. The establishment clause does not prevent publicly funded religious groups from conducting social service programs consistent with their deeply held beliefs or from sharing those beliefs with clients, as long as the program maintains a distinction between government-sponsored and religious activities and gives clients a genuine choice about their participation. Charitable choice allowed Cookman to translate its religious beliefs into compassionate action for women struggling to make welfare reform work. Between concerns and ideals, their example illuminates the middle ground of the possible.

■ Notes

The information in this chapter was gathered through the Congregations, Communities and Leadership Development Project, a study of church-based community outreach in the Philadelphia area directed by Ronald J. Sider and Heidi Rolland Unruh and sponsored by Eastern University.

1. Unless otherwise noted, quotations are taken from public speeches, author interviews, and field observations by the authors.

PART 2

The First Amendment Rights of Religious Organizations

The establishment clause of the First Amendment is only half of the constitutional story of religion. Equally important is the admonition that Congress pass no law "prohibiting the free exercise" of religion. While they logically can be treated as separate clauses, more often they are seen as related. The battle then becomes, which clause is subordinate to the other? Persons sympathetic to religion tend to see the free exercise clause as controlling, while more secular thinkers tend to think the opposite. That certainly is true in the context of faith-based initiatives. Legislators and other public officials are constitutionally mandated to take care that the funding of religious social service providers not establish or promote religion. But when the public funding of religious organizations is accompanied by restrictions to guard against church-state violations, it raises the corollary concern that such restrictions might undermine the First Amendment rights of those recipient organizations to live out their faith as they choose.

Indeed, the original charitable choice law was an attempt to resolve this tension in favor of religious organizations. While containing assurances that faith-based programs were to be implemented consistent with the establishment clause, charitable choice focused on protecting the free exercise rights of funded organizations. The acceptance of funds was not to affect or compromise the group's structural or organizational autonomy. They were to remain free to display religious artwork and imagery. Their freedom to express themselves religiously could not be muffled. Their right to hire persons in agreement with their mission was protected. In short, their access to public money was not to weaken their First Amendment right to religious exercise.

As the case studies in Part Two make clear, charitable choice has hardly had the desired effect; to the contrary, the tension between nonestablishment and free exercise is as acute as before. The result of that tension has been litigation challenging the rights of religious organizations. Perhaps equally significant, the specter of litigation has had a chilling effect on decisions to move forward with faith-based governmental partnerships. In some instances, governmental demands that make a grant contingent on a religious group's giving up of certain religious practices or expression is enough to drive the religious organization away from the governmentally sponsored program. At other times, the organization's refusal to give up overt manifestations or symbols of its religious character or identity renders the grant-administering official unwilling to do business with the religious nonprofit.

The issues surrounding how broadly or narrowly religious organizational autonomy extends are particularly contentious. For some religious organizations, their religious identity and mission rest on the ability to hire only people who share their faith; similarly, the program may be eviscerated if employees or volunteers are not free to share the Gospel or include religious activities in their programs. These practices are often central to evangelical groups' reason for being. They cannot forfeit such defining elements without losing their identity or purpose. Prior to charitable choice, such groups felt compelled to forego public programs and dollars. If acceptance of public contracts or grants is conditioned upon the sacrifice of the religious identity or mission vital to these groups, it would mean a return to the pre-1996 status quo. In other words, the result would be once again to exclude that category of religiously infused organizations from publicly sponsored social services.

The aim of Part Two is to shine some reason on the free exercise side of the constitutional equation. It does so through two contributions that confront the most explosive facets of this area. In Chapter 6, John Orr takes a more careful look at the California Supreme Court decision that denied Catholic Charities the exemption from the statutory requirement that it furnish contraceptive coverage to its employees as part of their health care coverage. Orr finds in the decision disturbing implications for socially active religious organizations whose articles of faith contradict or diverge from state law. In Chapter 7, Melissa Rogers parses the complicated issue of how acceptance of public funds impacts the hiring rights of religious organizations. While admitting that there currently is no clear constitutional precedent on point, Rogers weaves together a multifaceted argument that funded groups *should not* constitutionally be able to limit hiring to those applicants who pass the faith or denomination litmus test—at least on the basis of case law. These chapters raise many of the key constitutional considerations in analyzing how free exercise rights apply to the faith-based initiative, sometimes directly and sometimes implicitly:

What is the legal status of the right of religious entities that are recipients of public money to base hiring decisions on faith or religious compatibility? Faith-based groups and public officials are being sent conflicting messages on this question. The George W. Bush administration has issued numerous executive orders and pushed subsequent regulations that would protect the hiring autonomy of religious groups that take federal funds. Similarly, a survey conducted by the Roundtable on Religion and Social Welfare Policy indicated that, of those states with data on this issue, about half allowed faith-based contractors to make faith-based hiring choices (Ragan, Montiel, and Wright 2003, vi). Yet Melissa Rogers demonstrates that there is no easy answer. Moreover, the legal status of hiring decisions made on the basis of religious commitment is especially complicated by the wide assortment of state and municipal laws relating to employment rights.

To what extent is First Amendment freedom of association implicated by legal restrictions on, or challenges to, partnerships between faith-based organizations and government? The First Amendment offers certain constitutional protections to those who wish to associate with others with whom they share some commitment or interest, whether a political party, a social group, or a religious denomination. The right of association encompasses one's right to organize for political purposes, to speak by pooling resources with other like-minded individuals. How does that right of association apply to those of a shared faith who wish to band together in acts of social service (if at all)?

What does the free exercise of religion encompass and protect? Put another way, what is included in, or qualifies as, religious practice such that it falls within the protective rubric of the First Amendment? Is it only private religious practice that is protected? Corporate worship? Or does the free exercise of religion include collective social action that is not religious per se, but that grows directly out of what one believes to be a biblical mandate? How does the state (either judicially or legislatively) define key concepts such as religion, faith, and the church for constitutional purposes? Is the government qualified to render a definition? Can it avoid doing so? Should it be a matter of self-definition by the religious organization? Answers to these questions will shed significant light on the "neutrality" standard preferred by four members of the Supreme Court.

To what extent should the constitutional determination of First Amendment rights of publicly funded religious groups take into account the realities of the impact of that determination? Consider the potential impact of forcing "contraceptive equity" laws upon Catholic charities throughout the country. Should the litigation in New York acknowledge the fact that Catholic Charities receives millions of dollars in New York City health care and foster care contracts? A negative decision for Catholic Charities raises the possibility of driving faith-based groups from the public social services arena, thereby creating a hole in services for which the city might well lack suitable replacements or means of filling. Catholic-affiliated social services, hospitals, and schools across the country employ tens of thousands of individuals and serve millions. Should such pragmatic considerations inform the judicial determination of what qualifies as constitutionally protected religious exercise?

America's religious-secular divide tends to coalesce around these rights questions. Secularists already see religious organizations as the exclusive recipients of favorable tax treatment and other benefits denied their secular counterparts. Religious groups see themselves as victimized by an overreaching secular state that demands that they place their religious core aside if they are to take part. There will likely be no easy legal victories in this area, given the passion with which each side holds its convictions. But the answers to the above questions undoubtedly will play a central role in the future of the faith-based initiative.

6   Should Catholic Charities Have to Pay for Contraceptive Drugs?

John Orr

Catholic Charities of Sacramento serves a region that reaches all the way from Sacramento (in the middle of the state) to the Oregon border. It serves the state's capital city, a huge expanse of California's central farm belt, and one of California's most beautiful mountain recreational areas. Redding, located at the northern end of Sacramento Valley, bills itself as a magnet for hikers, campers, kayakers, and houseboaters. It has a substantial population of low-income residents (including retirees), lured to the area by the promise of low home prices. A few years ago, when a forest fire approached the northern boundary of Redding, the city discovered that it was also the home of impoverished forest dwellers.

Catholic Charities of Sacramento has been a major player in California's efforts to implement Congress's 1996 welfare reform laws. In Shasta County, it has helped to pioneer a series of "community tables," which unite public agencies, the area's community college, faith-based organizations, and other nonprofits in the development of cooperative welfare-to-work strategies. It holds and manages the contract for FaithWorks, a publicly funded interfaith project that has become a national model for faith-based welfare-to-work mentoring. Its publicly funded project to move Temporary Assistance for Needy Families participants from motels into affordable housing is regarded across the state as a radical innovation.

Now, however, Catholic Charities of Sacramento regards itself as being in serious trouble. In March 2004 the California Supreme Court rejected a request by Catholic Charities to be exempted from state legislation that requires it to include contraceptive devices and drugs in the health benefit plan it offers its employees. Now the organization's administrators believe that their ability to maintain their religious identity while serving the needs of Sacramento Valley's

89

low-income residents is being severely compromised. They must engage in activity that violates their Catholic conscience.

On July 20, 2000, Catholic Charities of Sacramento took its first step within the California court system to avoid this extraordinarily negative situation. It filed a complaint in the Sacramento Superior Court against the state's Department of Managed Health Care and Department of Insurance. *Catholic Charities of Sacramento v. Superior Court of Sacramento County* (2001) challenged the constitutionality of two laws that had recently been passed by the California State legislature—laws requiring that any organization in the state that offers prescription drug coverage as part of its menu of health care benefits or as a part of its liability insurance must cover costs of contraceptive drugs and devices. Since Catholic Charities currently does not offer liability insurance, its lawsuit focused only on mandates imposed by the Women's Contraceptive Equity Act (WCEA), which applies to contraceptive coverage with a California employer's health care benefits.

Litigating on behalf of Catholic Charities' twelve freestanding, diocesan-based affiliates, the Sacramento organization argued that Catholic Charities should be granted an exemption from the laws' provisions. The Catholic Church views artificial contraception as morally unacceptable. Since Catholic Charities is an integral part of the Catholic Church, Catholic Charities' lawyers argued, its employment practices and its insurance practices must be consistent with this teaching. Not to grant an exemption would be to violate both the establishment and free exercise clauses of the federal and state constitutions.

Supporters of Catholic Charities of Sacramento regard this lawsuit as a watershed event. Their rhetoric at times seems almost apocalyptic. Carol Hogan, associate director for pastoral projects and communications of the California Catholic Conference, for example, asserts that the case's outcome "may determine henceforth the scope of religious freedom in the state of California, and indeed, in America."[1] Rick Mockler, executive director of Catholic Charities of California, agrees. He argues that "[this case] is part of a much larger debate over the role of religion in public life, and over the nature of democracy in a pluralistic society. We believe that the current movement to privatize and restrict religious practice serves no one, and that a healthy society depends on the dynamic interplay of competing ideas, values and institutions." Speaking at a meeting of Los Angeles County's Faith-Based Coordinating Council, Ron Lopez, a senior administrator in Catholic Charities of Los Angeles, expressed indignation that his organization was being regarded, under WCEA, as a secular organization. "That is frightening for nonprofits like ours that have strong ties to faith communities."

Administrators of both Catholic and non-Catholic faith-based human services in California acknowledge that they have a big stake in the outcome of this lawsuit. In the era of charitable choice, initiated by Congress's 1996 welfare reform legislation, then expanded by President George W. Bush's "Equal

Protection of the Laws for Faith-Based and Community Organizations," they have been assured that they could maintain their systems of beliefs and governance while using federal funds to serve the poor. Faith-based organizations could "be themselves," even in the face of requirements that their publicly financed human services must be secular. For many of these administrators, *Catholic Charities of Sacramento v. Superior Court of Sacramento County* offers an opportunity to assess more precisely how far that guarantee reaches. When a faith-based organization's belief system, embodied in its employee benefit package, collides with a statewide gender discrimination law, which of these trumps? Does a law that limits gender-based discrimination in prescription drug plans trump Catholic Charities' demand that it be allowed to offer a prescription drug benefit package that is consistent with Catholic social teachings?

The case has created an occasion for one more significant test of a claim, regularly espoused by religiously affiliated nonprofits, that they should receive the same exemptions from federal and state antidiscrimination laws that are routinely afforded to sectarian organizations (congregations, religious denominations). Their services, their boards and administrators claim, are extensions of the beliefs and visions of their sponsoring sectarian organizations. Their charters and mission statements are grounded in religious beliefs. Their boards of directors are often led by clergy, or at least by members who share the religious orientation of the sponsoring sectarian organizations. Nevertheless, they are not routinely granted the same corporate privileges (and/or rights) that belong to "religious" or "ministerial" organizations.

There is a long history of litigation in state and federal courts, for example, that focuses on the asserted right of religiously affiliated nonprofits, such as congregations and denominational organizations, to utilize religious criteria in employing and dismissing staff members. Religiously affiliated nonprofits have generally prevailed in these efforts, but only on a case-by-case basis. Over and over, they have had to petition the courts to grant employment practice rights that they believe are theirs under the free exercise and establishment clauses of the state and federal constitutions.

Catholic Charities of Sacramento v. Superior Court of Sacramento County moves litigation about exemptions from state and federal discrimination laws into relatively uncharted territory. It raises the issue as to whether religiously affiliated social service nonprofits can legitimately claim an exemption from state-mandated employment benefit rules that are morally offensive to their religiously based self-identities and charters—in this case, requirements imposed by the California legislature mandating that California employers must pay for contraceptive devices and drugs as a part of their health benefit packages. Catholic Charities believes that it has identified convincing constitutional bases for demanding that exemption. California's attorney general, representing the state's Department of Managed Health Care and

Department of Insurance, rejects Catholic Charities' constitutional arguments. The attorney general's arguments have prevailed as the case has moved from the Sacramento Superior Court to the California Court of Appeals, and now to the California Supreme Court.

■ The Women's Contraceptive Equity Act

Catholic Charities' troubles date back to the 1993–1994 session of the California legislature. In that session, Assemblyman Robert Hertzberg initiated a years-long attempt to correct what he regarded as widespread discrimination against women employees in health care service plans and in disability insurance. With strong support from Planned Parenthood and the American College of Obstetricians and Gynecologists, Hertzberg observed that, when women are not granted access to prescription contraceptives, they are likely to experience a frightening array of health problems, and they are far more likely to engage in child abuse. Only women are discriminated against when contraception coverage is not available, because prescription contraceptive methods are used only by women.

Prior to the enactment of the Women's Contraceptive Equity Act, two predecessor bills that had been authored by Assemblyman Hertzberg reached the desk of Governor Pete Wilson. Both were vetoed. The first did not include a conscience clause, a fact that led the governor to observe that the bill failed to respect the free exercise rights of Catholic religious employers. The second included a broad conscience clause for religious employers, accompanied by a mandate that the state subsidize prescription contraceptives for all uninsured women whose incomes were below a qualifying threshold. Governor Wilson vetoed that bill because he believed that the threshold income minimum was set too high.

In 1999, Assemblyman Hertzberg succeeded in his efforts to move the WCEA through the legislature. That law, along with a parallel piece of legislation relating to disability insurance, he claimed, eliminated gender discrimination in the insurance industry by granting women access to prescription contraception coverage.

When the legislature was considering the WCEA, the California Catholic Conference and the California Association of Catholic Hospitals demanded that a conscience clause be included. They argued that, in the absence of an exemption from the requirements imposed by WCEA, Catholic human service nonprofits, Catholic health care organizations, Catholic universities, and some Catholic schools would be forced to pay for benefits that the Catholic Church regards as morally objectionable—even sinful.

The California legislature did not grant the exemption in the WCEA that the Catholic organizations wanted. It did, however, include an exemption for "religious organizations" that exhibit each of the following characteristics: their organizational mission is to inculcate religious values, they primarily employ persons who share their religious beliefs, they primarily serve persons who share their religious beliefs, and they are 6033(a)(2) nonprofits—a category that includes churches, temples, synagogues, mosques, and other sectarian organizations.

As measured by these criteria, the twelve diocesan-based affiliates of Catholic Charities in California (and their umbrella organization, Catholic Charities of California) did not qualify as exempt organizations. Catholic Charities service agencies do not attempt to proselytize, they do not use religious criteria in employing staff members, they do not discriminate religiously in providing services to recipients, their services are essentially secular, and they are independently incorporated as nonprofit public benefit corporations. Indeed, according to the American Civil Liberties Union, "Catholic Charities is the paradigm of a secular organization that is not exempt from state labor policy" (American Civil Liberties Union 2001, 5).

■ The Lawsuit

In its lawsuit, Catholic Charities of Sacramento asked the Superior Court of Sacramento County to grant an injunction, which would block the state from implementing the Women's Contraception Equity Act on grounds that it violated the free exercise and establishment clauses of the federal constitution and, also, the parallel (but allegedly "stricter") free exercise provisions of the California constitution. On September 26, 2001, the superior court tentatively rejected Catholic Charities' complaint, concluding that it is not likely that Catholic Charities will prevail on the merits of its constitutional challenges. After a ninety-minute hearing on September 25, 2001, in which both sides presented their cases, the judge commented that he had "about 20 to 22 inches worth of materials that were submitted. . . . And there are probably issues under the surface that aren't even discussed that are implicated by this ruling that are even deeper and broader. . . . I will reconsider everything that I've gone over and consider everything that's been said today and issue a final ruling" (*Catholic Charities of Sacramento v. Superior Court of Sacramento County,* filed July 20, 2000; oral argument September 25, 2001). With a speed that Catholic Charities' lawyers tagged as "abuse of discretion," in less than twenty-four hours the judge confirmed his rejection of Catholic Charities' complaint.

On November 20, 2001, Catholic Charities took its case to the Third Appellate District Court of Appeals, requesting that the Superior Court of Sacramento County be instructed to grant a preliminary injunction against the implementation of the WCEA. The appeals court was asked to consider whether the superior court erroneously interpreted and applied the state and federal constitutional free exercise and establishment provisions. The appeals court also rejected Catholic Charities' request, but granted permission for the organization to appeal its decision within the California Supreme Court. Now Catholic Charities' constitutional claims have been rejected by the California Supreme Court. Whether the case will be reviewed by the U.S. Supreme Court is, of course, an open question.

The Arguments: The Religious Employer Exemption

In the brief that Catholic Charities submitted to the California Supreme Court, the lead lawyer, James Sweeney, argued that the legislature had violated the establishment and the free exercise clauses of the California and federal constitutions when it assumed the authority to devise criteria for identifying which faith-based organizations are "religious" and which are "secular," based of factors that are unrelated to those organizations' charters, affiliations, and self-definitions.

Catholic Charities argued that the legislature did not have the authority or the competence to draw distinctions between "religious" and "secular" Catholic organizations. In support of this position, James Sweeney referred to the California Supreme Court's opinion in *Espinosa v. Rusk* (1980), in which the majority concluded that "to make distinctions as to that which is religious and that which is secular so as to subject the latter to regulation is necessarily a suspect effort." The justices observed that, in *Espinosa,* the lower court's conclusion that "the charitable activity of the church . . . [is] subject to regulation" was based on a biased "evangelical" and "spiritual" conception of religion. "This broad definition of secular is part of the problem," the California Supreme Court concluded. "[A]lthough the ordinance does not express any anti-religious effort or object, it is objectionable because it involves municipal officials in the definition of what is religious."

To determine whether particular Catholic organizations are eligible for the WCEA's religious exemption, Catholic Charities argued, public officials must decide whether employees affiliated with a Catholic organization share "religious tenets." They are forced to survey Catholic organizations' service records to determine if these organizations routinely serve non-Catholics. They are forced to identify which acts of justice and compassion should be deemed direct efforts to inculcate religious values and which should not.

When the legislature created its narrow definition of the WCEA's exemption for religious organizations, it gerrymandered a whole range of Catholic organizations out of that exemption. The legislature excluded Catholic social service agencies, Catholic health care organizations, and even some Catholic schools, all of which identify themselves as organizational extensions of the Catholic Church's mission to practice justice and compassion. Indeed,

Sweeney claimed, "[The] entirety of the Catholic Church could plausibly be ineligible for the exemption depending both upon the demographics of a particular diocese, the fortuitous nature of hiring patterns, and the particular application of the theological criteria used to define a 'religious employer'" (Catholic Charities 2001).

Catholic Charities accused the California legislature of knowingly crafting the WCEA's religious organization exemption to exclude Catholic organizations, whose professional social service practices, devised in accord with Catholic social teachings, prohibited the application of contraceptive drugs and devices. According to Sweeney, the authors and the sponsors of WCEA were blatant in expressing their disinterest in accommodating Roman Catholic social teachings. WCEA's sponsors and authors viewed Catholic social service agencies and hospitals as *the problem*. Their apparent intent was to "close the gap" in insurance coverage caused by the resistance of Catholic social service organizations to providing prescription drug benefits that pay for contraception drugs and devices.

Catholic Charities accused legislators of being uninterested in, and even hostile to, the religious freedom rights of Roman Catholic organizations. Throughout the process of enacting what finally became the Women's Contraceptive Equity Act, legislators repeatedly insinuated that Catholic social teachings about contraception did not deserve to be accommodated because they are widely ignored by Catholics and Catholic institutions. In *Catholic Charities of Sacramento v. Superior Court of Sacramento County* (2001), Senator Jacqueline Speier, for example, pointed out that "59 percent of all Catholic women of childbearing age practice contraception. Eighty-eight percent of Catholics believe in a New York Times poll that someone who practices artificial birth control can still be a good Catholic. I agree with that. I think it's time to do the right thing."

Speaking in defense of the Women's Contraceptive Equity Act, California's attorney general confirmed that the legislature had declined to enact an exemption as broad as the one that had been demanded by the California Catholic Conference and the California Association of Catholic Hospitals. The legislature's choice had been to grant an exemption only to those organizations whose essential character and purpose are religious, not to "secular institutions like [Catholic Charities] and the growing number of large hospitals and universities loosely affiliated with the Catholic Church." If the broader exemption had been adopted, the attorney general argued, the legislature

> would [have deprived] literally thousands of employees in this state of access to nondiscriminatory health and disability insurance coverage. It would also effectively permit such organizations [as Catholic Charities and Catholic hospitals] to impose their internal religious views on their largely non-Catholic employees, limiting the employees in the exercise of their own compelling free exercise interests.

According to the attorney general, the decision to narrow the definition of exempted religious organizations was not motivated by hostility to Catholic institutions. The legislature was not targeting Catholic institutions. Catholic Charities' assertion that the legislature willfully gerrymandered Catholic institutions out of the religious exemption was based on a misrepresentation of what was said in testimony before the Senate Insurance Committee and in letters to the legislature that spoke about the need "to close a gap" in the state's health insurance coverage. Katharine K. Kneer, who represented Planned Parenthood Affiliates of California and the California Planned Parenthood Education Fund at a hearing held by the Senate Insurance Committee, had been the individual who first spoke about closing a gap. She never referred to a "Catholic gap." Instead, she argued that the primary purpose of the WCEA was to close a gap in insurance coverage for contraception in prescription benefit plans. Catholic Charities erroneously interpreted this language as referring to a "Catholic gap," that is, to a gap comprising institutions that are affiliated with the Catholic Church.

The attorney general rejected Catholic Charities' claim that the necessity of distinguishing between "religious organizations" and "secular" (albeit religiously affiliated) nonprofits involves the state in prohibited acts of determining what is meant by such terms as "religious tenets" and "the inculcation of religious values." Catholic Charities, the attorney general claimed, was mistaken in arguing that these terms are always defined in the context of particular religious traditions, and thus that the state's determination of which religiously affiliated organizations are exempt from the WCEA's requirements inevitably entangles public agencies in religion. "Religious tenets" and "religious values" are terms that are not specific to particular faith traditions. They are general terms. It would be impossible to define "religious employer" without using them or something similar.

In the opinion issued by the California Supreme Court, the justices rejected Catholic Charities' claim that it had unfairly been targeted—that it had been victimized by legislative gerrymandering. The court noted that the legislature had attempted to address Catholic concerns while still affirming the public welfare goals embodied in the Women's Contraceptive Equity Act. The legislature had reached a defensible compromise when it agreed to permit religious employers to act consistently with their beliefs about artificial contraception, yet to exclude independently incorporated, religiously affiliated nonprofit agencies from sharing in that exemption.

The Arguments: Burdening Religion

According to Catholic Charities, the constitutional right to the free exercise of religion can be limited only by laws that are neutral, that are of general applicability, that advance interests of the highest order, and that are narrowly tailored to achieve those interests. The Women's Contraceptive Equity Act fails to meet all of these tests, because the design of the act's religious organization exemption specifically targets Catholic social teachings and the employment practices of Catholic nonprofits.

Catholic Charities asserted that, even if its claim did not stand up to federal constitutional free exercise tests, it received even stronger support from the free exercise language of the state constitution. Under Article 1, Section 4, of the California constitution, religious liberty rights can only be limited by laws that are directed toward the protection of the state's peace and safety and toward protection against licentious behavior. The WCEA is not such a law.

Consequently, Catholic Charities claims that the WCEA places an unconstitutional burden on Catholic social service agencies by coercing them to engage in conduct that is forbidden by Catholic social teachings, especially by forcing them to subsidize contraceptive programs that are regarded as sinful. Catholic agencies are forced into a situation where all available options are unacceptable: they can choose to engage in forbidden behavior by including the coverage of contraceptive drugs and devices in their health care benefit packages, or they can discontinue offering prescription drug benefits to their employees—an option that violates Catholic social teachings about economic justice.

In response, the attorney general argued in *Catholic Charities of Sacramento v. Superior Court of Sacramento County* (2001) that the analysis of Catholic Charities' claims "must begin and end with the United States' Supreme Court decision in *Employment Division v. Smith* [1990]." Before *Smith,* he observed, the courts had assumed that challenged laws could survive constitutional scrutiny only if they could be justified as the least restrictive means of furthering a compelling state interest. Before *Smith,* Catholic Charities' arguments might have been more cogent. After *Smith,* the Catholic Charities arguments had lost their force.

In *Smith,* the justices asserted, the challenged laws no longer have to be justified as the least-restrictive means of furthering a compelling state interest when they are: "(1) otherwise valid and constitutional laws in an area in which the state is free to regulate; and (2) neutral and of general applicability. Such statutes are constitutional even if they have the incidental effect of burdening a particular religious practice."

The Women's Contraceptive Equity Act, according to the attorney general, is a law that meets those tests. The state of California has the authority to prohibit discrimination in the health care benefit plans of employers. The law is neutral and is generally applicable to all insurers and employers. Its requirements fall equally on the state's corporate employers, whether or not these employers utilize religiously formulated reasons for their decisions concerning provision of contraceptive coverage.

The attorney general disagreed with Catholic Charities' assertion that the WCEA is not neutral because its requirements specifically target the Catholic

Church. The legislature's intent, on its face, was to prevent all of the state's employers and insurers from interfering with the personal decisions of women concerning issues related to sexual conduct and reproduction, not to close a so-called Catholic gap. The WCEA may indeed have an unequal impact on Catholic social service agencies, in light of the fact that Roman Catholic social teachings regard artificial contraception as morally unacceptable. But this fact alone does not substantiate Catholic Charities' conspiratorial theories that the legislature had targeted the Catholic Church.

Even if the California Supreme Court chooses not to use *Smith* as the relevant constitutional authority, the attorney general observed, the WCEA should still prevail. The legislature had a compelling state purpose when it formulated the WCEA's requirements for contraception coverage. Its stated intent was "to eliminate discriminatory insurance practices that had undermined the health and economic well-being of women." As evidence, the attorney general cited facts that had been presented in legislative hearings and that had been cited by legislators in debates—for example, that pregnancy can have life-threatening consequences to women's health, and that prescription contraceptives are the most effective means of birth control and therefore are an essential component of the prescription drug coverage that employers provide.

The attorney general rejected Catholic Charities' claim that its demand for an exemption from the WCEA's requirements is reinforced by "stricter" free exercise protections afforded by the California constitution. California courts have treated the state and federal free exercise clauses as interchangeable. California courts, since the beginning of the twentieth century, have acknowledged a need to practice restraint when they have been asked to adjudicate constitutional issues. They will answer constitutional issues only when they are forced to do so.

In the decision rendered by the California Court of Appeals, and subsequently by the California Supreme Court, the justices focused on Catholic Charities' constitutional claims. The Sacramento Superior Court had considered only questions of law, and it had concluded that Catholic Charities' complaint was not likely to succeed on the basis of the constitutional arguments that the organization had presented. The California Court of Appeals announced that it agreed with the Sacramento Superior Court's assessment. Contrary to Catholic Charities' arguments, adjudication of the kind of issues forwarded in *Catholic Charities of Sacramento v. Superior Court of Sacramento County* must begin and end with *Employment Division v. Smith*.

Ultimately, the California Supreme Court concurred that its decision would have to be based almost entirely on the U.S. Supreme Court's decision in *Smith*—that is, the ruling that sincerely held religious objections "do not excuse compliance with otherwise valid laws regulating matters the state is otherwise free to regulate." In its *Catholic Charities* decision, the California Supreme Court argued that the Women's Contraceptive Equity Act serves a compelling state interest in eliminating gender discrimination. Catholic Charities' right to express its moral reservations about the use of contraceptive devices and drugs is protected, because the organization is free to express its disapproval and to urge its employees not to use this component in their health benefit plan.

■ The Political/Constitutional Context

When *Catholic Charities of Sacramento v. Superior Court of Sacramento County* was filed during the summer of 2001, church-state scholars who had become aware of the case were intrigued. Congress's 1996 welfare reform legislation, through charitable choice, had affirmed the right of religiously affiliated nonprofits to use religious criteria in their employment practices—that is, to enjoy the same exemption from the Civil Rights Act's (Title VII) religious discrimination rule, which had been granted to "religious organizations." Was there a disconnect here? Why were religiously affiliated organizations being exempted from religious discrimination laws in their employment of staff members when they were being denied that same exemption in the area of employee insurance coverage? The occasion seemed made-to-order to test whether this disconnect could be eliminated.

Title VII of the Civil Rights Act of 1964 allowed religious organizations to be exempted from a general prohibition against religious employment discrimination by private sector organizations (e.g., employers, labor organizations, employment agencies). In a 1972 amendment of Title VII, Congress signaled that it wanted to apply the "religious organization" exemption to employers that would be engaged in a wide variety of activities, not just "ministerial" activities. The Civil Rights Act had initially applied its exemption from religious employment discrimination rules only to employers that were engaged in "religious observance and practice." The 1972 amendment removed the word "religious" as a qualifier, suggesting that the exemption would include religiously affiliated organizations involved in a wide range of activities.

Federal and state courts have generally been expansive in their interpretations of what kinds of faith-based organizations qualify for the Title VII exemption. As court after court has observed, there is no "bright line" or obvious boundary between organizations that qualify for the exemption and those that do not. The courts have chosen to proceed on a case-by-case basis. They have chosen to examine each organization in terms of its balance of secular and sacred elements. In 1987's *Corporation for the Presiding Bishop v. Amos,* the U.S. Supreme Court showed that it was willing to include even a religiously affiliated health club in the Title VII exemption, in spite of the fact that the club's day-to-day activities appeared to be essentially sectarian.

Whether Catholic Charities could ever have prevailed in an effort to establish an analogy between the Title VII exemption and its own demand to be exempted from the WCEA's requirements is, of course, unknown. Catholic Charities' lawyers simply chose not to develop that line of argument. Instead, they launched a broad-based, multifaceted challenge against the WCEA's "religious organization" exemption, arguing that denying Catholic Charities this exemption violated its free exercise rights and was an unconstitutional establishment of religion. The lawyers focused on the perceived intent of the legislature to target Catholic social service agencies, hospitals, and universities, arguing that the WCEA's religious organization exemption was based on an overly narrow spiritual, evangelical conception of religion. They contended that the WCEA inevitably involves state agencies in unconstitutional acts of specifying what does and does not constitute religion. They argued that the WCEA is not a neutral and generally applicable law and therefore that it should be subject to "strict scrutiny," that is, to a determination of whether it stands up to the tests that have been created by the U.S. Supreme Court to assess the law's compatibility with the First Amendment, or whether it stands up to free exercise tests spelled out in California's constitution.

The California Supreme Court's rejection of Catholic Charities' constitutional arguments was based substantially on the U.S. Supreme Court's decision in *Employment Division v. Smith* (1990). At issue in that case was the question as to whether the state of Oregon could use its antidrug laws to prosecute several members of a Native American religious group who used peyote as part of their worship rituals. The Court decided that the free exercise (freedom of religion) clause of the First Amendment does not excuse an individual from the obligation to comply with "valid and neutral laws of general applicability" (in areas where the state is free to regulate) just because those laws happen to place burdens on particular religious communities. The government's ability to protect the public against harmful conduct or its ability to carry out public policy, the justices argued, cannot depend on measuring whether "valid and neutral laws" differently affect the nation's religious communities' abilities to act in accord with their own belief systems:

> Precisely because "we are a cosmopolitan nation made up of people of almost every conceivable religious preference," and precisely because we value and protect that religious divergence, we cannot afford the luxury of deeming *presumptuously invalid,* as applied to the religious objector, every regulation of conduct that does not protect an interest of the highest order. . . . [Such a rule] would open the prospect of constitutionally required religious exemptions from civic obligations of almost every conceivable kind. The first amendment's protection of religious liberty does not require this.

In *Catholic Charities of Sacramento v. Superior Court of Sacramento County* (2004), the California Supreme Court concluded that the Women's

Contraceptive Equity Act is exactly what *Smith* was talking about. It is "a valid and constitutional law that is generally applicable and neutral with respect to religion." The WCEA's purpose is to eliminate gender discrimination in women's health insurance. The legislature's interest in preserving the public's health and well-being is compelling. Its effect on Catholic Charities is only incidental. It does not directly target Catholic Charities' beliefs about artificial contraception.

In basing its decision largely on *Smith,* the California Supreme Court opened old wounds. Among constitutional scholars and religious advocates who identify with strong protections for free exercise, *Smith* had always elicited anger. It is viewed as a step backward. It is viewed as a direct assault on the constitutional free exercise protections that had laboriously been constructed during the middle decades of the twentieth century. It is viewed as a legal opinion that grants the government broad cover for discriminating against the practices of religious groups.

Indeed, immediately after the U.S. Supreme Court issued its decision in *Smith* in 1990, a large coalition of constitutional scholars, public officials, and religious leaders requested a rehearing. When the Court refused, the coalition succeeded in getting Congress to pass the Religious Freedom Restoration Act (RFRA), which mandated that the government had to demonstrate "a compelling public reason" or state interest before burdening any religious group. It required that, when the government passes a law based on a compelling state interest, it must use means that are the "least restrictive" in their effects on religious communities.

The Religious Freedom Restoration Act faced its first test when the U.S. Supreme Court agreed to consider *City of Boerne v. P. F. Flores (Archbishop of San Antonio)* (1997). In this case, the archdiocese of San Antonio, under the RFRA, argued that the Roman Catholic Church was exempt from San Antonio zoning ordinances that prohibited it from demolishing part of a seventy-year-old building. The archdiocese claimed that the ordinances placed a burden on the Church's free exercise rights.

A broad coalition of religious and civil libertarian groups filed a brief in support of Archbishop Flores's appeal to the Religious Freedom Restoration Act. The coalition included representatives from the American Jewish Committee, Muslim Council, Christian Church, Episcopal Church, General Conference of Seventh-Day Adventists, American Humanist Association, Church of the Brethren, Church of Scientology, Southern Baptist Convention, Guru Gobind Sing Foundation, Hadassah, Mystic Temple of the Light, National Sikh Center, National Council of Churches, Peyote Way Church of God, Presbyterian Church, National Council on Islamic Affairs, Christian Science, Unitarian Church, United Methodist Church, and others. These groups were also joined by Americans for Democratic Action, People for the American Way, Americans United for Separation of Church and State, Americans for Religious Liberty, the

First Amendment Rights

Coalition for America, Concerned Women for America, and the Traditional Values Coalition.

In June 1997 the U.S. Supreme Court decided against the archbishop's position in the *Boerne* case, and in the course of its opinion it explicitly overturned the RFRA. Speaking for the majority, Justice John Paul Stevens observed:

> In my opinion, the Religious Freedom Restoration Act of 1993 . . . is a "law respecting an establishment of religion" that violates the first amendment of the Constitution. If the historic landmark on a hill in Boerne happened to be a museum or an art gallery owned by an atheist, it would not be eligible for an exemption from the city ordinance that forbid an enlargement of the structure. Because the landmark is owned by the Catholic Church, it is claimed that RFRA gives its owner a federal statutory entitlement to an exemption from a generally applicable, neutral civil law. Whether the Church would actually prevail under the statute or not, the statute has provided the Church with a legal weapon that no atheist or agnostic can obtain. The governmental preference for religion, as opposed to irreligion, is forbidden by the first amendment.

Responding to the Court's decision in *Boerne,* supporters of the RFRA continue to seek ways to restore stronger free exercise protections. Although viewed as a last resort, one of the options that is being discussed is a constitutional amendment.

Thus, in its appeal to the California Supreme Court, Catholic Charities had to contend with a U.S. Supreme Court ruling that angers advocates of strong free exercise protections. This is a difficult situation. There are many supporters of the now-defunct Religious Freedom Restoration Act who had hoped that the California Supreme Court would urge U.S. Supreme Court justices to narrow the range of cases to which *Smith* applies. But to prevail under *Smith,* Catholic Charities' lawyers would have had to convince the California Supreme Court justices that the WCEA's narrow definition of its religious organization exemption did in fact target Catholic social service agencies, that the WCEA was not "neutral and generally applicable," and/or that the California constitution offered free exercise protections that were stricter than those guaranteed in the federal constitution. In light of the fact that Catholic Charities had not succeeded in the Sacramento Superior Court or in the California Court of Appeals, it would have had to offer extraordinarily powerful reasons to convince the California Supreme Court justices that these lower courts were wrong.

Catholic Charities of Sacramento v. Superior Court of Sacramento County has provided the leaders of religiously affiliated organizations in California with an education about their constitutional rights. First and foremost, they will be far more aware of the limited reach of their state constitution, which is allegedly stricter than the U.S. Constitution in protecting religious liberty and guarding against the establishment of religion. Ever since welfare reform block grants arrived in California in 1996, there has been confusion about the impact of the "stricter" church-state provisions contained in the California constitution on the implementation of charitable choice. During interviews with researchers from the University of Southern California, for example, two county welfare agency administrators and one employee in the California Department of Social Services claimed that the state constitution prohibits federal block grant money from being distributed to religiously affiliated social service agencies and sectarian institutions. Three administrators of religiously affiliated organizations reported that they felt safe from government intrusion in their affairs because of the state constitution's "stricter" free exercise clause.

The *Catholic Charities* lawsuit is the first case, at least in recent years, in which a religiously affiliated nonprofit has appealed to the state constitution for church-state protections that are more extreme than those offered by the federal constitution. If the *Catholic Charities* case is reviewed by the U.S. Supreme Court, perhaps the justices will disagree with the California Supreme Court and will affirm Catholic Charities' assertions. But until it does, individuals associated with religiously affiliated nonprofits will undoubtedly be wary. Their eyes will be fixed on the First Amendment of the federal constitution alone. The California Supreme Court's decision has punctured their illusions about the authority of the California constitution in church-state affairs.

They will also be far more aware of ways in which, under *Smith,* general purpose, neutral laws can have the effect of circumscribing free exercise rights. Rick Mockler, executive director of Catholic Charities of California, is on the mark when he argues that the *Catholic Charities* lawsuit is right at the center of a public debate that relates to the privatization of religion and to the restriction of religious practice in a pluralistic society. The public perception is that, under charitable choice, faith-based organizations are expanding their influence—that the separation of church and state is being eroded, or at least radically redefined. Nevertheless, Catholic Charities feels threatened. The agency's ability to operate faithfully as a Catholic institution appears to be diminished by a general purpose law, the Women's Contraception Equity Act, the authority of which is being interpreted by the Superior Court of Sacramento County and by the California Court of Appeals through the lenses of *Smith.*

Whether Catholic Charities will ultimately prevail in this lawsuit, the case has focused our attention, once again, on the effects of *Smith.* In the years since the U.S. Supreme Court declared the Religious Freedom Restoration Act unconstitutional, public debate about *Smith* has diminished. But now, in the context of *Catholic Charities of California v. Superior Court of Sacramento County,* that debate will in all likelihood be ignited once again. The case bears on all sorts of issues that have emerged, under *Smith,* in the era of charitable choice. It concerns the ability of religiously affiliated nonprofits "to be themselves." It relates to tensions created when general purpose laws collide with the free exercise of religion. It tests the ability of religiously affiliated nonprofits to be exempt from state-mandated requirements that offend their religious sensibilities. These are important issues in American society. *Catholic Charities of Sacramento v. Superior Court of Sacramento County* is a case, I am certain, that will be regarded as pivotal in defining the church-state relational issues raised by the emerging prominence of religiously affiliated social service agencies in our public life.

■ Note

1. Unless otherwise noted, quotations are taken from public speeches and interviews by the author.

7 Federal Funding and Religion-Based Employment Decisions

MELISSA ROGERS

Should religious organizations be permitted to make employment decisions on the basis of religion with regard to federally funded jobs? This is one of the most discussed and divisive aspects of the faith-based initiative advanced by President George W. Bush. It is also one of the most dimly understood, at least in terms of how current law applies to it. In a recent legislative debate, for example, some members of Congress said that a federal statute permits religious organizations to hire on the basis of religion with regard to federally financed employment, while others said that that law did not apply when public funds were involved. Some claimed that the Supreme Court had already ruled that the Constitution required that religious organizations be afforded this right, while others asserted that the Court had said no such thing.

In this chapter I first seek to clarify a few of the issues that have surfaced in the legislative debate over this matter. I do so by considering the House of Representatives' debate over a particular bill: the overhaul of the Head Start program proposed by President Bush and House Republican leaders, titled the School Readiness Act of 2003.[1] I then offer a brief discussion of the issue as a federal constitutional and policy matter.

■ The School Readiness Act of 2003: The Overhaul of Head Start

In May 2003, House Republicans introduced legislation to overhaul the Head Start program, a federally funded day care program launched in the 1960s to prepare indigent children for kindergarten (Schemo 2003). This proposal im-

105

mediately led to bitter arguments between House Republican leaders and Democrats. Republican leaders argued that the bill would make the program more effective by providing for academic testing and allowing selected states to receive block grants to administer this traditionally local program. Democrats argued that these plans would result in cash-strapped states cutting program funding, and thus jeopardize the vital nonacademic components of the program, such as medical and dental care as well as nutritious meals

Another contentious item of debate was the provision of the bill that amended the statutory nondiscrimination provisions governing the Head Start program to allow religious organizations to discriminate on the basis of religion in federally funded employment. The Head Start nondiscrimination provisions were originally enacted in 1972, when Congress passed and President Richard Nixon signed into law further authorization and certain amendments to the statute that governs the Head Start program.[2] They state in relevant part: "The Secretary [of Health and Human Services] shall not provide financial assistance for any program, project, or activity under [the Head Start program] unless the grant or contract with respect thereto specifically provides that no person with responsibilities in the operation thereof will discriminate with respect to any such program, project, or activity because of race, creed, color, national origin, sex, political affiliation, or beliefs."[3]

This prohibition on discrimination on the basis of religion or creed reflects a tradition begun during the early New Deal period of implementing "a policy of equal opportunity in employment and training financed by federal funds."[4] As discussed in more detail below, Presidents Harry Truman, Dwight Eisenhower, and John Kennedy took actions that extended this policy, and a 1965 executive order signed by President Lyndon Johnson generally required all government contracting agencies to include in every government contract a requirement that the contractor not discriminate against any employee on the basis of "race, color, religion, or national origin."[5]

The George W. Bush White House has launched a campaign to amend restrictions like these so as to allow religious organizations to make religion-based distinctions in government-funded employment. In addition to promoting this policy through the Head Start overhaul, in 2002 President Bush issued an executive order that amends the 1965 executive order issued by President Johnson to allow religious organizations that are government contractors and subcontractors to make religion-based decisions with regard to federally funded jobs.[6] The policy of the Bush White House on this issue is explained in a document it has published titled *Protecting the Civil Rights and Religious Liberty of Faith-Based Organizations: Why Religious Hiring Rights Must Be Preserved*. In this publication, the Bush administration promises that it "will work to preserve the Title VII rights of organizations that receive government funds" to make employment decisions on the basis of religion and will "support changes to laws that currently prevent religious organizations that participate in [government-funded] programs from taking religion into account when hiring" (*Religious Hiring Rights*).

Title VII refers to the equal employment opportunity title of the Civil Rights Act of 1964, which applies to employers with fifteen or more employees in an industry affecting interstate commerce.[7] As discussed in more detail below, Title VII prohibits these employers from discriminating in employment on the basis of "race, color, religion, sex, or national origin,"[8] but it also exempts certain religious bodies from its prohibition on religious discrimination in employment.[9] Thus, in contrast to the nondiscrimination obligations that follow federal funding, an employer need not receive federal funds in order to be bound by the provisions of Title VII—it must simply employ the requisite number of employees in an industry affecting interstate commerce.

The conviction that a religious organization should have the right to use federal monies to create staff positions and then hire on the basis of religion to fill them was first prominently asserted during the 1996 debate over the welfare reform overhaul, which resulted in the original enactment of the charitable choice provisions.[10] These provisions allow religious organizations of all kinds, including churches and other pervasively religious groups, to compete for federal social service funds, and they promise that such organizations will be permitted to maintain their "religious character and freedom." With regard to employment practices, charitable choice contains a provision that is intended to allow religious organizations to make employment decisions on the basis of religion vis-à-vis government-funded jobs.[11] Thus, as shorthand, this article refers to this policy as the "charitable choice employment policy," a policy the Bush White House has embraced and extended.

As noted above, the House Republican leadership followed the White House's lead on the charitable choice employment policy by introducing a bill that would amend the nondiscrimination Head Start provisions to allow religious organizations to discriminate on the basis of religion in federally funded employment.[12] House Republican leaders explained that different statutes had different requirements on this issue, and "as we bring these [statutes that place nondiscriminatory conditions on federal funding] through our committee, like the Workforce Investment Act, like Head Start, [we are] going to provide some consistency."[13]

Many Democrats vehemently objected to this proposed statutory change. Representative Lynn Woolsey (D–Calif.) offered an amendment to strike this proposed change from the Republican leadership bill and thus leave the statute's nondiscrimination provisions intact. The Woolsey amendment was rejected by a vote of 231 to 199 and on July 25, 2003, the School Readiness Act passed the House by only 1 vote, 217 to 216.[14]

■ **The House Debate over the 2003 Head Start Overhaul**

During the House debate over the Head Start overhaul, the Woolsey amendment was the subject of fierce and confusing debate. In particular, there were disagreements over the legislative history of Title VII, its interpretation by the courts, and what, if anything, the Supreme Court had said about Title VII's application to this particular issue.

Legislative History of the 1972 Amendments to Title VII

Proponents of the Head Start overhaul argued during the July 2003 House debate that their "bill [did] not ignore or undermine civil rights laws," but rather "[brought] the Head Start program up to date with [civil rights laws]." In support of their argument in favor of the charitable choice employment policy, a member of Congress stated: "The Civil Rights Act was amended in 1972 by the Equal Employment Opportunity Act because Congress recognized that there needed to be a more defined relationship between church and state. Indeed, these changes were made in response to concerns that government might interfere with the affairs of religious organizations."[15]

The reference to the 1972 amendments to Title VII highlights an important change made during that year to an exemption for religious organizations from the act's prohibition on employment discrimination based on religion. As signed into law in 1964, this exemption was limited to employee positions carrying out "religious activities."[16] Under the Equal Employment Opportunity Act of 1972, however, the exemption was broadened to allow religious organizations to hire on the basis of religion in all employee positions. This particular exemption from Title VII is often referred to by shorthand as the "702 exemption."[17] As mentioned above, proponents of the charitable choice employment policy sometimes suggest that the legislative history behind this statutory change demonstrates that Congress expressed its intent to allow religious groups to discriminate on the basis of religion with regard to federally funded jobs. A review of the 1972 legislative history, however, reveals that this claim cannot be substantiated.

Senators Sam Ervin (D–N.C.) and James Allen (D–Ala.) introduced the 1972 amendment to the Title VII 702 exemption.[18] Among their many objections to the bill, these Southern senators opposed proposals to bring educational institutions, which previously had been exempt from the equal employment opportunity provisions of the act, under the purview of Title VII.[19] They also were specifically concerned that one of the effects of the proposed amendment bringing educational institutions under the act would be to prohibit religious educational institutions from engaging in religion-based hiring for staff positions that performed nonreligious activities.[20] Senator Allen stated: "Under the provisions of the bill, there would be nothing to prevent an atheist being forced upon a religious school to teach some subject other than theology."[21] While Senators Ervin and Allen were unsuccessful in their attempts to amend the bill to exempt educational and religious institutions from Title VII entirely, their amendment to broaden the 702 exemption to cover all employment positions of religious corporations, associations, educational institutions, and societies was successful.[22]

It is true, therefore, that these senators considered an institutionwide exemption for religious organizations from Title VII to be crucial to religious autonomy and freedom. It is often recalled, for example, that Senator Ervin repeatedly said that his amendment was designed "to take the political hands of Caesar off of the institutions of God, where they have no place to be."[23]

But what has not been recalled is that, in his argument for allowing religious organizations to make religion-based employment decisions institutionwide, Senator Ervin repeatedly used an example of a religious institution from his home state that, as he stressed, "[was] not supported in any respect by the Federal Government," but by individual religious adherents. He stated:

> We have a college in North Carolina known as Davidson College that is affiliated with the Southern Presbyterian Church. *Davidson College is supported by the fees of its students and by the voluntary contributions of people interested in its activities. It is not supported in any respect by the Federal Government.* . . . This college was founded and is controlled by people who believe in giving a Christian education to the students of the institution. . . . [It has] a regulation which says that any person who is chosen to be a full professor at the institution shall be a member of an Evangelical Christian Church.[24]

Ervin then asked Senator Allen, his colleague and supporter: Is there "anything immoral or ought [there] to be anything illegal in people who support a college devoted to giving a Christian education taking steps to assure that the youth who attend it should be instructed on any subject, whether religious or nonreligious, by teachers who are members of a Christian church?"[25] And in response to a question later in the debate, Ervin emphasized again that Davidson College was "supported by fees of the students and voluntary gifts of people who believe in giving the kind of education this institution gives."[26]

Senator Allen echoed this argument in his own statements, commenting: "Under our system of religious freedom, which would be violated by this EEOC bill, religious organizations have seen fit to use their own resources to establish church schools at every level of education—elementary, secondary, and institutions of higher education. They did so because they wanted youth taught in a religious atmosphere and by Christian instructors."[27] Senator Allen also quoted a statement by Senator Ervin: "If the members of the Presbyterian Church, or the members of the Catholic Church, or the members of the Lutheran Church, or the members of any other religious body see fit to

establish, through their own resources, an institution of learning for the instruction of youth, and they want the youth of that institution to be taught by
persons they regard as Christian professors, even in nonreligious subjects
such as mathematics or trigonometry or philosophy, they should have the un-
qualified right to do that."[28] Thus it appears that the outrage Senators Ervin
and Allen felt stemmed in part from the fact that the very schools people of
faith had established and sustained now would be subject to religious restrictions by the federal government.

In sum, the 1972 legislative history confirms that those who supported the
broadened 702 exemption expressed their belief that religious organizations
ought to be able to make religion-based decisions with regard to all of their staff
positions, but it also reveals that the issue of government funding wasn't a topic
of discussion on the floor of Congress save for references Senators Ervin and
Allen made to self-supporting religious institutions. The lead sponsors of the
702 amendment rallied support for their amendments by offering examples of
religious institutions they said did not receive government financial aid, but
were supported by private funds. Far from supporting the charitable choice employment policy, this evidence cuts against it. Thus, any suggestion that Congress in 1972 offered support for allowing religious organizations to make religion-based employment decisions with regard to government-funded positions
is simply incorrect. The legislative history does not support such a finding.[29]

Title VII 702 Exemption: Government Funds and Waiver

As noted above, during the Head Start debate there also was disagreement
about whether and how Title VII applied when a religious organization received government funding. Proponents of the charitable choice employment
policy argued that "nothing in title VII provides that a religious organization
loses its exemption because it receives federal funds," and thus that the Title
VII 702 exemption applied even when religious organizations receive federal
subsidies.[30] An opponent, however, stated: "Head Start programs are federally
funded and as such do not fall under the jurisdiction of the Title VII statute."[31]

Courts generally have ruled that a Title VII exemption cannot be waived
by the conduct of the religious organization (see, for example, *Little v. Wuerl*
1991) and a federal appellate court has specifically held that a religious organization does not waive its Title VII exemption when it accepts government
funds (*Hall v. Baptist Memorial Health Care Corporation* 2000). For a variety of reasons, however, these cases do not necessarily mean that a religious
organization will be able to discriminate on the basis of religion in government-funded employment.

For example, these cases do not preclude courts from finding that the
U.S. Constitution or a state constitution prohibits the government from allowing religious organizations to make religion-based decisions with regard to
government-funded jobs. The plaintiffs in all but one of the cases referred to

above do not appear to have made an attempt to prove that their particular jobs were funded by the government or to question the constitutionality of allowing religious discrimination in government-funded jobs.[32] In *Siegel v. Truett-McConnell College,* a case in which the plaintiff apparently made a constitutional claim that "his particular position as a teacher [was] not eligible for the exemption because the [religious institution] receive[d] substantial government funding," the court concluded: "The government does not directly pay for any one teacher's salary, including [the plaintiff's] salary" (*Siegel v. Truett-McConnell College* 1994, 1344). Thus, in the *Siegel* case, the court found that the facts before it were "distinguishable from the fact situation" in *Dodge v. Salvation Army* (1989), in which a religious organization made religion-based decisions regarding a job position that was substantially, if not entirely, subsidized by a government grant. Indeed, as discussed in more detail below, in the *Dodge* case the court ruled that the facts created constitutional concerns that had the effect of prohibiting religious discrimination with respect to such a job.

These cases also do not in any way preclude legislatures from choosing to condition the funding they provide on compliance with the requirement that organizations, including religious ones, refrain from discriminating on the basis of religion in government-funded programs. Congress, of course, has already passed these kinds of nondiscrimination provisions—they appear in statutes governing the Head Start program as well as other federally funded social services. When a religious organization receives government social service funding that is subject to a nondiscrimination obligation, it appears that a court would find that this nondiscrimination condition controls the use of government funds, notwithstanding the Title VII 702 exemption. As one court has recognized, a nondiscrimination obligation that is tied to government funding is "designed as an *independent* source of protection for persons who are discriminated against in state-funded programs and activities" (*Arriaga v. Loma Linda Univ.* 1992, 1561).

Furthermore, it should be noted that courts may determine in some cases that particular organizations are ineligible for the 702 exemption due to the amount and type of government funds they receive. As discussed below, direct government aid may be used only for nonreligious activities. Thus if an organization, even one that says it is religious, receives a large amount of such aid, a court could find that the organization is not "primarily religious," and thus ineligible for the 702 exemption.[33]

The Supreme Court's Decision in
Corporation of the Presiding Bishop v. Amos

A third area of dispute in the legislative debate was the significance of the 1987 U.S. Supreme Court case of *Corporation of the Presiding Bishop v. Amos.* One member of Congress claimed that the Supreme Court has "said there is a constitutional right, even when you get public funds, to keep your religious liberty to hire and fire who you want."[34] Opponents of the charitable choice employment policy disagreed.[35] Another representative took a more nuanced approach, arguing that "the Supreme Court decided the *Amos* case on grounds that support the constitutionality of the title VII exemption as applied to employees of religious organizations that receive Federal funds."[36] This member of Congress also referenced Justice William Brennan's concurring opinion in the case, stating: "Perhaps one of the greatest liberal Justices . . . recognized that preserving the title VII exemption when religious organizations engage in social services is a necessary element of religious freedom."[37]

In the *Amos* case, the Court unanimously rejected a constitutional challenge to the Title VII 702 exemption. The case involved a building engineer at a nonprofit facility run by the Mormon Church. The engineer was fired from his job because he failed to qualify for a "temple recommend," a "certificate that he is a member of the Church and eligible to attend its temples" (*Amos* 1987, 330). He sued, claiming discrimination on the basis of religion and arguing that the broadened Title VII 702 exemption violated the Constitution's prohibition on religious establishments.

The Court rejected the engineer's claim. First, the Supreme Court found that the exemption had the required secular purpose. "It is a significant burden on a religious organization to require it, on pain of substantial liability, to predict which of its activities a secular court will consider religious," the Court explained (*Amos* 1987, 336). If the exemption were limited to those positions performing "religious" activities (the pre-1972 version of the exemption), religious organizations might feel that they could be safe from litigation only if they hired those outside the faith for certain jobs, even though the organization believed the jobs to be religious in nature. The broadened amendment spared a religious organization this concern, thus freeing it to define and advance its mission. The Court noted that "it is a permissible legislative purpose to alleviate significant governmental interference with the ability of religious organizations to define and carry out their religious missions" (*Amos* 1987, 335). Second, the Court found that the exemption did not have the forbidden primary effect of advancing religion: "A law is not unconstitutional simply because it *allows* churches to advance religion, which is their very purpose. For a law to have forbidden 'effects' under *Lemon* [*v. Kurtzman* (1971)], it must be fair to say that the *government itself* has advanced religion through its own activities and influence" (*Amos* 1987, 337, emphasis in original).

Thus the Court ruled that Congress had acted within constitutional bounds when it passed the broadened Title VII exemption. Although the Court found the exemption to be permitted by the Constitution, it declined to reach the issue of whether the Title VII exemption was constitutionally required.[38]

What the Court in *Amos* clearly did not find, however, was that the Constitution required the government to allow religious organizations to discriminate in employment based on religion when government funds were at issue. The Court was silent on this question because there was no suggestion that the Mormon organization at issue received any financial assistance from the state. Indeed, Steven Green has noted that, at the oral argument in the *Amos* case, "counsel for both the government and the Mormon Church emphasiz[ed] that 'this is not a religious benefit[s] case' and that it involved 'no endorsement of [or] financial support for . . . religious affairs by government'" (Green 2002, 37).

Further, as other commentators have noted, a number of the Supreme Court's reasons for upholding the exemption in *Amos* do not apply to situations in which religion-based discrimination occurs in government-funded employment (Brownstein 1999). The Court in *Amos* was understandably concerned, for example, that religious organizations might have to guess which jobs a court might view as secular. But it is clear that jobs subsidized by government grants and contracts must cover nonreligious duties, which cuts out the guesswork for the religious organization.

Also, contrary to the suggestions of some congressional charitable choice proponents, it is not fair to suggest that Justice William Brennan would have supported the charitable choice employment policy. In another case that involved a religious school Justice Brennan remarked: "When a sectarian institution accepts state financial aid it becomes obligated under the equal protection clause of the fourteenth amendment not to discriminate in admissions policies and faculty selection" (*Lemon v. Kurtzman* 1971, 651, concurring opinion). Further, a review of Justice Brennan's record on church-state issues clearly reveals his strong opposition to one of the faith-based initiative's main goals—allowing government funds to flow to pervasively religious organizations. Brennan repeatedly expressed his concern that making government aid available to such groups, even for ostensibly secular purposes, would result either in governmental support for or excessive entanglement with religion.[39] Thus, Justice Brennan's solicitude for a broad right to autonomy on behalf of religious organizations should not be taken as support for allowing religious groups to make religion-based employment decisions regarding government-funded jobs.

■ **Federal Constitutional and Policy Issues**

In the 2003 Head Start overhaul debate, Congress also generally debated whether allowing religious organizations to make religion-based decisions in federally funded employment passes muster under the U.S. Constitution or is good public policy. In contrast to the matters discussed above, these issues cannot be adequately assessed simply by applying historical data or law—case law on this issue is in the early stages of development, and any assessment of the policy merits involves subjective value judgments. Furthermore, a much more extensive essay would be required to do justice to these complex and evolving issues.

Instead, the section that follows simply highlights some of the most important constitutional questions that surround this issue, questions that arise under the First Amendment's establishment clause when governmental direct aid (grants and contracts) is involved. The second section offers a brief analysis of the issue as a policy matter, focusing again on discrimination regarding jobs subsidized by direct aid.

Establishment Clause Issues

One way in which the charitable choice employment policy could run afoul of the establishment clause is if a court determines that, through this practice, the government is impermissibly financing religious indoctrination or other religious activities (*Mitchell v. Helms* 2000). This employment policy not only ensures that religious organizations have the ability to hire and fire on the basis of religion, it also ensures that religious organizations are able to continually evaluate the beliefs and behavior of employees to verify that such beliefs and behavior conform to specific religious tenets and teachings.[40] When the government directly subsidizes these kinds of activities, a court could find that government funds are subsidizing religion, which is constitutionally prohibited. Charitable choice proponents respond by saying that, although the policy they advocate allows religion-based determinations in employment, that does not mean that religious content is being integrated into social services funded by direct aid. But, even assuming that such services are devoid of religious content, this practice could still have the effect of sanctioning the use of government funds for religious activities in the ways described above.

A court confronting the charitable choice employment policy also would ask whether the policy advances religion in other ways. When direct aid is used to create additional jobs within a religious organization and the organization hires only those of a certain faith, the primary effect would seem to be strengthening the religious nature of the organization and extending its influence (Brownstein 1999). Because the government directly subsidizes these positions, that promotion of religion could be attributed to the government and thus be found unconstitutional (*Lemon v. Kurtzman* 1971). Indeed, the only court to have squarely faced this issue so far ruled in an unreported decision that, when an employment position within the religious organization was funded "substantially, if not exclusively" by the government, "allowing the [religious organization] to choose the person to fill or maintain the position based on religious preference clearly has the effect of advancing religion and is unconstitutional" (*Dodge v. Salvation Army* 1989, 10–11).

Charitable choice proponents argue that the *Dodge* case and various legal tests and presumptions in this area reflect older Supreme Court doctrine that has since been discarded.[41] While the Court has significantly relaxed some traditional rules that govern the flow of government financial aid to religious bodies in recent decades, the Court continues to examine whether such aid has the effect of advancing religion and a Court majority continues to read the First Amendment to include a ban on the use of direct subsidies for religious activities.[42]

Another approach a court may use in its examination of this issue would be to consider whether the government has endorsed religion (*County of Allegheny v. ACLU* 1989). The method for determining whether the government has endorsed religion asks whether a hypothetical "reasonable observer" who is aware of relevant history and context, including some legal principles, would view the government's action as having the purpose or the effect of endorsing religion (*Capitol Square Review and Advisory Bd. v. Pinette* 1995, 780, J. O'Connor concurring in part and concurring in the judgment). Some would say this reasonable observer would not perceive governmental endorsement here because the observer would view a religious organization's religion-based hiring as simply the continuation of the hiring practices it was permitted to employ before it received government funds. But others would say that an understanding of past practice would not preclude the reasonable observer from concluding that the state had endorsed religion by allowing religious groups to exercise this policy vis-à-vis government-funded jobs. In short, judgments in these situations could rest heavily on the way in which particular judges interpret the views of the reasonable observer.[43]

The ultimate judicial outcome is difficult to predict because the issues are fairly novel and the current Supreme Court is badly fractured over related doctrine. To further complicate the matter, there is likely to be significant change in the composition of the Court in the near future. For now at least, this practice rests on shaky legal ground. Thus, those who engage in it will make attractive targets for lawsuits.[44]

Policy Issues

The first issue that must be emphasized in any discussion of the policy debate is what the debate is *not* about. As noted above, it is not about whether religious organizations can engage in religion-based hiring with regard to privately funded jobs, even privately funded jobs within organizations that also receive government funds. Some may want to fight these battles, but they are outliers. Instead, the debate is about whether religious organizations should be able to engage in religion-based discrimination with respect to government-funded jobs.[45] As noted above, this section focuses only on discrimination regarding jobs directly subsidized by government aid.

The involvement of federal direct aid invokes the longstanding policy of providing equal opportunity in federally financed employment, regardless of religion or creed.[46] This policy, which was begun during the early New Deal period, "was established by congressional and executive action" and "extended not only to direct federal employment and employment by government contractors, but to employment and training opportunities provided by grant-in-aid programs as well."[47] Through a 1941 executive order, for example, President Franklin Roosevelt required all defense contracts to contain "a provision obligating the contractor not to discriminate against any worker because of race, creed, color, or national origin" (Executive Order no. 8802, 1941).

Subsequent presidents made their own contributions to this tradition, including President Harry Truman who, in 1951, took "[a] major step" by "iss[uing] a series of executive orders directing certain government agencies to include nondiscrimination clauses in their contracts."[48] In an executive order in 1961 establishing a presidential committee on equal employment opportunity, President Kennedy observed: "It is the plain and positive obligation of the United States Government to promote and ensure equal opportunity for all qualified persons, without regard to race, creed, color, or national origin, employed or seeking employment with the Federal Government and on government contracts" (Executive Order no. 10925, 1961). Finally, as mentioned earlier, a 1965 executive order signed by President Lyndon Johnson generally required all government contracting agencies to include in every government contract a requirement that the contractor not discriminate against any employee on the basis of "race, creed, color or national origin" (Executive Order no. 11246, 1965).

These actions took the commendable steps of identifying certain personal characteristics that were sometimes used as screens to deny otherwise qualified people jobs, and ensuring that those characteristics would not disqualify or diminish citizens' opportunities in jobs that their tax dollars were used to support. Because religion is a category that is recognized for special protection under the Constitution, the inclusion of religion among those protected classes is particularly easy to justify.

For these and other reasons, most would agree that this general policy of prohibiting employment discrimination on the basis of religion in federally funded employment is positive. So, the question becomes, is there any reason to deviate from this policy when religious organizations are the recipients of direct aid?

Proponents of the charitable choice employment policy offer numerous reasons to do so.[49] First, proponents say that groups like the Sierra Club retain the freedom to hire environmentalists when they have government contracts, and that there is no difference between that kind of mission-based hiring and religious organizations' religion-based hiring. Thus, they say, these types of employment practices should be treated the same.

But the American tradition of religious freedom is based on the conviction that religion sometimes must be treated differently. While the state is free to promote secular causes, for example, it cannot promote religion. Even if the charitable choice employment policy is found not to violate the letter of the constitutional ban on governmental promotion of religion, it violates its spirit. By sanctioning and directly subsidizing religious discrimination in employment, the promotion of religion that results seems to bear the government's stamp of approval. And, when the state authorizes a process whereby people are disqualified from holding government-funded jobs because they aren't the "right" religion, the government plays a key role in making religion relevant to citizens' standing in the political community, which is inconsistent with constitutional and policy values (*Allegheny County v. ACLU* 1989).

If one were to focus solely on these special limits, it could appear that religion is being subjected to "worse" treatment than secular pursuits. But such a narrow focus ignores the other side of the coin, where the government often observes special limits that result in special accommodation for religion and only religion. The federal Religious Freedom Restoration Act, for example, prohibits unnecessary and substantial burdens on religious exercise and provides no similar protections for any secular activity.[50] All of these special limits are intended to work together to ensure that the government leaves religion alone, neither advancing nor interfering with it.

Another argument offered in favor of charitable choice is that the government must provide welfare beneficiaries with both secular and religious choices, and therefore the charitable choice employment policy is needed to attract the participation of religious organizations. This argument certainly has some rhetorical appeal, but it is misleading. It suggests that it has been or is national policy to ensure that the government funds an array of religious and nonreligious choices for beneficiaries of government largesse. There is no such national policy commitment. Indeed, the Establishment Clause precludes the government from directly funding religion. Once again, this is not to slight religion, but to recognize that government support for religion not only violates the government's obligation of neutrality, it also ultimately robs religion of its independence and vitality.

In defense of the charitable choice employment policy, a proponent also has argued that these "hiring rights are essential even when a faith-centered organization separates by location or time (and pays for with private money) [religious activities] from its government-funded program." The reasons for this include the fact that, "by experience these organizations have learned that religious activities are important to the success of a social service program even when voluntary, privately funded, and segregated from 'secular' government-funded activities." Charitable choice proponents argue that "forced religious diversity has the effect of stifling religious expression within the agency, creating a climate where employees fear offending other staff with their religious speech or practices" (Esbeck 2003, 77).

Despite the caveats, these comments highlight the fact that the charitable choice employment policy tends to enable the very things the Constitution and good public policy seek to prohibit. Religious expression should be restrained in the government-funded program, but charitable choice is apt to work against that goal. Similarly, the government program should be secular, but the charitable choice employment policy threatens that objective. None of this is to say that religious people will seek to violate the law. The point is that charitable choice sends mixed messages and creates standards that may be confusing and otherwise difficult to follow.[51]

Third, proponents of the charitable choice employment policy claim that, if this policy is not adopted, it will hurt the poor and needy. To accept this claim, one must first believe that the work of religious providers who discriminate on the basis of religion in hiring is superior to the work of religious and secular social service providers that do not do so. But the jury is still out on that question. Further, even if one were to assume that these programs were the most successful, it would not necessarily resolve the issue. As the foregoing illustrates, there are strong interests in ensuring that the government does not promote religion or deny equal opportunity in government-funded employment, even if this would result in a denial of government funding for some of the programs that are the most efficacious.

Another argument offered by proponents of the charitable choice employment policy is that requiring religious organizations to refrain from religious discrimination in government-funded jobs would require a widespread change in current partnerships between religious organizations and government. In the context of direct aid, however, it appears that nondiscrimination has been the dominant norm, at least until recently. In any case, to minimize disruption, any new provisions attaching nondiscrimination conditions to government grants and contracts should not apply to individuals who were employed by religious organizations previous to the date on which the government money was awarded.[52]

Fifth, proponents of the charitable choice employment policy argue that the decision of religious groups to select staff that share their religious convictions is not an act of intolerance but a positive assertion of their freedom. One need not believe these decisions are based in intolerance to believe that they are improper. Title VII's 702 exemption clearly permits religious groups to make employment decisions on the basis of religion; thus, this basic act has been deemed lawful and good policy. The controversy, once again, arises only when the government is asked to subsidize it. When government funds are extended to religious groups, the focus cannot be on freedom or religious autonomy alone anymore—accountability to the government and the common good suddenly has a crucial place in the analysis.

Moreover, our government has prohibited various forms of employment discrimination for at least two independent reasons. We as a nation have objected not only to animus that lurks behind discrimination, but also to its exclusionary impact.[53] Even when an employment distinction is made without any animus, it still means that the door was closed on an otherwise-qualified applicant. When government grants and contracts are involved, the equities weigh strongly on the side of preventing such exclusionary impact tied to religion, even assuming no animus exists. In sum, there appears to be no persuasive reason to deviate from the longstanding policy against religious discrimination in federally funded employment, and many reasons to retain it.

■ Conclusion

This issue is basically a legal frontier. For decades, some of the religious groups that were most committed to religion-based hiring were the same ones that were considered "pervasively" religious and thus ineligible to apply for government grants and contracts.[54] Furthermore, statutes and regulations often restricted all groups, including religious ones, from engaging in religious discrimination in federally funded employment. Thus, these issues were rarely raised in court. Now, however, the Bush administration is actively encouraging groups that engage in this practice to participate in government-funded social service programs by adopting regulations and promoting legislation that would allow them to continue the practice with respect to government-funded jobs. This in turn presents some unprecedented issues that courts must now resolve.

Because this issue is critical to those on all sides, the legal parameters that are articulated by lower courts will be viewed as tentative until the Supreme Court squarely addresses this issue. As noted above, further complicating the matter is the fact that the Court is badly fractured on some of the relevant issues and that it is likely to experience a significant degree of personnel change in the near future. Thus, while it is possible to clear away some of the distortion and misunderstanding that surrounds the issue at this time, a significant amount of uncertainty is likely to linger for years to come.

■ Notes

I would like to thank Alan Brownstein, Steve Green, and Kent Greenawalt for their very helpful comments and suggestions on an earlier draft of this chapter.
    1. H.R. 2210 (108th Cong. 1st Sess).
    2. See *Conference Report on Economic Opportunity Amendments of 1972,* report no. 92-1086 (September 5, 1972); *Conference Report on Economic Opportunity Amendments of 1972,* report no. 92-987 (July 26, 1972).

3. 42 U.S.C. Sec. 9849(a) (2005).

4. *Legislative History of Titles VII and XI of the Civil Rights Act of 1964,* U.S. Equal Employment Opportunity Commission 1 (1968, hereinafter "1964 Legislative History").

5. Executive Order no. 11246, entitled "Equal Employment Opportunity," 30 Fed. Register 12319 (September 24, 1965). President Johnson amended this order in 1967 to add a prohibition on discrimination on account of sex and to substitute the term "religion" for the term "creed." Executive Order no. 11375, 32 Fed. Register 14303-14304 (October 17, 1967).

6. Executive Order no. 13279, entitled "Equal Protection of the Laws for Faith-based and Community Organizations" (December 12, 2002).

7. 42 U.S.C. Section 2000e(b) (2005).

8. 42 U.S.C. Section 2000e-2 (2005).

9. 42 U.S.C. Section 2000e-1(a) (2005).

10. 42 U.S.C. Section 604a (2005).

11. 42 U.S.C. Section 604a(f) (2005).

12. H.R. 2210, Section 654(a)(2).

13. Comments of Representative John Boehner (R–Ohio), 149 Cong. Rec. at H7574 (July 2, 2003).

14. Dan Oshinsky, *New Head Start Plan Passes by One Vote,* States News Service (July 25, 2003).

15. Comments of Representative Marsha Blackburn (R–Tenn.), 149 Cong. Rec. at H7572 (July 24, 2003). Although Representative Blackburn spoke of a need to bring the Head Start nondiscrimination provisions "up to date" with the Title VII 702 exemption, the nondiscrimination provisions of the Head Start program were added to the statute in 1972, the same year the 702 exemption was amended to broaden it. See endnote 2.

16. Section 702 of the Civil Rights Act of 1964, P.L. 88-352, 78 Stat. 241 (1964) (reprinted in U.S.C.C.A.N. at 287)(exemption limited to employee positions "connected with the carrying on by such [religious] corporation[s], association[s] or societ[ies] of [their] religious activities"). Other Title VII exemptions also address hiring on the basis of religion, see 42 U.S.C. Section 2000e-2(e)(1) and Section 2000e-2(e)(2), but this chapter focuses on the 702 exemption, which is considered the most relevant one for religious social service providers.

17. Ibid.

18. See generally Legislative History of the Equal Employment Opportunity Act of 1972 (H.R. 1746, P.L. 92-261) Amending Title VII of the Civil Rights Act of 1964 (prepared by the Subcommittee on Labor of the Committee on Labor and Public Welfare, U.S. Senate, November 1972) (hereinafter "1972 Congressional Legislative History").

19. See generally 1972 Congressional Legislative History, 843–853, 1211–1231. See also Section 702 of the Civil Rights Act of 1964, P.L. 88-352, 78 Stat. 241 (1964).

20. Senators Ervin and Allen reacted vehemently against the proposed deletion of the blanket exemption of educational institutions from the coverage of Title VII that was part of the 1964 Act and against a proposal to add the words "educational institution" to the existing 702 exemption for religious corporations, associations, or societies. See generally 1972 Congressional Legislative History at 843–854. Senator Ervin explained that he believed that this would not only modify the 702 exemption, but also the Section 2000e-2(e)(2) exemption for educational institutions, so that they covered only employment positions within such educational institutions that were involved in "religious activities." Ibid. at 851.

21. 1972 Congressional Legislative History (Debate over Amendment no. 809) at 844. Amendment number 809 proposed to allow religious institutions to discriminate on the basis of religion with respect to all staff positions. Ibid. at 789.

22. See ibid. at 1845 (Equal Employment Opportunity Act of 1972—Conference Report, March 6, 1972).

23. Ibid. at 1645 (Debate over Amendment no. 809).

24. Ibid. at 848 (Debate over Amendment No. 809) (emphasis added).

25. Ibid. at 848–49.

26. Ibid. at 849.

27. Ibid. at 1255 (Debate on Amendment No. 815). Amendment No. 815 proposed to exempt religious organizations and educational institutions completely from Title VII coverage. 1972 Congressional Legislative History at 881. Senator Allen made similar remarks during debate over amendment number 809. Allen stated: "Under the provisions of the bill, there would be nothing to prevent an atheist being forced upon a religious school to teach some subject other than theology." Ibid. at 844.

28. Ibid. at 1256. Further, Senator Allen repeatedly objected to the fact that the bill would give the EEOC oversight of "church-supported schools." See, e.g., ibid. at 845 and 846 (Debate on Amendment no. 809), 1107.

29. If presented with this evidence from legislative history, would a court find that Congress expressed its intent that the exemption should *not* apply to government-funded positions? As noted above, the 1972 Congress did not debate this issue or otherwise formally address it. For this and other reasons, it seems unlikely that a court would find such Congressional intent based solely on the remarks of Senators Ervin and Allen. See generally *Garcia v. United States,* 469 U.S. 70, 76 (1984); Steven K. Green, "Religious Discrimination, Public Funding and Constitutional Values," 30 *Hastings Con. Law Quarterly* 1 (2002).

30. See Comments of Representative Marilyn Musgrave (R-Colo.), 149 Cong. Rec. at H7587 (July 24, 2003).

31. Comments of Representative Sheila Jackson Lee (D–Tex.), 149 Cong. Rec. at H7574 (July 24, 2003).

32. *Hall v. Baptist Memorial Health Care Corp.,* 215 F.3d 618 (6th Cir. 2000); *Young v. Shawnee Mission Medical Center,* 1988 U.S. Dist. LEXIS 12248 (D. Kan. 1988); *Arriaga v. Loma Linda Univ.,* 10 Cal. App. 4th 1556 (Calif. Ct. App. 1992).

33. See *EEOC v. Townley Eng. & Mfg. Co.,* 859 F.2d 610, 618 (9th Cir. 1988) ("All significant religious and secular characteristics must be weighed to determine whether the corporation's purpose and character are primarily religious" and thus eligible for the 702 exemption).

34. Comments of Representative Mark Souder (R–Ind.), 149 Cong. Rec. at H7573 (July 24, 2003).

35. See generally Comments of Representatives Chet Edwards (D-Tex.), Barney Frank (D-Mass.), and Robert C. Scott (D-Va.) in debate over Woolsey amendment to H.R. 2210, 149 Cong. Rec. H7572–7575 (July 24, 2003).

36. Comments of Representative Peter Hoekstra (R–Mich.), 149 Cong. Rec. at H7584 (July 24, 2003).

37. Ibid.

38. "We have no occasion to pass on the argument . . . that the exemption to which [the religious organization is] entitled under [Section] 702 is required by the Free Exercise Clause." *Amos,* 483 U.S. at 339 n.17.

39. See, e.g., *Lemon v. Kurtzman,* 403 U.S. 602 (1971) (J. Brennan, concurring); *Meek v. Pettinger,* 421 U.S. 349 (1975)(J. Brennan concurring in part and dissenting in part); *Wolman v. Walter,* 433 U.S. 229 (1977) (J. Brennan, concurring in part and dis-

senting in part); *Mueller v. Allen,* 463 U.S. 388 (1983) (J. Brennan, dissenting); *Aguilar v. Felton,* 473 U.S. 402 (1985). Furthermore, in *Amos,* Justice Brennan wrote a separate opinion concurring in the judgment to emphasize that he believed the judgment in the case rested on the fact that it involved a challenge to the practices of a nonprofit organization. *Corporation of Presiding Bishop v. Amos,* 483 U.S. at 340–346. His opinion in this case, and his statements in other court opinions, suggests that he would have been wary of extending this principle to other contexts, including a context in which nonprofit organizations received direct government aid.

40. Conversation with Professor Alan E. Brownstein.

41. Charitable choice proponents specifically criticize the *Dodge* decision for relying principally on the *Lemon v. Kurtzman* case rather than the more recently decided *Amos* case. It is understandable, however, that the *Dodge* court looked not only to the *Amos* case, but also to other cases, such as *Lemon,* in which government funds were involved.

And, although charitable choice proponents argue that the *Dodge* case has been criticized by another federal district court in the *Siegel v. Truett-McConnell College* case, the *Siegel* court did not criticize the *Dodge* decision; it distinguished *Dodge* based on the facts. *Siegel v. Truett-McConnell,* 13 F. Supp. 2d at 1344.

42. See *Agostini v. Felton,* 521 U.S. 203 (1997); *Mitchell v. Helms,* 530 U.S. 793 (2000). Moreover, although charitable choice proponents emphasize that the traditional "pervasively sectarian" test that prohibits aid from flowing to religious institutions like houses of worship has been rejected by four members of the current Court (*Mitchell v. Helms,* 2000), that is not necessarily relevant to the issue of whether *any* religious organization may make religion-based employment decisions regarding government-funded jobs.

43. Charitable choice proponents argue that the employment policy they favor is similar to the policy reflected in a federal statute that has already been found constitutional. They cite the "Hill-Burton Act," a federal statute that provides financial aid to hospitals, including religious affiliated ones, but also includes a special provision relating to abortions and sterilization procedures. 42 U.S.C. Section 291 et seq. (2005). This special provision, known as the "Church Amendment," states that the government cannot condition the money on the willingness of a hospital or its staff to perform or facilitate these procedures if doing so would be contrary to the individual's or entity's religious or moral convictions. See 42 U.S.C. Section 300a-7 (2005).

But this act differs from the charitable choice employment policy in important ways. Under the Hill-Burton Act, Congress declined to force certain organizations to choose between being eligible for federal funds and having to perform or assist in acts that would shock their religious or moral consciences. Requiring religious organizations that have elected to administer a secular program to make secular decisions regarding government-funded jobs is not such a burdensome requirement. Similarly, under the provisions of Hill-Burton, the government merely allows religious organizations not to act, whereas under the charitable choice employment policy, the government takes affirmative steps that further explicitly religious activities.

In another effort to argue that the employment policy they advocate is constitutional, charitable choice proponents cite a state court decision in which a court decided that neither the federal nor the state constitution was violated when the Salvation Army received state and federal grants for a drug treatment program and continued to enjoy an exemption from paying unemployment compensation benefits. See *Saucier v. Employment Security,* 954 P.2d 285, 286 (Wash. App. 1998). State law exempted the Salvation Army from paying unemployment compensation taxes because of its status as a church, and the Salvation Army later received state and federal grant funds to perform certain social services. In its brief opinion, the court in *Saucier* separately analyzed the constitutionality of these two government actions, finding a secular purpose from the exemption and a different secular purpose for the drug program.

Under charitable choice, however, the government ties the funding and the exemption together in a single program, creating a much stronger case that the government is promoting or endorsing religion. Further, the issue in *Saucier* appeared to be whether the religious organization as a whole could continue to enjoy the exemption or not. See *Saucier*, 954 P.2d at 286. But in the charitable choice context, the debate is not about whether a religious organization as a whole can enjoy the Title VII 702 exemption. In other words, the charitable choice debate is not about what a religious organization can do regarding privately funded jobs, but about what the religious organization can do vis-à-vis government-funded jobs.

44. While the Supreme Court has never addressed the specific issue of whether it is constitutional to allow religious organizations to discriminate on the basis of religion in government-funded jobs, the Supreme Court *has* rejected a religious institution's argument that conditioning federal financial assistance on compliance with certain statutory nondiscrimination requirements violates the First Amendment. See *Grove City College v. Bell*, 465 U.S. 555 (1984). Further, a recent case decided by the Court lends additional support to the notion that the application of such nondiscrimination conditions to religious institutions does not violate the Free Exercise or Free Speech Clauses. See *Locke v. Davey*, 124 S. Ct. 1307 (2004).

45. It is beyond the scope of this chapter to address cases involving job positions that are partially funded by the government and partially funded by the state, cases that pose a host of difficult questions. See Brownstein 1999.

46. See 1964 Legislative History at 1.

47. Ibid.

48. Ibid. at 3.

49. The pro–charitable choice arguments discussed in this section may be found in the White House booklet, *Religious Hiring Rights*, and in the record of a 2003 hearing on the National and Community Service Act before the House Subcommittee on Select Education of the Committee on Education and the Workforce (April 1, 2003).

50. See 42 U.S.C. Section 2000bb et seq. (2005). Allowing the placement of religious tests on government-funded jobs closely connects the state to a process that favors religion over nonreligion and particular faiths over others.

51. While some have argued that Congress intended with the Religious Freedom Restoration Act (RFRA) (42 U.S.C. 2000bb et seq. [2005]) to block laws such as religious nondiscrimination provisions that follow government funding to religious organizations the evidence contradicts that assertion. RFRA's legislative history states: "Parties may challenge, under the Religious Freedom Restoration Act, the denial of benefits to themselves as in *Sherber[t]*. The act does not, however, create rights beyond those recognized in *Sherbert*." *Religious Freedom Restoration Act of 1993*, Report of the Senate Committee on the Judiciary, Senate Report no. 103-111 (July 27, 1993) at Section V(g). The *Sherbert* case involved a denial of unemployment compensation to an individual worker because she refused to work on her Sabbath, a very different kind of situation than that at issue in a charitable choice program. See *Sherbert v. Verner*, 374 U.S. 398 (1963). Indeed, some of RFRA's chief supporters, such as Representative Jerrold Nadler (D-N.Y.), also have been some of the strongest opponents of the charitable choice employment policy. Many opponents of this employment policy view it as a violation of the Establishment Clause, and RFRA explicitly

states that it is not to "be construed to affect, interpret, or in any way address that portion of the First Amendment prohibiting laws respecting the establishment of religion" 42 U.S.C. Section 2000bb-4 (2005).

52. See, e.g., National and Community Service Grant Program, 42 U.S.C. Section 12635 (2005); Domestic Volunteer Services, 42 U.S.C. Section 5057 (2005).

53. Conversation with Professor Alan E. Brownstein.

54. See, e.g., *Bowen v. Kendrick*, 487 U.S. 589 (1988).

PART 3

Balancing Pragmatic and Theoretical Considerations

The participation of faith-based groups in the public social services enterprise is still rather modest in dollar terms relative to the entire social service universe. This should not overshadow the reality in which faith-based groups now find themselves, with the assistance of public funds, engaged in the delivery of services of every kind. The faith-based initiative has mushroomed into a wide-ranging, multifaceted effort that defies easy categorization or description. Partnerships between government and the religious sector have moved into new and uncharted areas of social service delivery. Governments at all levels are employing new forms of religious nonprofits as partners to provide virtually every imaginable type of social service. As a consequence, the ways in which religion intersects with program services are new as well. In short, it is far more difficult to categorize or generalize as to the nature and shape of faith-based initiatives, the role of faith in service provision, or the actors taking part.

Accordingly, the constitutional questions presented are more difficult as well. Parts One and Two canvassed the main elements, respectively, of the establishment clause and free exercise debates surrounding faith-based ventures. Part Three seeks to go further, exploring the tension between pragmatic and theoretical concerns that adds layers to the constitutional dialogue. The chapters here consider whether resolution of the constitutional church-state dilemma might hinge on more than text, interpretation, and precedent. Namely, to what extent should constitutional analysis be enriched or informed by practice and theory? On one hand, are there philosophical or theoretical objectives that impact constitutional considerations? On the other hand, should practical questions of policy efficacy influence the constitutional debate? Or are these factors the business of legislatures rather than judges? Even if it can be determined that the policies produce good results, should those determinations trump constitutional questions?

In Chapter 8, on faith-based initiatives in the black church, Frank Pryor and David Ryden explore this intersection of the theoretical and the practical. First the authors examine the communitarian indictment of modern liberal constitutionalism as overly attentive to individual rights at the expense of the common good. They suggest that the faith-based movement is as much about building civil society through the revitalization of community as it is about religion. That government should see fit to tap into black churches as potential allies is simply a realistic acknowledgment of the church's central role as the glue of society in poor, stressed, urban communities. Program effectiveness is likely to be achieved by going through those community presences best situated to access difficult-to-reach constituencies; those are black congregations.

Yet the authors also admit the theoretical dangers that surface when government involvement reaches into corners of society that traditionally have stood apart from and against government. Indeed, one classic justification for the need for intermediate civil society is that it constitutes a buffer of protection between the individual and the overbearing state. This concern especially resonates with the black church, which has long been a prophetic voice piquing the conscience of the state on behalf of a dispossessed minority. Thus public funding of black congregations runs the real risk that the state will co-opt a presence that must be free when necessary to protest and object to governmental action (or nonaction). In the end, however, the authors suggest that pragmatism overwhelms all other considerations for black clergy and congregations. The constitutional church-state objections to taking public money are too abstract to concern many black churches, given the stark needs of minority urban communities and the dearth of resources available to meet them.

In Chapter 9, Mary Segers likewise focuses on both theoretical and practical dimensions of faith-based policy, specifically on how faith-based collaborations relate to federalism. The theoretical justifications for the federalist arrangement certainly are on display in faith-based developments at the state level. Around twenty states have created their own faith-based offices or liaisons. Other states have implemented faith-based activity even in the absence of a formal office.

The variety of faith-based approaches across the country raises important and sometimes problematic questions of both practice and principle. On the practical level, how faith-based programs look and work is reflective of the particular state or region in which they are found. Moreover, the policy effectiveness of faith-based efforts is heavily dependent on details of states' faith-based approaches. Segers's analysis on a statewide level of the New Jersey faith-based initiative, which is very much a reflection of a state that is ethnically and racially diverse, urban, and pluralistic, makes this point. Faith-based programs adopt an approach well suited to the state's demographic makeup, much in the mold of the traditional, pre–charitable choice model of religious nonprofit involvement in government work. Great care has been taken to ensure that religion does not bleed into the social services. As a result, the faith-based initiative in New Jersey, while effectively bringing in faith-based new players, has also avoided generating controversy around potential constitutional failings or conflict between religious and secular forces.

It is at this point where constitutional principle and practice intersect. How the differences between the states are viewed relative to the U.S. Constitution depends upon one's broader understanding of the Constitution. Some would read the First Amendment religion clauses more restrictively, requiring greater separation of church and state at all levels of government. The result would be a more uniform understanding of the federal establishment clause limits on governmental-religious interaction. Those limits would trickle downward, narrowing the outer constitutional margins within which the fifty states' policies toward religious nonprofits must fit.

Alternatively, the establishment clause might be interpreted in a more permissive fashion, setting loose boundaries and allowing for a more porous wall of separation. This more accommodating view is based on the realization that real and significant differences continue to exist from state to state and region to region; it suggests that constitutional dictates should at some level be shaped and molded to fit the people who are governed by it. In short, this perspective would prefer that there be some latitude for adopting more flexible legal standards that allow state policy to fit the real differences that persist between states and regions.

In sum, does the principle of federalism allow for more elastic constitutional standards to govern church-state partnerships under the First Amendment so as to take these differences into account? The answer to this question is further complicated by state constitutions and Blaine amendments prohibiting aid to religious institutions.

In Chapter 10, Joyce Keyes-Williams likewise focuses on practical considerations. Her examination of a congregation-based multiservice ministry considers whether the twin objectives of preservation of the religious character of the provider and protection of individual religious liberty rights can be simultaneously realized. She concludes that the latter may well be subordinated to the former. Constitutional problems are likely to go unnoticed, since a church that is doing demonstrably good things via social service and has strong ties to local government officials is not likely to be the target of complaints.

Part Three, then, examines the degree to which practical considerations ought to trump constitutional ones, or how controlling theoretical concerns ought to be. In short, the effort to balance practice and principle in arriving at workable constitutional guidelines is sure to be a complicated one. Moreover, it is difficult to predict how the U.S. Supreme Court might ultimately strike this balance, since the dynamic among the Court's personnel parallels this divide. Atop this divided court sits Justice Sandra Day O'Connor, the ultimate minimalist jurist. O'Connor has demonstrated a strong aversion to broad-based, rule-driven outcomes, instead adopting a cautious, incremental, case-specific style of deciding cases. But unlike the others in the minimalist, pragmatic camp of justices, O'Connor is equally likely to reach outcomes that are conservative or liberal. The fact that she is the decisive vote in church-state cases (where the Court usually is divided along the lines described above) means that the future of this area of constitutional doctrine is highly unpredictable. In the end, a careful eye must be kept on Justice O'Connor as the competing pulls of theory and pragmatism play out on the subject of faith-based initiatives.

8 Serving the Inner City: Social Programs in Black Churches

Frank A. Pryor III and David K. Ryden

> The Negro churches were the birthplaces of Negro schools and all
> agencies which seek to promote the intelligence of the [Negro] masses.
> . . . [C]onsequently all movements for social betterment are apt to
> centre in the Negro church.
> —*W. E. B. Du Bois*, The Philadelphia Negro, *1899*

The enactment of charitable choice legislation by the Clinton administration
and the push by George W. Bush to expand faith-based initiatives have not
been adequately situated in the context of African American politics. Both the
popular media coverage and scholarly analysis framing faith-based programs
have neglected two decades of devolutionary politics and its deleterious impact on the bottom third of the black population who reside in major U.S.
cities.[1] Indeed, faith-based proposals mark a significant alteration in the historical reliance by Congress on social service delivery by secular and governmental entities at the local level of government.

The asserted benefits and drawbacks of faith-based programs are most
acute within the framework of black clergy and congregations. Hence the
merits of faith-based social services have been hotly debated within black circles. For some, the historically rich activism of black churches in the realm of
social service uniquely qualifies them to apply government resources to improve the neighborhoods they serve. For others, the parallel political activism
of the black church and its moral authority as a prophetic presence inevitably
will be compromised by taking on the government as its partner.

■ Outreach to Black Communities on Faith-Based Initiatives

The charitable choice rules embedded in the 1996 welfare reform advanced the
possibilities for faith-based social service providers to compete on equal terms

with secular organizations for government funds to underwrite community outreach. Charitable choice encouraged states to utilize faith-based organizations in serving the poor and needy; it required that the government consider religious organizations for contracts, grants, and vouchers on the same basis as any other nongovernmental provider. It sought to make state and local government rules and practices for buying services more hospitable and less hostile to faith-based groups. While welfare reform shifted ultimate responsibility for social welfare from the federal government to the states, charitable choice heightened both the visibility and the role of religiously based services providers as viable collaborators (Cnaan, Weinburg, and Boddie 1999, x–xi).

The initial impact of charitable choice was modest. It generally remained under the radar screen, without producing a major shift in public monies flowing to private religious charities (Chaves 1999, 7). Things changed dramatically with the elevation of faith-based politics as a significant campaign issue in the 2000 presidential election, and with President Bush's subsequent creation of the White House Office of Faith-Based and Community Initiatives (WHOFBCI). Faith-based legislative proposals produced a hotly contested and contentious policy battle. After a bruising public debate, the bill ultimately stalled in the Senate. This did not stop President Bush from aggressively employing other tactics to achieve results. He issued executive orders extending charitable choice to encompass housing programs, hunger relief, employment training, ex-offender rehabilitation programs, and youth mentoring programs. At the heart of the faith-based element of Bush's domestic policy agenda was the notion that charities, voluntary organizations, and churches could and should play a critical role in assisting the poor.

On one level, Bush's efforts were uncontroversial. Groups like Catholic Charities and Lutheran Social Services were longtime beneficiaries of substantial government largess. In turn, they made a point to incorporate separately from their churches, and typically took care to remove overt religiosity from their services and surroundings. But Bush clearly envisioned moving beyond existing models of faith-based governmental collaboration. The faith-based initiative contemplated a contracting system open to unabashedly religious groups, where they would not be expected to abandon their religiosity upon entering the governmental contracting sphere. Bush asserted:

> The indispensable and transforming work of faith-based and other charitable service groups must be encouraged. . . . Religious groups should have the fullest opportunity permitted by law to compete on a level playing field, so long as they achieve valid public purposes, like curbing crime, conquering addiction, strengthening families, and overcoming poverty. (White House 2001)

A key piece of the president's faith-based agenda was outreach to black churches and leaders. As president-elect, he promptly arranged a meeting with black ministers from across the country to stir up enthusiasm for faith-based social service provision. To head the WHOFBCI, Bush selected John DiIulio, who had strong ties to black clergy and urban, minority neighborhoods. A faith-based Capitol Hill summit that accompanied the introduction of legislation in the House in early 2001 was aimed almost exclusively at African American religious leaders. Throughout his presidency, Bush touted the need to empower black churches to take advantage of public funds for bringing badly needed social services to their communities. Even as he approached reelection, Bush's outreach efforts continued; in early 2004, he marked Martin Luther King's birthday by promoting faith-based initiatives at an inner-city black church in New Orleans.

■ Why the Black Church?

The Bush administration's appeal to black churches and their leaders made sense as substantive policy from a number of angles. First and foremost, African Americans are in many ways the most religious group of citizens in the United States. According to a Gallup Poll, 82 percent of blacks (versus 67 percent of whites) are church members; 82 percent of blacks (versus 55 percent of whites) say that religion is "very important in their life"; and 86 percent of blacks (versus 60 percent of whites) believe that religion "can answer all or most of today's problems" (Gallup 1995, 4).

Moreover, the black churches are broadly connected to black communities overall. Institutionally, the black church's presence in the community is anchored in eight major denominations: African Methodist Episcopal, African Methodist Episcopal Zion, Christian Methodist Episcopal, Church of God in Christ, National Baptist Convention of America, National Baptist Convention USA, National Missionary Baptist Convention, and Progressive National Baptist Convention (see Table 8.1). The National Baptist Convention is the largest denomination of black Christians in the United States, with approximately 33,000 churches and 8.2 million members in 1999. These denominations in sum include over 66,000 churches and more than 24 million members (DiIulio 1999, 129–130). This represents almost 60 percent of the African American population nationwide.

These denominations historically have been successful in addressing a variety of community concerns in black America. Eric Lincoln and Lawrence Mamiya write: "The black church has no challenger as the cultural womb of the black community. Not only did it give birth to new institutions such as schools, banks, insurance companies, and low income housing, it also provided an arena for political activities" (1990, 8). In other words, the black church has occupied historically, and continues to occupy, an unparalleled position as a foundational social institution in the African American community.

Table 8.1   Majority Black Denominations, 1999

Denomination	Congregations	Members
National Baptist Convention USA	33,000	8,200,000
National Baptist Convention of America	2,500	3,500,000
African Methodist Episcopal	8,100	3,500,000
National Missionary Baptist Convention	N/A	2,500,000
Progressive National Baptist Convention	2,000	2,500,000
Church of God in Christ	15,300	2,400,000
African Methodist Episcopal Zion	3,100	1,200,000
Christian Methodist Episcopal	2,300	700,000
Total	66,300	24,500,000

Source: Data collected from the respective websites of each denomination.
Note: N/A = data not available.

Studies confirm the strong social service mission of black churches. Lincoln and Mayima's 1990 survey of 2,100 black churches found that almost two-thirds had one or more social outreach programs. Two-thirds of black church leaders surveyed in the National Black Church Family Project claimed to have at least one community outreach program, with four in ten having at least three such programs (Owens 2000, 9). An examination of black churches in Atlanta found that 85 percent engaged in some form of outreach beyond pastoral or education ministries (Ryden 2003, 255). These studies indicate that black churches are significantly more involved than their white counterparts in providing programs for the poor (Chaves and Higgins 1992, 425–440).

In short, the functions of black churches extend far beyond their role as spiritual center or house of worship. Rather, they are an integral source of social structure and stability in the communities where they are found. Harold Dean Trulear has called them the "centers of neighborhood and community life" (2000, 10). For some, this attentiveness to the social and economic needs of those they serve means black churches are ideally suited to create community in those neighborhoods where community has been lost. As the most permanent institutional presence in urban neighborhoods, black churches are thought to have a capacity to bind together individuals, groups, and society in ways that neither the state nor secular providers can match. Hard-to-reach populations, distrustful of the state or of other outside organizations, may be more accepting of the church located just down the street.

Given the expansive social outreach role of the black churches, it is not surprising that black clergy and churches are more open to the potential of governmental collaboration. In the National Congregational Study, 64 percent of black congregations, compared to only 28 percent of white ones, expressed an interest in receiving public funds for their programs. The study concluded that predominantly black congregations were "five times more likely than other congregations to seek public support for social service activities" (Chaves 1999, 3). In short, the fit between the Bush proposal and black churches seemed to be a confluence of opportunity and interest. This was especially true in light of the detrimental impact on the funding of social service programs from two decades of devolutionary politics.[2] Black churches appeared well situated to take advantage of currently constructed faith-based initiatives to undo some of that effect.

■ The Reasons for Skepticism

There was hardly a universal embrace of faith-based opportunities among African American leaders. Much of the opposition among black leadership to the Bush initiative stemmed from deep-seated suspicions regarding ulterior political motives. For good reason, many wondered if the faith-based outreach was primarily designed as a vote-getting mechanism. After all, the black vote for Bush in the 2000 presidential election did not even rise to double digits. Charges of intimidation and disqualification of black voters, especially in Florida, left a widespread residue of resentment toward Bush. The substantial black turnout in Florida, and the fact that a handful of votes would have altered the outcome, left Bush an illegitimate president in the eyes of many black voters. Indeed, it is hard to overstate the animosity many blacks held toward Bush in the wake of the 2000 presidential election. It was unsurprising, then, that Bush's appeal to black religious leaders was met with appreciable skepticism in many corners.

But the caution that many blacks exhibited toward the Bush faith-based policy extended beyond mere political distrust. Charitable choice and the Bush faith-based initiative only amplified long-standing philosophical differences within the black community regarding the appropriateness of the churches' falling in with the state. Just as the potential benefits of faith-based collaboration arose out of the unique position of the church in black communities, so too did the hesitancy grow out of the black church's equally important role as political and moral voice. Black churches provide political direction and leadership, serving as a catalyst for black cultural identity (Chang et al. 1994). This political dimension—the church's prophetic presence in the face of a society that so often has been dismissive of the needs of black communities—produces a wariness toward the state as a formal ally.

The prophetic role of the black church as voice of opposition to unjust public policy surfaced during the debate surrounding charitable choice and the 1996 welfare legislation. The Congressional Black Caucus (CBC), the National Association for the Advancement of Colored People (NAACP), and liberal religious leaders rejected charitable choice on grounds that it was attached to an inherently unjust welfare bill. How could African American religious leaders and churches chase funds made available under a law that was seen by many as depriving urban minorities of badly needed public assistance? Charitable choice was viewed as "cover" for an effort by a conservative Republican-led government to shrink its commitment to poor blacks. Under the pretense of devolution and privatization, the state was pushing its responsibility for care of the poor onto an already overburdened faith community (Ryden 2003, 256). The prophetic, oppositional role of black churches compelled their opposition to charitable choice, and to the Bush faith-based program that was its logical extension.

The churches' traditional role as political catalyst raised the concern that joint action with the state would undermine their ability to speak and act prophetically. The danger was that the lure of public funds for badly underresourced religious institutions would compromise the clarity of their moral voices, that they would be more timid in condemning ongoing injustices or inequities aimed at black people. The fear was that the faith-based ventures would prove to be the latest form of political patronage, through which funds would be dispensed to religious leaders in exchange for their political support, acquiescence, or silence.

■ The Fault Lines, Constitutional and Political

The multiple roles described above have produced fault lines within the black leadership generally, and black clergy more specifically, on faith-based proposals. More liberal congregations out of the civil rights tradition have vocally opposed the bill (Milbank 2000; Nolan 2004), while conservative religious leaders have welcomed the president's attention (Sherman 1997, 6). For example, when Bush as president-elect hosted a meeting of black ministers to discuss his initiative, it proved highly controversial and divisive. The largest representation at the meeting came from clergy already sympathetic to charitable choice, while civil rights leaders and representatives of the Congress of National Black Churches complained loudly that they were being excluded (Ryden 2003, 258).

Likewise, black voices have been heard on both sides of the constitutional debate. On one hand, there has traditionally existed among black churches and their leaders a more porous wall of separation between church and state than in other religious traditions. Black preachers are less disposed to treat the establishment clause as a pristine wall separating politics from church business. Many are accustomed to seasoning their worship and preaching with some political spice. Consequently, many black clergy are relatively unconcerned about constitutional objections to collaboration between the public and religious sectors. They view charitable choice as having resolved the church-state issues for religious groups willing to partner with the government (Trulear 2000, 17).

Other groups, such as the Congressional Black Caucus, have vigorously attacked faith-based efforts on constitutional grounds. The CBC even hosted conferences devoted to the topic, charging that charitable choice and other faith-based proposals impermissibly allow discrimination in the hiring realm on the basis of religious belief. For some black leaders, their opposition grew out of their strong Baptist affiliation. The Baptist Joint Committee on Public Affairs termed charitable choice a "frontal assault" on the establishment clause of the First Amendment (Baptist Joint Committee 2000). Studies showed that the interest in pursuing charitable choice funds was markedly lower among black Baptist congregations than black congregations as a whole (Chaves 1999).

Questions abound when it comes to the constitutionality of government-sponsored faith-based social services. But those questions are especially acute when considered within the black church framework. This is because black churches have the most to gain *and* the most to lose from such partnerships. On one hand, the case for allowing black churches to participate in government-sponsored social programs is more compelling than it is for white churches. The reasons for channeling social services through black churches are especially convincing, given the central place they occupy in poorer, urban communities. They are uniquely situated to get government benefits into the hands of those who need them most, especially when the potential recipients are young black men who are deeply distrustful of the government. Those public programs that employ churches to serve poor and at-risk populations might well be looked upon more sympathetically by judges called upon to weigh their constitutional merits (Ryden 2003, 267–268).

At the same time, the dangers that accompany church-state partnerships are amplified when the church is a black church. The perils of partnering with government are multifold, from losing the clarity of one's primary mission and prophetic voice, to undermining the spiritual element of the service, to excessive dependence on government money. Because of the special position of black churches in society at large, the impact were these dangers to materialize would be great. While affiliations with government hold out promise for black religious groups hoping to positively influence their communities, such partnerships are fraught with dangers, legally and organizationally. The question remains as to whether churches taking public funds are able to navigate these dangers.

■ The Philadelphia Experience

This section briefly examines the demonstrated potential of black churches to address some of the more intractable problems confronting the neediest and most vulnerable black communities. Despite the reservations of many black leaders, a number of churches have abandoned their initial opposition to welfare reform to collaborate with the state. A growing number of black churches are courting, and receiving, public funds to assist in their social service delivery efforts (see generally Ryden 2003).

This section especially focuses on faith-based institutions operating at the congregational level in black urban Philadelphia. Philadelphia is the nation's fifth largest city, with 1.5 million people in 2000. It also ranks fourth in black population, with 656,000 citizens, representing 43 percent of the city's total population. Of an estimated 2,000 congregations in Philadelphia, black congregations compose about 55 percent, or 1,100 (*Census 2000 Brief* 2001, 7). The programs highlighted below were part of a multichurch study of black urban megachurch congregations in predominantly African American north central Philadelphia.[3] They are located in impoverished neighborhoods, sharing similar socioeconomic status across census tracts. The churches have memberships ranging from 2,000 to 8,000, with 90 percent of the congregants living in the city. This discussion recounts how these churches avail themselves of government funds to enhance a variety of social service programs they operate.

Black churches in Philadelphia have played a significant role in structuring community life, dating back to the establishment of the Free African Society and the founding of Mother Bethel African Methodist Episcopal (AME) Church by Richard Allen in 1787 (Frazier 1964, 30–34). In that tradition, the contemporary urban black megachurches in the Philadelphia study sponsor an impressive array of programs and services: self-help programs, drug and alcohol prevention, job counseling and placement, emergency housing, after-school programs, family counseling, parenting skills, study groups, food pantries, graduate equivalency diploma (GED) classes, summer and recreational programs for teens, health screening programs, and more. They provide a range of social programs for needy children and adults, and willingly accept federal funds through separately established nonprofit 501(c)(3) organizations (a separately incorporated, affiliated nonprofit organization meeting the requirements of Section 501[c][3] of the Internal Revenue Code). Many churches also collaborate with other congregations, community organizations, and government agencies in social service delivery. One pastor in the study noted, "I want this church to be more than an entity in the neighborhood. I envision the mission of this church as addressing the physical needs of the community in addition to providing spiritual nourishment" (personal interview A1, September 10, 2002).[4]

One church in the study built a $700,000 community learning center with ten classrooms that are used for mentoring, day care, and an after-school program that enrolls about 100 elementary school students per semester. A primary goal of this program is to use innovative approaches to bridge the digital divide in students' access to computers, technology, and online resources. The program's state-of-the-art computer lab houses over twenty computers for enhancing basic writing, reading comprehension, and math skills. Partnering with the National Urban League, this church strives to ensure that underserved young people acquire the skills, experience, and resources they need to succeed in the digital age. While the main focus is the development of the youth in the community, adult computer services are offered as well.

The church also provides a drug and alcohol support program, matching participants with the tools to overcome their abuse habits. A referral program directs program participants to the appropriate therapeutic professionals to address any needs beyond the church's capabilities. Substance abuse recovery groups meet weekly, along with drug prevention awareness groups for children. The church also provides an emergency food pantry that feeds 15,000 people annually.

Overall, the faith element manifests itself in several ways. Most of the staff are church members and prayer is part of afternoon activities for both staff and children. While the physical and material services are important, there is a sense of opportunity for a spiritual transformation, a chance to change life circumstances through a relationship with a "higher power." One case worker in the program proclaimed that "the spirit of the Lord permeates all that we do here" (personal interview, P9).

Since 1995, another church has served as a subcontractor for the Philadelphia Workforce Development Corporation. The program is in its seventh cycle, having received over $700,000 in contractual fees. It prepares participants for office work by training them in computer literacy, secretarial science, typing, and résumé building. The church also participated in a state-sponsored welfare-to-work program that received $1.7 million and successfully transitioned 250 Temporary Assistance for Needy Families (TANF) recipients into employment. The church also established a credit union, which provides a range of financial services to residents of north central Philadelphia in neighborhoods where other financial institutions have refused to do business.

A third church in the Philadelphia study received a four-year $1 million contract to operate a job retention program, which includes job training and placement. A prominent and nationally known pastor in the study candidly admitted, "What we do requires federal funds. We simply can't provide the range of services with private and foundation money. The need is such that we need a combination of the three" (personal interview B1, July 23, 2002).

In collaboration with Big Brothers Big Sisters of America (BBBS), Public/Private Ventures, and Pew Charitable Trusts, over forty black churches in Philadelphia are participating in the Amachi Mentoring Program, an initiative for African American children of jailed parents. Its goal is to match young people with adults from churches across the city in an effort to break the cycle of incarceration. Mentors work on life skills and assist youth in establishing positive behavior patterns. The mentoring effort is multipronged: corporate sponsors provide career guidance, academic mentors offer tutorial assistance, and community members emphasize socialization and interpersonal skills (Goode 2002).

In existence since November 2000, Amachi is led by former Philadelphia mayor W. Wilson Goode, who was the first African American elected mayor of the city, serving from 1983 to 1991. He currently is director for faith-based initiatives at Public/Private Ventures in Philadelphia. The mentoring program grew out of research confirming that children of incarcerated adults run a high risk of similar outcomes. For African American children with parents in jail or prison, the likelihood is greater still that they will end up embroiled in the criminal justice system. There are currently 45,000 African American children in Philadelphia whose parents either are in jail or have recently been released (Goode 2002).

As of mid-2002, Amachi had matched over 500 children with adult mentors, with a goal of doubling that figure. BBBS had an effective model of mentoring, but has had limited access to African American children in the city. Its pursuit of partnerships with the churches was an intentional effort to satisfy this unmet need. The black churches were seen as an untapped resource for providing role models who could offer leadership, guidance, and direction to young people who did not receive this in their own homes (Goode 2002).

Early assessments of the Amachi Mentoring Program are encouraging. According to Goode, antisocial activities such as drug and alcohol abuse and fighting are down; academic performance, attitudes, and behaviors are improving, and relationships with friends and family are characterized as more positive. Improved self-concept, delinquency prevention, and social and cultural enrichment were all considered by-products of the mentoring relationship (Goode 2002).

Many church leaders who were interviewed as part of the Philadelphia study see these collaborative efforts with government as a victory for the African American community. One pastor who has run nonprofit organizations in Philadelphia for over thirty years has more recently focused on aiding church leaders in navigating the processes of applying for federal social service funding. He claimed at a July 4, 2001, block party held at a Philadelphia church and attended by President Bush: "It is more effective working through the churches because they have on-going relationships with the people in the community."

Rarely are questions of church-state separation an issue for the church leaders interviewed in this study. With charitable choice expansion in legislative limbo, black congregations are receiving federal funding through federal agencies that have faith-based centers: Housing and Urban Development, Health and Human Services, Education, Justice, and Labor. One pastor noted,

"We set up our separate nonprofit organization, and take it from there. On the religious side, our prophetic message is not muted, but we keep the two separate, and the government stays out of our business" (personal interview, W2, September 10, 2002). Another stated more directly, "Our prophetic message does not get compromised at all because we take government money for the social services we provide. Blacks have always depended on the government and our churches" (personal interview, C1, July 25, 2002). In sum, black clergy in Philadelphia are highly pragmatic when it comes to government funding of faith-based social services; the current set of governmental relationships is simply one way of empowering their churches to carry out their mission to the needy.

■ Why We Can't Wait

At the national level, the Bush administration's efforts to reach out to black pastors through the White House Office of Faith-Based and Community Initiatives appears to have created a partisan divide within black clergy and with other black leadership. Attacked by traditional civil rights leadership, that outreach effort included such notables as Bishop T. D. Jakes in Dallas (Potter's House Ministries), Reverend Kirby-John Caldwell in Houston (Windsor United Methodist Church), Reverend Eugene Rivers of Boston (Azusa Christian Community), and many others. Even before Bush entered the White House, conservative black religious leaders such as John Perkins, Tony Evans, and Gerald Austin were outspoken critics of the welfare system and supported reform, including charitable choice (Sherman 1997, 6). Reverend Floyd Flake, a former Democratic congressman from New York and director of a series of social service programs in his AME church in Queens, actually resigned from the Congressional Black Caucus over its opposition to charitable choice (Brookings Institution 2000).

Ron Walters, head of the African American Leadership Institute at the University of Maryland, notes, "The debate over faith-based [initiatives] is beginning to drive a wedge [between] the traditional civil rights leadership and the leaders of black churches" (Leonard 2001, A01). Among those who came out strongly against the faith-based initiative were Jesse L. Jackson Sr. (Rainbow/PUSH), Reverend Al Sharpton (National Action Network), former congressman Kweisi Mfume (NAACP), Marc Moriel (National Urban League), and the Congressional Black Caucus. They viewed the policy initiative as an attempt to weaken black churches and reduce the Democratic hold on the black vote. When President-elect Bush met with black clergy in Austin, the event was derided by some as "an end run around the traditional civil rights groups and their leaders" (Milbank 2000, A01). The exclusion of clergy hailing from large liberal black churches only reinforced the belief that Bush was cynically wooing African American voters upset over the alleged voting rights injustices in Florida and elsewhere in the 2000 presidential election. According to Jesse Jackson, "The same forces that sought to deny us [Blacks] the right to vote in Florida now are trying to neutralize the strength and the voice of black churches. It's all about voter suppression . . . and the black clergy should watch out because money is seductive" (Leonard 2001, A01).

Some outspoken critics of the election, however, have grown receptive to the initiative. Reverend Walter Fauntroy is an African American Baptist minister and former Democratic delegate to Congress from the District of Columbia who led an inaugural protest over the election of President Bush. In explaining his openness to the Bush proposal, Fauntroy explained that he "was not about to walk away from an election in 2000 I thought we won and say to the president, 'Dispense the money wisely, it's all yours.' Not when we have people and institutions at risk and churches that can get the job done" (Leonard 2001, A01).

Critics of the faith-based plan accuse Fauntroy and others like him of being pawns in a patron-client relationship. Their silence with respect to Republican policies that are unfriendly to blacks is the implicit quid pro quo for their receipt of federal funds. As Reverend Al Sharpton charges:

> We have a responsibility to be prophets to Pharaoh, not subsidized by Pharaoh. If he [Bush] wants to put money through the churches to develop communities, then fine. But if he's going to buy the silence of those of us that are supposed to tell it like it is, then it's nothing but a payoff and we ought to reject that payoff. And we ought to render unto Caesar what is Caesar's, and render to God what is God's. (Black Think Tank II 2001, 14)

Frederick C. Harris offers a more academic and less polemic explanation, noting that

> political elites have used public funding of church-based ministries to build political alliances with black ministers. At times, these alliances have compromised the ability of activist ministers who receive funding to speak out on political matters that may be in conflict with political elites who are supportive of their faith-based efforts. . . . Public funding of churches through programs such as charitable choice has the potential to undermine the civic tradition of church-based black activism by rewarding funding to activist ministers and churches who might be induced into accepting funding in exchange for their public support of candidates and policy initiatives. (2002, 15)

But supporters and recipients of faith-based public funds offer a different perspective. In so doing, they lay bare the dilemma presented by faith-based initiatives as means of empowerment and community control for the more disadvantaged end of the African American community. Bishop T. D. Jakes contends:

> While we grapple with and wrestle with the intention of the President and
> the faith-based initiative . . . I think it distracts us from the greater opportu-
> nity . . . of getting control of our own communities and creating our [own]
> opportunity from this leveraged position to reach our own people and reha-
> bilitate them through the auspices and economy that is provided from the
> government to the church. It gives power back to the community and we can
> regulate that power to our advantage. (cited in Harris 2002)

But Jakes offers little on how this "leveraged" position would translate into
tangible benefits from the government. Nor does he specify how it might
counteract a discriminatory social structure that arguably was responsible, at
least in part, for the marginalized status of many black Americans. Adolph
Reed articulates the critique:

> It is absurd to present neighborhood and church initiatives as appropriate re-
> sponses to the effects of government-supported disinvestment; labor market
> segmentation; widespread and well-documented patterns of discrimination
> in employment and housing, as well as in the trajectory of direct and indirect
> public spending; and an all-out corporate assault on the social wage. (1999,
> 127)

In a political landscape with few policy options for impoverished blacks,
Jakes and other proponents interpret faith-based initiatives as an opportunity
for blacks to seize control of their communities, and to enhance their self-
determination in the process. In contrast, Sharpton and other adversaries of
the faith-based initiatives accuse the black middle class and clergy of prop-
ping up what Reed labels the "social management apparatus." Reed contends
that genuine black activism in addressing the predicament of economic and
social marginalization has been neutralized by the emergence of black offi-
cialdom, of which black clergy are a part. He argues that "[they] vie for the
right to rationalize an externally generated agenda to the black community"
(Reed 1999, 69–71).

Beneath the political fray, the Philadelphia experience with faith-based
initiatives renders this abstract debate largely irrelevant. For many black
clergy and church members in Philadelphia, access to federal money at the
congregational level is welcome as churches seek to make themselves relevant to the needs of a marginalized community.

While the anecdotal evidence from the programs described above is encouraging, the ultimate success and structural impact of faith-based programs
await more in-depth empirical analysis. Until then, opportunities for faith-
based organizations to avail themselves of public funds present a difficult
choice for black churches. Government grants and contracts are an appealing
source of funds for churches committed to expanding their services. But participation in such programs may be seen as condoning the poverty politics of
their primary political sponsors. It remains for black churches to decide

whether they can reconcile the prophetic and social service dimensions of their character.

The balance to be struck is a difficult one. Churches must be able to collaborate without losing the power to confront. In the end, faith-based programs provide an opportunity for black churches to influence their neighborhoods through active engagement. This demands that they add to, not abandon, past practices. It means supplementing their role as petitioner of the state with active participation. Appeals to government for justice must be combined with proactive cooperation with government to implement policy. It means not only legal or political advocacy, but also the pursuit of change in society through service made possible by government (Ryden 2003, 268).

Churches need to be fully cognizant of the constitutional restraints and implications of entering the state-sponsored social services sphere. Indeed, it may be that the emerging role of black urban megachurches in Philadelphia and other major cities institutionalizes short-term survival needs at the expense of long-term social justice, and not a coupling of the two. But in an era of center-right politics and the accompanying devolution movement, black advocates of the faith-based initiative contend that those on the bottom rung cannot wait.

■ Notes

1. Devolution is the shifting of power, authority, and responsibility for programs and services from the federal government to state and local governments while reducing federal aid in an effort to reverse or reshape the welfare state: "Devolution is the antithesis of the welfare state in which the central government assumes full responsibility for the social and health needs of individuals with low income. In the United States, the process of devolution has resulted in the replacement of federal allocations for social services by smaller block grants to the states. The states, in turn, ask counties and cities to do more with less and engage nonprofit organizations in the provision of services" (Cnaan, Weinburg, and Boddie 1999, x).

2. According to the U.S. Conference of Mayors during the Reagan administration, federal funds as a percentage of city budget were reduced from 18 percent in 1980 to 6.4 percent in 1987, a drop of 64 percent (Gunther 1990, 254).

3. The Hartford Institute for Religion Research characterizes the megachurch as a cluster of congregations with (1) regular weekly attendance in excess of 2000 persons; (2) a charismatic, authoritative senior minister; (3) an active seven-day-a-week congregational community; (4) a multitude of social and outreach ministries; and (5) a complex differentiated organizational structure (http://hirr.hartsem.edu/index.html). Urban megachurches were selected for this study because of their commitment to remain in their inner-city locations. As such, they ensure social stability for inner-city neighborhoods in transition. Large congregations have also expressed a greater willingness to take advantage of charitable choice opportunities because of their organizational capacity (Chaves 1999, 1). Furthermore, these congregations are viewed as trendsetters in the contemporary Christian world, with many smaller or mid-sized

churches looking to the programmatic characteristics of the megachurch for clues about what their congregation should be doing to help the black community.

The social power and influence of the megachurch is considerable, as Scott Thumma observes: "In order to understand fully the dynamics of mega-churches, they must be seen as a collective social phenomena. The rise of hundreds of these large churches in the last several decades implies that this new pattern of congregational life has a particular resonance to and fit with changes in modern American society and culture. . . . [T]his analysis offers a possible explanation of the symbolic significance of the mega-church phenomenon both for the spiritual lives of its members and its relationship to modern society" (http://hirr.hartsem.edu/index.html).

4. The personal interviews referenced here and in the following sections were conducted by Frank A. Pryor. The identities of the interviewees have remained confidential at their request.

Drawing on Tradition: New Jersey's Statewide Initiative

MARY C. SEGERS

Two years after passage of the 1996 welfare reform law (the Personal Responsibility and Work Opportunity Reconciliation Act) and three years before President George W. Bush established the White House Office of Faith-Based and Community Initiatives (WHOFBCI), New Jersey under Governor Christine Todd Whitman launched a faith-based community development initiative. Originally conceived as a division of the Department of Community Affairs, the New Jersey Office of Faith-Based Initiatives (OFBI) is a partnership between state government and private funders such as J. P. Morgan–Chase Manhattan Bank, Public Service Gas and Electric (the state's largest utility), and the Center for Non-Profit Corporations. In its five years of existence, the OFBI has funded over 140 grantees in most of the state's twenty-one counties.

New Jersey offers an instructive example of a faith-based initiative. In contrast to the 1996 charitable law, the Garden State follows traditional patterns of governmental funding of nonprofit social service agencies such as Catholic Charities and Lutheran Social Services. Its policy requires that a funded program be an incorporated entity, a 501(c)(3) nonprofit group (a separately incorporated, affiliated nonprofit organization meeting the requirements of Section 501[c][3] of the Internal Revenue Code). It also stipulates that faith-based groups cannot proselytize and must follow civil rights laws in their personnel practices. As a result, the New Jersey faith-based initiative has avoided the thorny First Amendment religious establishment issues that have dogged President Bush's faith-based initiative.

This does not mean that the New Jersey faith-based initiative has not encountered difficulties. In 2002, during the transition to the new Democratic administration of Governor James E. McGreevey, it became clear that the program had been subject to financial mismanagement and improper auditing. In response, Governor McGreevey moved the OFBI from Consumer Affairs to the Department of State. Secretary of State Regena Thomas in turn replaced the leadership of the program and began a proactive campaign for more assistance from federal agencies. Democrats Thomas and McGreevey cooperated with federal administrative agencies and the WHOFBCI, in part because of severe state budgetary cutbacks. They hoped federal funds would ease the 40 percent cut in the $5 million annual budget of the New Jersey OFBI.

In this chapter I examine the inception and development of the New Jersey initiative, some of the programs it has funded, as well as some of the difficulties it has encountered. My tentative assessments require drawing some comparisons with President Bush's proposed initiative, and a thorough understanding of the political culture of New Jersey and its impact on the establishment and implementation of the policy.

■ President Bush's Faith-Based Initiative: A Brief Overview

On January 29, 2001, nine days after his inauguration, President George W. Bush introduced a major public policy initiative, proposing to facilitate the flow of government funds to churches and other religious groups that offer social service programs to the needy. Calling this faith-based initiative the cornerstone of his agenda of "compassionate conservatism," the president sought to promote contributions to religious organizations while encouraging those groups to adopt a wider range of social services with the help of federal funds. The president described his initiative in these terms: "We're in the process of implementing and expanding 'charitable choice'—the principle already established in federal law that faith-based organizations should not suffer discrimination when they compete for contracts to provide social services. Government should never fund the teaching of faith, but it should support the good works of the faithful" (Bush 2001).

Indeed, charitable choice was not new. It first appeared as a little noted provision in the 1996 welfare reform law,[1] sponsored by then-senator John Ashcroft (R–Mo.). One of Ashcroft's goals in proposing charitable choice was "to encourage faith-based organizations to expand their involvement in the welfare reform effort by providing assurances that their religious integrity would be protected" (Ashcroft and Carlson-Thies 1996). Calling it a constitutionally permissible partnership between government and the churches, Ashcroft had argued that charitable choice would protect simultaneously the rights of faith-based providers and the religious liberty of the individuals they serve.

Amid the furor over the broader welfare reform, charitable choice garnered little attention. Even following the law's passage, charitable choice was something of a "sleeper." During the Clinton administration, federal administrators largely ignored it. Its implementation at the state level was sporadic at best, nonexistent at worst. Nevertheless, both Al Gore and George W. Bush explicitly touted the notion of faith-based collaborations on the 2000 presidential campaign trail. Once elected, President Bush followed through by establishing the White House Office of Faith-Based and Community Initiatives to implement that campaign position.

Stated briefly, charitable choice is a legislative provision designed to remove unnecessary barriers to the receipt of certain federal funds by faith-based organizations that provide social services. According to the Department of Health and Human Service's website (http://www.hhs.gov/faith/choice/html), charitable choice rests on four principles:

- *A level playing field.* Faith-based providers are eligible to compete for funds on the same basis as other providers, their religious character neither favoring nor disadvantaging them.
- *Respect for the integrity of faith-based organizations.* The religious character of faith-based providers is protected by their retaining control over the definition, development, practice, and expression of their religious beliefs. Government cannot require a religious provider receiving funds to alter its form of internal governance or remove religious art, icons, scripture, or other symbols to be a program participant.
- *Protecting client rights.* In rendering assistance, religious organizations cannot discriminate or deny admission to the program on the basis of one's religious beliefs, affiliation, or refusal to actively participate in religious practices or activities. If one objects to the religious character of a program, an equivalent secular alternative must be provided.
- *Church-state separation.* The government funds must be used to fulfill the public social service goals of the program, and no direct government funding can be diverted to inherently religious activities such as worship, sectarian instruction, and proselytization.

The Bush faith-based initiative encountered stiff resistance almost immediately, from opponents on left and right. The ensuing controversy and the ultimate demise of congressional efforts to implement the president's faith-based initiative are complex but fascinating stories beyond the scope of this chapter.[2] In the face of congressional failure to enact new legislation, President Bush resorted to executive orders to implement further charitable choice provisions. The Bush administration has made significant progress on the faith-based initiative, quietly and without public controversy, by assertive use of administrative action and the executive branch bureaucracy. This silent revolution may be the most important success of the Bush faith-based initiative (Tenpas 2002, 13–16).

■ The Political Culture of New Jersey

The New Jersey faith-based initiative announced by Governor Whitman in January 1998 was both similar to and different from the federal proposal. One cannot understand the political reasons that spawned the governor's policy without some sense of the political culture of the Garden State. New Jersey is the ninth most populous and the most densely populated state in the nation.[3] There are 566 municipalities in the state and no county land remains unincorporated. Sandwiched between the large metropolises of New York and Philadelphia, Jerseyans have a strong penchant for home rule and local control. Jersey voters are also independent-minded: the state's U.S. senators are Democrats (Jon Corzine and Frank Lautenberg), but Republicans controlled the governor's office and both houses of the state legislature from 1993–2001. Nationally, the state's fifteen electoral votes went to Clinton (over Dole) in 1996 and to Gore (over Bush) in 2000.

The old industrial character of the Garden State is evident in its major cities: Newark, Trenton, Elizabeth, Jersey City, Camden, and Paterson. But three decades of changing demographics have left it predominantly suburban. The state is so varied and complex racially and ethnically that it has been called a virtual "microcosm of the United States, with urban, suburban and rural areas, significant blue-collar ethnic areas as well as sizable black and Hispanic populations" (Burnbauer and Dodson 1990, 7).

The state's population of 8,414,000 increased 8.6 percent over the 1990 census figure (7,748,000). Of the total population, 13.6 percent are African American, 5.7 percent Asian, and 13.3 percent Hispanic (with large numbers of Mexicans, Puerto Ricans, and Cubans) (U.S. Census Bureau 2001, 26–27). During the 1990s, the state's growing Asian and Arab populations produced a corresponding increase in the Muslims and Hindus in the state. Earlier immigrant groups are also well represented: Italians, Irish, Polish, and other eastern European nationalities. New Jersey's religious makeup is 46 percent Catholic, 26 percent Protestant, 6 percent Jewish, 1 percent Muslim, and 5 percent atheist/agnostic.[4] In short, the state is tremendously diverse. This variety, coupled with the state's population density, demands that Jerseyans learn to live with one another peacefully, cooperate, and respect others' religious beliefs.

Religious conservatives have a significant presence in New Jersey. They range from Catholic traditionalists and charismatics to conservative evangelicals. Religious conservatives usually unite around prolife issues, working toward such abortion restrictions as parental notification and late-term abortion bans. They have succeeded in electing actively prolife state legislators, and have reelected Representative Chris Smith (R–N.J.) to Congress from the fourth congressional district. Smith has introduced numerous antiabortion measures in the House and is perhaps the most prominent legislator in Washington associated with the issue. The state as a whole is generally moderate to left-leaning on abortion. It is one of the few states that funds the abortions of poor women; its last five governors (three Democrats and two Republicans) have been prochoice.

On the constitutional level, the New Jersey constitution goes well beyond the U.S. Constitution in those provisions related to religion. Religious freedom and rights of conscience are protected under Article 1, paragraph 3, while Article 1, paragraph 4, forbids religious establishment and the use of religious or racial tests for public office. Article 1, paragraph 5, is a broad yet specific rejection of all forms of discrimination. Most significant, the state constitution prohibits public funding of houses of worship. Article 1, paragraph 3, states that no person shall "be obliged to pay tithes, taxes, or other rates for building or repairing any church or churches, place or places of worship, or for the maintenance of any minister or ministry, contrary to what he believes to be right or has deliberately and voluntarily engaged to perform." This language is pertinent to whether public funds can be granted to faith-based organizations under New Jersey law.[5]

Article 1, paragraph 5, also contains a nondiscrimination clause stating that "no person shall be denied the enjoyment of any civil or military right, nor be discriminated against in the exercise of any civil or military right, nor be segregated in the militia or in the public schools, because of religious principles, race, color, ancestry or national origin." Unsurprisingly, the New Jersey faith-based initiative requires that faith-based organizations receiving funds not discriminate in hiring on the basis of faith or creed.

In sum, religious freedom and church-state separation are enshrined firmly in New Jersey's constitution. Indeed, church-state relations are generally calm in the Garden State. The more salient and controversial issues in New Jersey politics concern the environment, urban sprawl, traffic congestion, racial justice, and education (the New Jersey Supreme Court ordered assistance to twenty-eight poor, largely inner-city school districts). The paramount issue for most New Jerseyans is taxes; local government relies very heavily on property taxes, and the state reluctantly instituted an income tax in the 1970s.

This unique political culture provides the contextual backdrop for New Jersey's faith-based initiative. In contrast to other states or on the federal level, the initiative has not provoked major church-state controversy. Governor Whitman's faith-based community development initiative generated little opposition, in part because the program has been small, with budget allocations of $5 million per year for the first several years. Another factor is Jerseyans' recognition that churches in inner-city and poor rural areas are neighbors that provide valuable social services and need funding to do so. Third, the diversity of New Jersey works to defuse controversy. The tremendous ethnic and religious variety of the state, coupled with its population density, underscores the need for toleration in a highly pluralistic environment. Jerseyans as a result have a strong tendency to respect and accept one another's religious traditions.

Finally, the structure and format of the state's faith-based policy enabled it to avoid the fate of the Bush plan.

■ The New Jersey Faith-Based Initiative

New Jersey's faith-based program was one of the first in the country, antedating President Bush's initiative. Governor Whitman proposed the faith-based community development initiative in her second inaugural address, in January 1998. Whitman was first elected New Jersey governor in 1993, but her victory was marred by her campaign strategist Ed Rollins's boast that he had given black clergy "street money" to suppress urban votes—a factor he claimed was decisive in her victory. Whitman adamantly denied knowledge of such actions, but her first gubernatorial term opened with questions about her relationship to black citizens and voters.

When she ran for reelection four years later, Governor Whitman approached various clergy, including many black pastors, for ideas and assistance in shaping new urban initiatives. By this time, the initial effects of the 1996 welfare reform were playing out in New Jersey, as people being pushed off welfare rolls turned to local churches for assistance. As a result, clergy asked Whitman for state aid to assist them in meeting the rising demand for social services. On January 20, 1998, coming off a narrow reelection victory, the governor stated in her inaugural address:

> Talking bricks and mortar isn't enough. Our cities also need another kind of renewal; a renewal of faith, hope, and confidence. That's why I've launched a Faith-Based Community Development Initiative. We will expand our support of religious organizations that are already building shopping centers, offering job training, and providing childcare in their communities. I am proud to announce a State commitment of $5 million for this initiative. (cited in Peterson 2002, 3)

The state legislature quickly approved Whitman's initiative and allocated $5 million to the new Office of Faith-Based Initiatives. Those programs receiving grants from the OFBI have covered a broad range of services: nonprofit health care services, transitional housing programs, food pantries, after-school safe haven programs, tutoring services, homeowner education programs, soup kitchens, drug rehabilitation programs, midnight basketball programs, homes for mothers with AIDS and their children, and community centers for the elderly. Isaiah House in East Orange received state funding to lease minivans to transport teenagers—of whom Isaiah House has physical custody—to sports and cultural events. In Cherry Hill, the Jewish Community Center received a similar grant for minivans to transport the elderly to shopping centers (Williams-Alston 2002).

In accordance with the state constitution, the OFBI does not fund houses of worship. Programs must incorporate as 501(c)(3) nonprofits to qualify for funding. Under the authorizing legislation, faith-based organizations are defined and limited by the following:

- They have been created by a community of faith and maintain a relationship with it.
- They have a separate 501(c)(3) nonprofit status.
- They have a special impact on neighborhood stability.
- They provide services to low- to moderate-income families.
- They do not proselytize.
- Grants cannot support construction or "bricks and mortar" projects.
- Recipients must comply with civil rights laws in hiring practices, and avoid nepotism and other questionable employment practices.

In addition to grant allocation, the OFBI hosts conferences to aid small churches with accounting, grant writing, and training for board membership (the board of directors of the social service program must be separate from the board for the mosque, church, or synagogue). The need for technical assistance is so great that the OFBI has developed the Faith-Based Training Institute to provide more frequent training sessions. Learning how to incorporate as a nonprofit, select board members, run board meetings—these are essential for small faith communities who provide neighborhood social services. The goal is to equip them with the requisite skills to build capacity and enhance their ability to apply for and implement grants from other sources.

The OFBI has, from the start, intentionally avoided some facets that triggered major criticisms of the Bush initiative. It explicitly prohibits proselytization or sectarian teaching. It mandates nondiscriminatory hiring in accordance with civil rights laws and the state constitution. It mandates on-site monitoring requirements with both announced and unannounced visits. It also coordinates with the Department of Health and Human Services to assist people transitioning from welfare rolls to work.

Over the five years of its existence, the OFBI has allocated a total of $17.5 million to 142 groups. In addition, the annual conferences and training workshops conducted by the OFBI likely enable some of these faith-based groups to apply for federal funding made available under President Bush's initiative.

■ Select Profiles of Funding Recipients

The New Jersey OFBI announced its first round of grants in December 1998, distributing $3.6 million among thirty-seven faith-based organizations across the state to fund a host of neighborhood revitalization and social service programs. Those groups funded included Christian, Jewish, Muslim, and several interfaith organizations. The United Jewish Federation–MetroWest received $150,000 to expand statewide programs that help senior citizens in need through services such as home-delivered meals and preventative health care. Waris, a Muslim organization based in Irvington, New Jersey, received $150,000 to assist people making the transition from welfare to work by offering training in workplace literacy, computer skills, and job placement services. In Perth Amboy, Cathedral Community Development Corporation Vision 2000 was awarded $140,000 to expand its "trackless trolley" that provides transportation to and from the city's downtown business district, provide support services for the homeless, and train people coming off welfare (http://www.state.nj.us/dca/98annual/aisle2.pdf). Three grant recipients in particular—Isaiah House, New Community, and Faith Fellowship Community Development Corporation—provide a better sense of the New Jersey faith-based initiative.

Isaiah House

One of the first grant recipients under the New Jersey policy was Isaiah House, an interfaith group in East Orange, a largely black Newark suburb. Isaiah House received $120,000 to expand its programs to help people overcome substance abuse and find jobs. Groups included in the first round of grants received funding at approximately the same level for three years. Following its initial three-year term, Isaiah House received another $75,000 for employment counseling and training for the hard-to-employ.

As a nonprofit agency for children and families, Isaiah House is community based and supported. Its focus is on the homeless, many of whom have HIV or AIDS. In operation since 1988, the organization is the lone shelter in the area, and provides temporary lodging, food, social, and financial services for over 100 families a year. Isaiah House also houses teenage girls, maintains a food pantry, and furnishes prenatal outreach, child care, and HIV services. Many clients are mothers with AIDS and their children. Part of Isaiah House's initial grant was used to lease minivans for transportation of clients to clinical and educational service programs (http://www.isaiahhouse.org).[6] Isaiah House has received a number of awards; in 2000, the Department of Housing and Urban Development included Isaiah House in its "Top 100 Best Practices in the Country."

Isaiah House is ecumenical in fact and in spirit. It has a diverse staff from a range of major faiths—Christians, Jews, Muslims, and Hindus. Many staff members are veiled in accordance with religious custom. While Isaiah House acknowledges religious holidays in its newsletters, there is no prayer or worship services on the premises. One staff member remarked that a faith dimension operates mostly at the board and senior staff level; that is, it provides the reason and motivation for the pursuit of funding and delivery of social services to a needy population.

New Community

New Community in Newark is the largest community development corporation in the United States and New Jersey's largest nonprofit housing corporation. Founded in 1968 by Reverend William J. Linder and a group of Newark residents, New Community was a direct response to the Newark riots of 1967. Since its inception, New Community has been a major contributor to urban revitalization, especially in the Central Ward, which was devastated by the 1967 disorders.

New Community owns and manages 3,000 units of affordable housing and employs 2,300 people (93 percent of whom are minorities). It operates eight "Babyland" child care centers, community-based health care programs, job training, and education programs. In 1990 it persuaded Pathmark, a major supermarket chain, to move to Newark, establishing the first supermarket in Newark's Central Ward in twenty-five years. That shopping center also attracted a Dunkin' Donuts, a Nathan's, a copy center, and a pharmacy. New Community runs a job training and continuing education facility, a large welfare-to-work program, and charter schools. It has continued to expand; its facilities, services, and programs, which now extend beyond Newark into Jersey City and Englewood Cliffs, provide for the needs of over 50,000 people on a daily basis.

New Community's mission is "to help residents of inner cities improve the quality of their lives to reflect individual God-given dignity and personal achievement." This mission initially played out in a focus on decent affordable housing, with the first housing development opening in 1975. The organization then sought to use new housing to spur neighborhood revitalization. To promote a sense of ownership and pride, New Community developed a process for community participation, actively involving residents in the design and management of new housing. In 2000 the OFBI awarded New Community a $75,000 grant for welfare-to-work services. Even with net assets of $300 million, New Community relies on grants and funding from outside sources to carry on its many activities (http://www.newcommunity.org).[7]

In 2003, New Community celebrated its thirty-fifth anniversary at Queen of Angels parish in the Central Ward. In his remarks, founder Reverend Linder spoke of New Community's origins in the civil rights movement, and the challenges ahead. In those comments, one can discern the faith-based foundational values of the organization. The faith commitments of New Community and its staff are worked out in practical ways on a daily basis. As New Community serves "communities that are most economically in need while fostering a sense of self-reliance and determination," faith-generated values are on display and imparted to those served. Reverend Linder described the corporation as "you and I and people from communities and neighborhoods working together and rebuilding brick by brick. . . . This is my mission and your mission" (cited in Flores 2003, 16). Through all its activities, New Community conveys a religious worldview grounded in personal dignity, social interdependence, and the importance of community.

Faith Fellowship Community Development Corporation

Faith Fellowship Community Development Corporation (FFCDC) is a faith-based nonprofit organization whose programs and services are aimed at addressing the personal needs of community residents who require assistance to improve the quality of life for themselves and their families. It is an offshoot of Faith Fellowship Ministries World Outreach Center, a megachurch of over 6,000 congregants in central New Jersey. Begun in the early 1980s by Pastors David and Diane Demola, this nondenominational church is a "regional Christian Church" with members from Pennsylvania, Staten Island, Brooklyn, and all points in northern, central, and southern Jersey.

Faith Fellowship is a melding of the traditional and modern. Part basilica and part corporate headquarters, it is located in a modern, spacious corporate park next to the Middlesex County Fire Academy. The church and its attached buildings contain three kitchens, a large lecture hall that also services wedding receptions, a large conference room, and well-equipped classrooms. The large basketball gym is home court to a dozen teen basketball teams. The buildings include a baby day care room, a chapel, the large sanctuary for services, a bookstore, and a computer room for the church's in-house computer system. The space includes a television room equipped for distance learning, an office for printing (the church prints all its books, booklets, and publications), and a "Holy Grounds" coffee shop on the premises (an attractive stop for those people commuting to church from significant distances for services). A small school is being phased out in favor of Agapeland Daycare, a child care and early literacy program for which FFCDC received an OFBI grant of $47,500 in 2001 (Bulluck 2002).[8]

The megachurch connection means that FFCDC is already a well-established nonprofit well acquainted with the business of grantsmanship and programs. The relative sophistication of the corporation is evident in its leadership. Reverend Clarence Bulluck brings both business and church volunteer experience to his work as executive director of FFCDC. He not only worked for twenty-seven years in sales and marketing for AT&T, but also has been a volunteer in the church ministry for two-thirds of that time. An ordained minister, Bulluck is politically astute and knowledgeable. He started FFCDC in 2001, when he took advantage of state-sponsored training workshops and learned how to establish a tax-exempt 501(c)(3). He is assisted by Julie Vasquez, program coordinator, who has a background in social work and business and is fluent in Spanish.

The church and corporation are separate 501(c)(3) organizations with separate boards of directors and tax identification numbers. The church has a "vision" statement; the corporation's mission statement states in secular language what it hopes to accomplish with its social services. Only the corporation is audited by federal and state governments. Clearly, the pastors and clergy of the church do not wish the government to tell them how to spend charitable donations. In short, the church and the corporation coexist in a "separate but equal" partnership. The close ties are exemplified in the fact that all volunteers come out of the Faith Fellowship Ministries congregation.

Faith Fellowship Community Development Corporation seeks to enhance the quality of life for low- to moderate-income residents through self-sustaining community initiatives. It aims to accomplish community goals more effectively by developing strategic partnerships with public and community organizations, churches, corporations, and governmental agencies. Many in the congregation come from old New Jersey municipalities (Plainfield, Perth Amboy, Newark) that have fallen on hard times financially. FFCDC's programs target the needs of these people—through education in financial literacy, first-time home-buyer programs, and home maintenance programs. FFCDC operates job fairs, health fairs, services to ex-offenders, youth after-school programs, and early literacy learning programs. Its fairs attract banks, realtors, government agencies such as Freddie Mac and Fannie Mae, and local employers. Reverend Bulluck is clear about FFCDC's mission, which is "not running soup kitchens" but rather as "the feet on the street" (Bulluck 2002).

Faith Fellowship Community Development Corporation understands the constraints of the faith-based initiative in New Jersey: no religious proselytizing and no religious hiring. While the church and the corporation are two distinct organizations, the corporation depends on the church for its volunteers. Consequently there is a sense of the corporation as the "works" part and the church as the "faith" part. The theology that underpins the church spills over into the good work that trained volunteers carry out in the corporation's programs. The biblical call to stewardship and service is reflected in practical efforts to help low- to moderate-income people buy homes, learn sound financial practices, obtain high school diplomas and learn English as a second language, and develop entrepreneurial initiatives. Finally, Reverend Bulluck stresses the importance of professional practices: developing a track record of success on stated goals and objectives, and careful record keeping and reporting to granting agencies, whether public or private.

* * *

These grant recipients demonstrate how groups that diverge in their religious dimension nevertheless pursue their faith-based mission through the OFBI. Isaiah House is interfaith and ecumenical in staffing and orientation. New Community is a community development corporation led by a Catholic priest and informed by incarnational theology. Faith Fellowship Community Development Corporation is a nondenominational Christian megachurch whose activities reflect the duty of all Christians to do good works. All have succeeded within the constraints of the OFBI without compromising their mission or character.

■ Lessons from New Jersey

So what lessons can be derived from the New Jersey faith-based initiative? First, it is difficult to quarrel with public funding for minivans so the Jewish Community Center in Cherry Hill can transport the elderly to shopping centers. And what is objectionable about using public funds to supply vehicles to Isaiah House in East Orange for mothers with AIDS and their children? The theoretical strictures of church-state separation recede when we consider the practical operation of these programs. The plain fact is that small, nonprofit organizations are desperate for funding to enable them to meet the needs of the poor and the dispossessed.

Second, assistance to faith-based neighborhood organizations that help build "social capital" is difficult to oppose. One recipient of a faith-based grant emphasizes the positive, beneficial effects of the program, pointing to the lasting capacity improvement for these small nonprofits and church-related groups: "The net beneficial effect is not so much the grants themselves (these are important, to be sure, but they come and go) but the building of the capacity to network and acquire the skills to manage such programs and to attract future funding. This is why the New Jersey Faith-Based Training Institute is so important" (confidential interview, August 2, 2002).

Third, communitarians and advocates of civil society emphasize the localism and personal contacts of such faith-based programs and social services. The point of contact is not an impersonal federal bureaucracy, but neighborhoods and communities where people know and trust one another. As one state official remarked, "This program works because these faith-based organizations are neighbors of the people they serve. They encourage self-sufficiency and self-improvement while giving people the support they need to improve their lives" (Kenny 2001). Program benefits come with civic bonds and connectedness that hopefully will remain once the benefits have ended.

I have yet to hear anything negative about the New Jersey OFBI. In this, it is quite unlike the controversial federal initiative. Hence it is worthwhile to conclude with a comparison of the New Jersey and Bush faith-based initiatives. First, there are similarities in political context. Both programs have political origins. As noted above, Governor Whitman needed to mend fences with New Jersey's African American community after the controversy surrounding her first election, in 1993. In the case of President Bush's policy, the faith-based initiative was an important piece of his agenda of "compassionate conservatism." While Bush, from all appearances, is sincere in his belief in the power of religious groups to effect personal transformation through social service, it would be naive to ignore the potential political benefits of the Bush faith-based policy. Like Whitman, President Bush is attempting to woo certain constituencies, namely African Americans and Roman Catholics. In the 2000 election, African Americans preferred Gore to Bush by nine to one. Providing assistance to social programs run by small black churches that serve mostly black communities might garner for President Bush more support among black voters. Catholics essentially split their 2000 vote, with 50 percent supporting Gore compared to 47 percent supporting Bush. Catholics are a crucial demographic group, concentrated in seventeen states with large electoral votes. Moreover, the Roman Catholic Church is the largest single nongovernmental provider of social services in the country. Hence, easing the path of government funding to faith-based service programs also could generate more support for President Bush among Catholic voters.[9]

But the New Jersey and Bush policies are very different in other respects. First, Whitman provided funding to back the New Jersey initiative, committing $5 million in the first year and raising money from private corporations to fund future grants. In contrast, the Bush administration provided little in new funds to back the federal initiative. The president simply sought to make faith-based organizations eligible on equal terms with other nonprofits to compete for existing contracts and funds. This left Bush vulnerable to criticism from established faith-based organizations such as Catholic Charities (Formicola and Segers 2002).

Second, the constitutional issues are much less acute in the New Jersey case. The state constitution clearly rules out direct public funding of houses of worship. Accordingly, the OFBI will only fund religious organizations that form independent corporations. The policy also stipulates that faith-based groups cannot proselytize, and the nondiscrimination clause of the constitution compels that faith-based organizations receiving public funds not discriminate in hiring on the basis of faith or creed. In comparison, the Bush initiative has raised a host of questions about direct government assistance to churches, synagogues, and mosques. Neither charitable choice nor the Bush plan requires churches to set up separate 501(c)(3) organizations. This raises the concern that more easily commingled funds might be used to pay for overtly religious activities. Critics also worry that the Bush administration's policy rides roughshod over civil rights laws forbidding discrimination in hiring. Finally, some suspect that the Bush initiative is part of a broader agenda: to further weaken church-state separation and embrace church-state partnerships, cooperation, and accommodation.

When the New Jersey law was formulated, it focused on community development corporations as well as church-based groups. It also emphasized state funding and private sector contributions rather than federal funds. Finally, it was drafted in accordance with a state constitution that is stricter than the federal constitution on issues of religious freedom, church-state separation, and nondiscriminatory hiring.

On a practical level, the faith-based organizations profiled in this chapter are successful in serving the needy and the disadvantaged while complying with the requirements of the New Jersey faith-based initiative. Each set up a separate, independent corporation; they carefully avoid proselytizing or religious instruction; none conduct worship services as part of their programs; they obey state civil rights law in hiring.

Thus the New Jersey policy is much more in line with the long-standing practices of public funding of faith-based providers such as Lutheran Services or Catholic Charities. The important role of religious organizations in providing social services is recognized. The New Jersey case lends support to this traditional approach. It is noncontroversial and well accepted, and has the added appeal of avoiding the thorny First Amendment issues concerning religious establishment and religious liberty that have dogged the Bush administration's faith-based initiative.

New Jersey adopted the traditional approach to more carefully comply with a state constitution that is stricter than the U.S. Constitution in barring funding of churches or church ministries and prohibiting discrimination on the basis of faith or creed. New Jersey is also a microcosm of the nation's religious and ethnic diversity; this pluralism necessitates public policies that respect religious freedom and church-state separation and avoid sectarian strife.

The New Jersey case reveals a pluralistic state that is wary of government endorsement of religion, and that has taken pains to avoid entanglement with the provision of services by faith-based organizations. The state has adopted a more practical approach to social services for the needy. Faith-based groups are grateful recipients of public funding and have not experienced undue burdens in their free exercise of religion.

The Bush administration can learn from the Garden State how better to use faith-based groups to build community. New Jersey got there first—with a noncontroversial program to fund faith-based providers of essential social services. The point must be stressed: faith-based initiatives are part of a welfare reform designed to free people from poverty, not a strategy to effect major changes in church-state relations.

■ Notes

1. P.L. 104-193, the Personal Responsibility and Work Opportunity Reconciliation Act, enacted August 22, 1996, Sec. 104.

2. For a detailed inside account of that story, see Jo Renee Formicola, Mary C. Segers, and Paul Weber, *Faith-based Initiatives and the Bush Administration: The Good, the Bad, and the Ugly* (Lanham, Md.: Rowman and Littlefield, 2003); and Black, Koopman, and Ryden, 2004.

3. New Jersey is a very small state in size. It ranks forty-sixth among the states with a total area of 8,224 square miles. According to the 2000 census, the population per square mile of land is 1,134.2 persons. See U.S. Census Bureau 2001, 26–27. See also League of Women Voters of New Jersey 1969.

4. These figures are from the *Star-Ledger*/Eagleton Poll, September 2001. I am indebted to Cliff Zukin of the Eagleton Institute of Politics, Rutgers University, for supplying this information. A category of "Other" would include religious groups under 1 percent, such as Mormons, Hindus, and Bahai.

5. The original Blaine amendment was a federal constitutional amendment proposed by Representative James G. Blaine of Maine in 1875 (it was part of a nineteenth-century U.S. reaction to large waves of Catholic immigration and the creation of a parochial school system in the country). The Blaine amendment never won congressional approval, but similar "little Blaine amendments" appeared in state constitutions, partly because Congress required them in state constitutions as a condition for admission to the Union. New Jersey does not have a Blaine amendment prohibiting the use of public funds to support religious instruction. However, the state constitution does have a provision that allows for transportation of students attending private schools (Art. 8, Sec. 4, para. 3). I am indebted to G. Alan Tarr, professor of political science and director of the Center for State Constitutional Studies, Rutgers University, for information on the New Jersey Constitution. For the Blaine amendment generally, see Philip Hamburger, *Separation of Church and State* (Cambridge: Harvard University Press, 2002), 297–298, 324–325; John T. McGreevy, *Catholicism and American Freedom* (New York: W. W. Norton, 2003), 91–93; John Witte, *Religion and the American Constitutional Experiment* (Boulder: Westview, 2000), 87, 301; and James Hennesey, *American Catholics: A History of the Roman Catholic Community in the United States* (New York: Oxford University Press, 1981), 182–187.

6. This description is also based on information provided by El-Rhonda Williams-Alson, executive director of the New Jersey Office of Faith-Based Initiatives.

7. Also I am relying on a packet of information about the New Community Corporation distributed by Monsignor William J. Linder at the March 2001 annual meeting of the American Society for Public Administration held at Rutgers University in Newark.

8. Unless otherwise noted, all references are to this interview.

9. Here, it is interesting to note that the Catholic bishops were very critical of the 1996 welfare reform act and fought vigorously to modify what they saw as some of the more egregious features of the legislation. However, five years later, they were among the more ardent supporters of charitable choice and the president's faith-based initiative. See Formicola and Segers 2002.

10 Congregations as Service Providers: Devolution in California

JOYCE KEYES-WILLIAMS

This chapter tells the story of how one church acts out its faith in serving the community and city at large.[1] This congregation, referred to here by the pseudonym "A Tranquil Place" (ATP), is well known for its "ministries of help" to community members in the city of Oakland. It provides basic needs assistance, and works in collaboration with other area churches, nonprofits, businesses, and government agencies to address crime, advance education, and empower all people "regardless of age, race, class, and religion."

Devolution provides the broader context within which the story of ATP develops. After a brief overview of charitable choice, I conclude with an examination of ATP in light of the constitutional debate surrounding charitable choice.

■ Background

Almost a decade has passed since the enactment of the welfare reform law known as the Personal Responsibility and Work Opportunity Reconciliation Act of 1996. This is long enough to critically examine implementation efforts by states and counties and to see its impact on local human service providers. In their *First Look* at welfare reform, the Federalism Group of the Rockefeller Institute of Government noted, "Although devolution to the states is widely discussed in describing the welfare reforms now underway, the real federalism story of welfare reform is *local*" (Nathan and Gais 1999, 35).[2] The report, authored by Richard Nathan and Thomas Gais, highlights major developments in transfer of welfare and related human service program responsibilities to local entities.[3]

161

The "policy mantra of the 1990s" was a "new era of devolution" in which federal policymakers looked to all types of nongovernmental organizations (including faith-based organizations [FBOs] and congregations)[4] "to build human, economic, and social capital necessary to bring about change" (de Vita 1999, 216). In particular, nonprofit providers have been drafted to help alleviate poverty by encouraging employment and strengthening families and reducing long-term welfare dependency.

Robert Wineburg states that social policy programs "are being sent from the federal government to the states and then are implemented at the local level based on the view that the individual and corresponding voluntary and religiously based set of services are the best vehicles to handle the problem of welfare and poverty" (2001, 5). Wineburg recasts "devolution" as "*devilu-tion*" to expose how the "language of good and evil" entered the public discourse of social welfare policy in the early 1980s through the 1990s. He claims that the ideas of conservative intellectuals such as George Gilder and Charles Murray converged with religious televangelists Jerry Falwell and Pat Robertson to impact the course of social welfare policymaking. By focusing on the failures of the federal welfare bureaucracy to adequately provide much-needed services for the poor, they viewed states and local governments as better suited for a greater role in solving many of the country's social problems. Grassroots organizations were on the ground in the trenches meeting community needs, and were preferable to the government as providers of social services. At the same time, the notion of personal responsibility was implanted in the minds of recipients of assistance.

Lester Salamon anticipated this direction of government in his discussion about the nonprofit sector in general, and the rise of a "third-party" government in particular. In his book *Partners in Public Service,* Salamon describes privatization and the broader trend toward devolution:

> Significant transformation has taken place in the way federal government goes about its business—a shift from direct to indirect or "third-party" government, from a situation in which the federal government ran its own programs to one in which it increasingly relies on a wide variety of "third parties"—states, cities, special districts, banks, hospitals, manufacturers—to carry out its purposes. (1995, 9)

Richard Nathan, director of the Rockefeller Institute of Government, takes privatization a step further in his remarks about the faith-based initiative. He notes that "non-profit groups provide most social services and community development programs. . . . It's not privatization; it's non-profitization" (Fois 2002).

In sum, devolution and privatization have altered views of the nature and role of the federal welfare state, leaving the federal government often functioning as a "broker" managing contracts rather than providing direct service. Devolution has historical antecedents and remains an ongoing trend. The concept is deeply rooted in the constitutional debates over federal versus state responsibilities in particular public policy areas. Devolution provides the broader context within which the charitable choice legislation and faith-based initiatives are situated.

■ A Brief Overview of Charitable Choice

Collaborative efforts between the government and faith-based groups in welfare and related human service delivery are not a new phenomenon. Prior to the passage of charitable choice, faith-based organizations (i.e., predominately large organizations such as Catholic Charities, Lutheran Social Services, and the Salvation Army) did, in fact, obtain substantial financial contracts directly from government agencies to provide human services. However, these organizations, because of their religious affiliations, were required to establish a separate nonprofit organization—designated as a 501(c)(3) under the Internal Revenue Code—to receive government funding.

Charitable choice removed this requirement and expanded the list of eligible service providers to include more overtly sectarian institutions. Critics have contended that this statutorily favors openly religious organizations over others, but the main controversy lies in whether including smaller, local "houses of worship" as service providers unconstitutionally links government to intensely religious organizations. The fear is that direct funding to congregations is likely to result in the intermingling of public money with congregational funds, leading to the advancement of religion.

But simultaneously balancing the interests of faith-based organizations and government may not always be feasible. Indeed, charitable choice fails to address what constitutes undue pressure or proselytizing. Supporters of charitable choice point to the benefits of increasing the alternative solutions to help poor people become self-sufficient. Furthermore, not only are beneficiaries of services denied genuine choice, but congregations are also constrained in their ability to provide a range of diverse services.

On the flip side, tangible public support of faith-based organizations may conflict with the government's constitutional mandate to provide nondiscriminatory services to the needy. It may be unrealistic to legally require government officials to respect the religious character and identity of government-funded FBOs and not to interfere in their organizational operations. As is always the case with government contracts, direct oversight of faith-based contractees is not always possible. In short, managing the relationships between government agencies and FBOs is much more complex than the mere awarding of a contract.

Nevertheless, the framers of charitable choice included careful protections for FBOs and articulated certain rights of beneficiaries of services. The controversial charitable choice provision outlined the specific goals and rules of the relationship between government agencies and FBOs. The three main goals of charitable choice were to (1) encourage states to expand the involvement of community and FBOs in antipoverty efforts, (2) protect the religious integrity and character of faith-based organizations that accept government funding for social services, and (3) protect the religious freedom of beneficiaries (Solomon and Vlissides 2001, 9). Additionally, the rules that govern the funding of FBOs clearly reinforce those goals and the protections on both sides of the service delivery relationship. But the law appears to be at odds with itself in insisting that "pervasively sectarian" institutions ought to receive funds while simultaneously protecting the religious freedom of service recipients.

Scholars have questioned the feasibility of realizing both interests simultaneously. In theory, the rules delineate what *is* and *is not* acceptable. In reality, the dynamics between FBOs and the government play out quite differently. The establishment clause states that "Congress shall make no law respecting an establishment of religion, or prohibiting the free exercise thereof." The extent to which the establishment clause limits "government action promoting religion" is at the forefront of the constitutional debate of charitable choice. Ira Lupu and Robert Tuttle, legal scholars at George Washington Law School, assert that partnerships between government and FBOs are contentious because "our constitutional law, at varying times and in varying degrees, has imposed limits on government's authority to finance the delivery of social services with sectarian institutions" (2002, 1). They characterize the period from the late 1940s into the 1970s as strictly separationist, when the establishment clause was interpreted to disfavor any government involvement in religion. From the 1980s to the present, there has been a discernible movement toward "neutrality," with the courts allowing governmental involvement with religion provided that government does not discriminate against any particular religion.

Lupu and Tuttle argue that the current legal tensions with charitable choice exist primarily around whether employers can discriminate in their hiring based on religious beliefs, since "FBOs are frequently exempt from the federal prohibition on religious discrimination in employment, but not in every federal program" (2002, 2). While the legal obstacles to faith-based partnerships appear complex and challenging, considering a specific case in light of charitable choice brings understanding from a practical standpoint and adds insight to this multifaceted debate.

■ The Context of the Case Study: Oakland, California

Oakland is the largest city in Alameda County in the East Bay Area of the northern region. According to the state's finance department, Oakland is California's eighth largest city, with 408,800 residents. Alameda County ranks seventh in population size of counties (with approximately 1.5 million inhabitants), and also is the seventh fastest-growing county in California. The dramatic growth in population has been accompanied by unprecedented stress on city and county officials and residents, as a result of crowded living conditions and inadequate job supply. Densely populated cities often experience an increase in such social problems as crime rates, unemployment, and overcrowding in rental housing and public classrooms. Certainly this has been the case in Oakland.

Oakland also has been hit hard by U.S. economic restructuring over the past two decades. Its east and west sides have high concentrations of crime, drug traffic, and prostitution, and other illegal activities prevail. In his narrative of church-based community organizing in the Bay Area, Richard Wood describes how the loss of manufacturing jobs transformed East Oakland from "a belt of solid blue collar neighborhoods [into] an area of concentrated poverty and shuttered factories" (1997, 1). Today, main streets are filled with abandoned retail stores and dilapidated buildings, with homeless individuals making their beds at the entrances of these establishments.

The discouraging situation was clarified in a 2000 report by the Community and Economic Development Agency, a local research and development organization. The agency's study confirmed Oakland's housing woes, identifying six major housing problems facing the city: population fluctuations, lack of jobs, large concentrations of low- and moderate-income households, inability to maintain stable housing due to increased costs and fixed income, inability to afford homeownership, and overcrowding in rental units.

Oakland's crime rates remain well above the national averages in each of the major crime indicators, as Table 10.1 indicates. This gruesome picture has

Table 10.1   Oakland's Crime Rates Versus National Averages, 2001

	National Average	Oakland, California
Population	114,967	373,215
Violent crimes per 100,000 population, total	506.0	1,349.9
Murder	5.5	21.4
Forcible rape	32.0	85.7
Robbery	144.9	516.9
Aggravated assault	323.6	725.9
Property crimes per 100,000 population, total	3,650.1	5,364.8
Burglary	728.4	939.4
Larceny-theft	2,475.3	3,122.1
Motor vehicle theft	414.2	1,303.3
Arson	32.2	N/A

Source: 2001 FBI Uniform Crime Reports.
Note: N/A = data not available.

threatened the safety of city and county residents, raising serious concerns for city and county officials.

A number of church leaders joined together to address the crime issue and speak with a united voice. Like most community organizations, they believed the city needed more resources devoted to issues of poverty, homelessness, and recreation for youth. One pastor echoed this sentiment when he stated that "the problem is not police and crime. The problem is economics. The problem is education. The problem is family structure." A common theme in the stories of grassroots, community-based organizations is the lack of resources and educational opportunities. This case study examines one congregation, A Tranquil Place, that took up the fight against crime and poverty in its neighborhood.

■ Description of the Case Study: A Tranquil Place

A Tranquil Place is situated in the heart of inner-city East Oakland. Its mission is to "express . . . love for Jesus through fervent prayer, worship, anointed prophetic preaching as well as outreach and the demonstration of the power of the Holy Spirit, all within the context of a caring environment of faith as [they] grow together into the stature of Christ and pass this vision on to succeeding generations." The 2,000-member congregation was established in 1965 with the goal to "serve [the] generation[s] by the will of God as inspired by Genesis 49: 9–10," the story of Jacob blessing his sons, who go on to establish the twelve tribes of Israel.

ATP is very active in helping the homeless and disadvantaged in the city. Its services include an emergency housing shelter called Mercy Ministries, a food and clothing distribution center, after-school care and tutorial programs, health fairs that provide free physical exams and eye and dental checkups, block parties and "marches for righteousness" in the neighborhood, a counseling center, a Bible college, and international missions. ATP also participates in "Adopt-a-Cop" and chaplaincy programs run by Oakland Police and Clergy Together, a collaborative project of law enforcement and clergy to address crime in their neighborhoods.

ATP has three generations of leaders involved in the ministry. Pastor Daniel's mother (Reverend Valerie) founded ATP after she migrated to California from Vancouver, Canada, following the Great Depression and the death of her husband in World War II. Pastor Daniel's son and daughter-in-law are the college ministry leaders, while his daughter and son-in-law are the youth and children's ministry directors. Both adult children of the senior pastors (Daniel and Mary) are also raising their children in the church and "look forward to passing the 'spiritual mantle' on to them to carry on their work," according to Pastor Daniel's son.

Pastor Daniel believes the church should not be "a sleeping giant in the community." Therefore, he has become involved with the police department and mayor's office in the "war against poverty and drugs" campaign and other movements to address East Oakland's most pressing social ills. His love and compassion for people of all backgrounds have led one follower to describe him as being on a mission to "unify the body of Christ." Pastor Daniel's desire for unity between churches and denominations led him to organize monthly corporate prayer meetings for local pastors. He firmly believes that breaking down walls of separation begins with the leadership. Hence, ATP serves as the lead congregation in initiating multicultural and interracial reconciliation in the surrounding religious and secular communities.

The acute crime problems have led local residents to call on their ministers to act. Heightened citizen concerns drove leaders to organize a "Pray the Bay" event involving thirty different Christian congregations of various denominations (Jaime 2001). All eight counties surrounding Alameda County sent representatives to join with local Oakland churches. The ministers walked through the city and prayed, sometimes stopping to pray with individuals. Prior to the event, mailers were sent to area pastors, which read: "Gather in the name of the Lord. Coming Together to Promote Unity. Coming Together to Be a Blessing. Coming Together to Increase the Daily Prayer Presence Over Our Neighborhoods, Work Places, & Schools." Attendees emphasized "the responsibility of the church of Jesus Christ" to unite to "reclaim their city from the kingdom of darkness." ATP was one of the lead congregations helping to organize the event. Some critics have wondered, in light of the strong biblical message, whether ATP is the type of FBO to which the government should look to carry out social services. The answer to this question lies in part in the history of the relationship between government and church leaders.

■ A Historical Account of ATP Community Outreach

ATP has had a strong presence in Oakland since the late 1960s. It had a humble beginning, with a congregation numbering about twenty renting a storefront for worship. Pastor Valerie said, "It soon became evident, following the prolonged battle with City Hall over the use permits for a facility, that this . . . diverse body of people had been uniquely called to" teaching people about "the grace of God" and "His desire to bless and fully restore His children." In 1967, ATP opened a Bible college to equip ministers and lay people for "effective leadership within local assemblies as well as cross-cultural and community involvement." A focus on international missions also began in the early years of ATP ministries with the launching of missionary endeavors in Hong Kong, Japan, Israel, and China. Eventually ATP expanded its ministries into eastern Europe, taking medical supplies into Romania and holding crusades throughout the region. Leadership conferences, church plantings, and Bible colleges were established to train pastors and leaders in assisting people. From its very beginnings, ATP offered services to everyone who expressed the need for help.

In 1970, ATP expanded by purchasing three storefronts in East Oakland. Located next to the church, these storefronts functioned as offices and classrooms. A fellowship coffee shop was opened as was a twenty-four-hour hotline for those needing emergency assistance. In 1973, ATP hosted the first national meeting of Exodus, a ministry to people leaving the homosexual lifestyle. Pastor Valerie also experienced a serious illness and what she describes as a miraculous healing after being paralyzed for more than a year. Taking this as a sign from God to expand ATP's ministries and services, she joined forces with her son.

By 1977, ATP had about 700 attendees each week. By this time, city officials were well acquainted with ATP, and supported its expansion efforts. ATP purchased apartment complexes and dwellings across the street and next to the church to provide ministers and other individuals with affordable housing. In 1979, ATP purchased an old movie theater in East Oakland, which it converted into its permanent facility, complete with a sanctuary with a seating capacity of a thousand, a gymnasium, a fully equipped kitchen, and numerous classrooms. In the early 1980s the church purchased a nearby Mobil station to serve as a neighborhood food and clothing distribution center.

In the early 1980s, ATP aligned with other Bay Area churches "in an effort to unite ministries throughout the city." In 1985 the murder of a church member propelled the community into the spotlight. ATP took a major role in comforting neighbors in the immediate surrounding area. This led to "new forums . . . to share the love and life that Jesus offers, compared to the hopelessness that comes through violence, drugs and crime." The March for Righteousness began, and soon rippled out through the city's east side. Daniel, the current senior pastor, described it as a way to take a "visible stand against sin in our city and offer practical help for hurting people in our community."

The husband-and-wife team of Daniel and Mary were installed as senior pastors in 1985, where they currently remain. Meanwhile, the church continued to increase its community involvement. Block parties were organized in drug-ridden city neighborhoods. These events were marked by original "worship and praise music" and games, as well as offerings of clothing, food, and spiritual help. The block parties were an especially "effective way of spreading hope and building bridges of communication" between the church and neighbors in the community. On any given Saturday, there were likely to be three or four block parties occurring in various neighborhoods. As a result, ATP had become very visible throughout the city.

ATP also partnered with city and county government agencies on a host of projects. On several occasions, it brought together coalitions of local churches, community organizations, businesses, law enforcement officers, and government agencies to address the city's problems. Public officials at the local, state, and federal levels have recognized the contributions of ATP in the community. It has worked with public health, city, and county agencies on community health fairs to assist the underserved (mainly Spanish-speaking immigrants) with various health needs. ATP also cosponsored a homeless shelter in the face of the lack of affordable housing.

ATP's current emphasis on unity grew out of racial reconciliation meetings that it hosted in the early 1980s. Eight hundred Christian leaders from around the city gathered together to pray for Oakland. Today over fifty churches are represented at monthly prayer gatherings for clergy—the East Bay pastors' prayer meeting. ATP also held open public meetings to discuss the region's problems and what churches might do. The meetings were a reflection of the desires of local ministries to make a reality Jesus' prayer of John 17 for protection for his followers from the "evil one."[5]

Intentionally focused outreach ministry to various ethnic groups in and around ATP continued to evolve in the late 1980s and early 1990s. Special services for Spanish, Filipino, Samoan-speakers, and Ethiopians were established, as pastors responded to the rush of immigrants settling in the area. Although ATP continued to gather as a congregation on Sunday mornings, other meeting times also were established for groups to fellowship, worship, and pray in their native languages. The pastors felt it important to preserve distinctive cultures and to create environments where individuals could worship in ways and languages consistent with their culture. One pastor spoke proudly of ATP's efforts to reach out to everyone:

> This type of outreach primarily provides multiple doors of entry into fellowship with the church but more importantly with Jesus Christ. Our local body continues to become not only multiracial, but also multicultural as people from many nations become part of the membership. Currently, we have over fifty nations [who] are represented among congregants at ATP.

National flags decorate the sanctuary walls. Once every several months there is a "multicultural day," where the church celebrates its diversity and oneness in Christ. The services incorporate music from different countries and individuals dress up in traditional garb. Following worship, a dinner is hosted in the fellowship hall featuring an assortment of ethnic dishes. In the weeks leading up to the "Celebration Sunday," special emphasis is placed on reaching out to friends, family, and others who do not normally attend church.

These events demonstrate the purposefulness of ATP in reaching out to all people in the surrounding neighborhoods. Serving people without regard for race or ethnicity is the bedrock of the congregation. ATP acts on what it considers a "holistic understanding of the gospel of the kingdom of God." Its goals from the very beginning were to help anyone in need through "material support, as well as a new life through faith in Jesus."

The past decade has seen the congregation move into other types of community involvement. An alternative school for the Oakland Unified School District is housed at ATP. Students who attend either are awaiting disciplinary hearings or for some other reason are unable to function in conventional educational settings (due to language barriers, severe emotional problems, and so on). An associate pastor remarks that "the Lord has allowed us to teach a spiritual values class which is a miracle in most public school settings." The curriculum incorporates religious materials, but presents it in a practical way by instructing students in the principles of compassion, commitment, personal responsibility, and community applied to everyday life issues.

ATP also hosts the Parent Empowerment Program (PEP), sponsored by World Vision International. World Vision is a Christian humanitarian organization that provides emergency relief, education, health care, economic development, and promotion of justice in more than 100 countries (World Vision 2002). PEP trains parents of elementary school–age children how to work within their school system and how to teach them spiritual values in parenting. In addition, ATP maintains a ministry for inmates in North County Jail and San Quentin and Santa Rita Prisons. Teams of church members conduct visitation on a regular basis. Released inmates also may receive follow-up counseling from trained counseling staff at ATP. ATP's close working relationship with the Oakland Police Department through the "Adopt-a-Cop" program enables it to serve as advocate for inmates in matters involving local law enforcement. Moreover, ATP maintains a chaplaincy program of prayer and visitation at two Alameda County hospitals. In nursing homes, special services are frequently arranged for residents to attend. Music is provided, along with preaching, prayer, and communion.

Finally, ATP cosponsors safety programs for elementary public schools at its church facilities. Community leaders, police, church members, and neighborhood residents gather to talk about ways to keep their neighborhoods safe. These public meetings are important open forums. In one meeting, citizens shared both their appreciation for and complaints with local law enforcement agents firsthand. The police in turn solicited community members to work with them to better perform their jobs. As one attendee described it, "We cannot fight crime and violence alone; the only way is to have an open, honest dialogue about real issues to really communicate the problems in our city. A nonthreatening environment is required and here at ATP this is made possible."

ATP is well known for convening different groups and diverse sectors of society to collectively pursue problem solving. Most attendees find such meetings central to successfully attacking the social problems that plague the city neighborhoods. In sum, ATP has maintained an impressive history of service, not only to its church members, but to the community as well. At first glance, it appears that the services and programs offered are all positive with no negative effects. But how does ATP fare in terms of the constitutional issues raised in the FBO-government relationship?

■ Analysis of the Case in Light of Charitable Choice

Several aspects of the ATP case study implicate constitutional themes of nondiscriminatory service provision on the one hand, and the protection of the religious identity and character of the FBO on the other. Maintaining the balance between these two facets is complex. This congregation made an intentional effort from its beginnings to reach out to diverse ethnic populations and create a culture of inclusiveness and acceptance. Yet one might question whether it could require people to sit through a religious message while they are simultaneously receiving a meal or clothing. From firsthand observations, homeless people attending the services did not seem concerned about the message. Indeed, most ignored the announcements over the loudspeaker encouraging them to pray with a staff member if interested in spiritual guidance. The primary focus was on the enjoyment of a good-portioned, warm meal.

Likewise, teaching spiritual values in parenting classes seems harmless—that is, if the parent is interested in a spiritual perspective that incorporates the study of religious texts into the learning process. But which spiritual perspective will the class curriculum follow? PEP candidly applies Christian teachings and principles to issues of poverty. The vision, mission, and core values are all linked to a biblical worldview.

As to individuals' religious freedoms, no one voiced a complaint with how ATP offers its services (i.e., material support with a strong "Gospel message"). The evangelical thrust is evident in the comment of the founding pastor about block parties allowing the church to "share the love and life that Jesus offers." This and similarly religious remarks about taking "a visible stand against sin in our city" might suggest that ATP's viewpoint is for the most part evangelistic. The concern is that ATP subtly pressures recipients to commit to its faith tradition. Is the sharing of the Gospel inextricably linked to how ATP thinks about and approaches the problems people face? It implicates the important and yet unclarified question of what rises to impermissible proselytizing.

ATP also pushed the boundaries of the establishment clause prohibition on government promotion of religion. The collaboration of ATP's alternative school with the public school system is the most striking illustration. The school enrolls students who have disciplinary or other problems with integrating into a normal school setting. Students are referred by city and county agencies, as well as juvenile courts. An associate pastor admits that "spiritual values" are taught in class. Students are taught from a religious perspective how to apply principles such as compassion, commitment, responsibility, and community to their lives, as religious texts are incorporated into class lessons and exercises. These practices raise serious constitutional questions. Critics argue that government, by directing young people to an explicitly religious learning environment, is endorsing religion.

Finally, there are potential problems with the health fairs that ATP provides in conjunction with the city, county, and other community-based organizations. ATP provides a host of activities for children—games, face painting, puppet shows, drama skits, and music. For adults, free health screening services include eye exams, dental checkups, blood pressure and weight readings, and blood tests for cholesterol and tuberculosis. But members of ATP also distribute Christian literature and share the Gospel of Christ. Some contend that local government officials need to draw clearer lines to prevent mixed signals as a result of these collaborative efforts. As of yet, however, no complaints have been lodged against ATP.

A real tension exists between implementing the rules of charitable choice while enabling FBOs and government agencies to work in tandem to address pressing social problems. First, the beneficiaries of ATP activities are fully aware of the Christian nature of ATP and are often drawn to the organization precisely because of it. They trust, and therefore are willing to participate in, programs offered by the local church rather than a public school or a county health clinic. When approached by church members about block parties and health clinics, community residents enthusiastically responded; the response was much less favorable when a school official informed residents about free parenting classes. Indeed, when congregation members went door-to-door to advertise the same events, the overall interest of individuals in attending increased. Residents apparently trust ATP more than their public counterparts, although more systematic research is needed on the role that trust plays in connecting needed public services to needy clientele.

As a general matter, ATP respects the wishes of individual participants in its activities, despite its strong Christian message in service provision. It is careful to obtain consent from recipients of services, usually asking individuals if they would like prayer or to visit other church programs. There is no compulsion to participate in religious activities. If there are coercive religious pressures emanating from ATP in service delivery, they were not reflected in complaints or in my observations.

There are three important reasons why the partnerships between ATP and local government agencies have proved relatively successful, without generating serious First Amendment religious establishment problems. First, the agreements and communications between the parties have fostered a clear understanding of the relationship and the respective roles played by each actor. In particular, the public forums held at ATP have allowed representatives of a host of organizations to meet to flesh out differences on the most important issues facing the city. Second, ATP has had a long working relationship both with city and county government officials, as well as with other organizations in the city. These historical ties have fostered a much needed level of trust in the FBO-government relationship. Finally, governmental support of ATP has not come in the form of a direct grant, check, or other financial partnership. Rather it has come in the form of client referrals and other indirect means of support. As a result, ATP has maintained full autonomy and flexibility over its organizational operations and reduced accountability to those agencies.

■ Conclusion

Charitable choice promised to preserve the character and identity of faith-based organizations while simultaneously protecting the religious rights of beneficiaries of services. This is no small task, given the natural tension between these twin demands. From ATP's example, it is difficult to find fault in how faith-based organizations do their business when they have a strong congregational presence in the neighborhood and similarly strong ties to public offices, business leaders, and other grassroots nonprofits. Its well established and long-standing working relationships with local law enforcement, public schools, health care organizations, and the business establishment allow ATP to carry out a full range of services and programs largely free of restraint. This suggests a disconnect between the practical issues that exist on the ground and the theoretical problems posed by establishment doctrine. ATP, as a well-respected organization, appears relatively free to provide programs and services at its discretion without causing major constitutional concerns for either participants or its friends in government.

■ Notes

1. Names of persons have been changed to maintain their confidentiality. Ethnographic research methods were employed: face-to-face interviews with church leaders, direct observation of (and where appropriate, participation in) activities such as meetings and classes, and a review of documents for background information. Initially, I sought to understand the perceptions of government officials about the role of churches in addressing Oakland's most needy citizens. After conversations with individuals in grassroots and civic organizations, government agencies, and churches, the focus shifted to the congregations and their community outreach efforts.

2. A basic dictionary search offers this definition of the term *devolution:* "transference (as of rights, power, property or responsibility) to another; especially: the surrender of powers to local authority by a central government" (http://www.merriam-webster.com).

3. For the purposes of this chapter, *first-order devolution* refers to the federal government looking to the states to handle welfare responsibilities; *second-order devolution* refers to the subsequent shifting of responsibility to the counties to carry out welfare services; *third-order devolution* refers to county governments looking to nonprofits and other local entities to deliver services; and *fourth-order devolution* refers to yet another level of refinement within nonprofit organizations, such as congregations being called upon to become more involved in the delivery of public welfare services.

4. The term "faith-based organizations" has been used extensively and loosely in the scholarly literature, policy circles, and public discourse to include a diverse group of organizations with religious or spiritual origins. Jim Castelli and John McCarthy's typology (1998) categorizes FBOs into three groupings: national networks, congregations, and freestanding institutions, each with its distinct characteristics. National networks are the social service arms of denominations, while congregations are the local, community bodies organized around religious worship. Freestanding religious organizations are those institutions incorporated separately from congregations and national networks.

5. This biblical passage in John 17 is Jesus' prayer for His followers before His death. Jesus prays to God for their safety "from the evil one" as He leaves the earth. The Scripture reads: "My prayer for all of them is that they will be one, just as you and I are one, Father—that just as you are in me and I am in you, so they will be in us, and the world will believe you sent me" (New Living Translation). Jesus speaks of the "oneness" in hearts and actions of the twelve disciples who walked with Him and for those who accept Him thereafter.

PART 4

Conclusion

11 Past, Present, Future: Final Reflections on Faith-Based Programs

JEFFREY POLET AND DAVID K. RYDEN

The passage of the first charitable choice legislation in 1996 did little to raise the profile of faith-based nonprofit collaboration with government. Charitable choice did not exactly revolutionize the delivery of social services; indeed, its tangible impact in cultivating greater partnerships between the public and religious sectors was modest at best. There were relatively few takers among religious charities and churches, due to a lack of awareness of the law itself (Charitable Choice Compliance 2000; Sherman 2000). An almost complete lack of knowledge of the law among pastors—one survey had only 3 percent of them even knowing what charitable choice was (Chaves 1999, 7)—was matched by ignorance on the public side. In the majority of states, little or nothing was done to implement charitable choice programs, largely because local and state officials themselves did not know of or understand the law (Charitable Choice Compliance 2000). Though charitable choice was the governing law for federal welfare block grants, the federal government did little to apply the rules to its grant making or to require states receiving funds to adjust their rules to comply. The limited familiarity with charitable choice on both sides of the contracting relationship ensured that its reach was limited and sporadic. The extension of charitable choice rules to other federal grant programs did little to alter the anonymity and ignorance surrounding the law.

Following George W. Bush's election in 2000, however, the evidence on virtually every front reveals roiling activity surrounding faith-based activities. One measure of that activity is in the *increased awareness of charitable choice and faith-based opportunities*. One demonstrable repercussion of the high-profile scrap over the Bush legislative plan is the degree to which actors, both private and public, have been made aware of charitable choice. The debate increased public awareness of the potential of religious agencies as collaborators with the government in delivering social services. It had the salutary effect of informing large numbers of actors, both public and private, that there already were charitable choice laws on the books. In the wake of the debate over the Bush plan, those seeking to advance religious-based social welfare service delivery under the auspices of charitable choice are likely to find a much more informed and intelligent audience within and outside of government.

The momentum in faith-based partnerships is evident in actual increases in the numbers of faith-based programs and public funds flowing to those programs. Concerted administrative efforts indeed may have begun to reshape how bureaucratic cultures perceive faith-based organizations (FBOs) as potential partners. John Green and Amy Sherman's 2002 cataloguing survey of new publicly funded faith-based programs in fifteen states revealed a sizable upswing in their numbers, more than 700 contracts totaling $125 million. While this is a relatively modest sum within the universe of all government social spending, it is still a considerable increase over past amounts. Moreover, that trend has only strengthened. In 2003 the amount of federal money flowing from the original five federal faith-based cabinet centers to faith-based groups was $1.1 billion, a substantial increase over the previous year. The creation of new faith-based programs continues unabated. Hardly a week went by in late 2002 and early 2003 without a report of some new state program that melded public dollars with faith-based delivery.

A number of states have opened state-level equivalents of the White House Office of Faith-Based and Community Initiatives (WHOFBCI), as have approximately 180 mid-sized and large cities. At the state and local levels, therefore, governors and mayors friendly to faith-based organizations can similarly use executive power to direct agencies to implement charitable choice-type programs. Select state legislatures are likely to move forward, as are state attorneys general, who can issue opinions and lead efforts to educate public officials on faith-based programs (O'Keefe 2002).

Collaborations between the government and the religious sector are no longer the exception. From all appearances, they have taken on a momentum that is unlikely to subside anytime soon. In short, faith-based programs will continue with or without additional federal charitable choice legislation. If in fact public officials responsible for contracting with the private sector are beginning to look at faith-based organizations differently and in a more friendly light, then the faith-based phenomenon is likely to be a long-term development. It enhances the possibility that, even without supporting legislation, faith-based partnerships will continue beyond the present Bush administration.

■ The Faith-Based Initiative and Establishment Clause Issues

These tangible measures of faith-based advances suggest proponents may have lost the legislative battle but won the religion-in-government war. If a central aim of the Bush plan was to increase the presence of religious groups in the delivery of government social services, the initiative must be judged a legitimate success. However, a final marker of the initiative's forward movement is less heartening for its backers: the marked rise in the litigation and judicial activity in the wake of the Bush plan. The long-term viability of faith-based partnerships will depend in no small part on the legal proceedings and challenges that have arisen following the public attention given the Bush faith-based agenda. Lawsuits involving publicly funded faith-based social programs were virtually nonexistent before Bush elevated the issue. Indeed, charitable choice had been the law of the land for five years without a direct challenge to its constitutionality. Since faith-based initiatives were thrust into the limelight in 2000, a flurry of lawsuits have arisen. On one hand, advocacy groups and faith-based opponents have turned aggressively to litigation in an effort to stem the tide of greater church-state interaction. On the flip side, religious providers also are litigating issues relating to those rights they hope to retain even as government contractees. Some of these cases have yielded decisions at the trial level and are now proceeding up the appellate ladder. Others are in the earliest stages of litigation. These lawsuits can be expected to yield precedents more clearly defining both the lines of acceptable religious establishment and the extent of religious exercise rights.

These factors reinforce several striking realities. First, faith-based initiatives have engaged in a fresh way the arduous struggle to locate the appropriate place for religion in the policy and political arenas. Second, charitable choice and the Bush faith-based efforts have failed to settle the major legal and constitutional questions regarding interaction between government and the religious sector. On the contrary, significant dimensions of the underlying church-state dilemma remain unresolved. Finally, the debate over faith-based initiatives is likely to be part of the political conversation for years to come. As the United States continues its ongoing effort to navigate and negotiate the relationship between religion, politics, and culture, the legal status of faith-based initiatives is likely to be at the epicenter of that debate.

A related consideration is whether the courts are the best forum for a thorough constitutional examination of the faith-based initiative. Should we take solace in, or be concerned by, the fact that, after the faith-based bill stalled in the legislature, the focus is now on the courts? Which is the better venue for hashing out the constitutional considerations, the legislative or judicial chamber? This issue divides the authors of this book. David Ryden contends that the courts and the litigation process, because they are the least encumbered by debilitating political pressures, are most likely to yield a constructive and thoughtful resolution of complex constitutional issues. The judicial context allows for evidentiary presentations at trial and a fully briefed and argued appellate argument before a panel of experienced and sophisticated judges. For Ryden, this is the closest thing to an adequate forum for exploring the appropriate place for religious groups in public policy making. As the legal challenges to the Bush administration's executive moves mature, reasoned legal analysis free of demagoguery will inform the debate. In the courts, there is at least a chance that the constitutional merits and failings can be weighed reflectively and insightfully. Furthermore, if the courts take a relatively permissive approach to faith-based partnerships, it need not preempt the legislative task. Rather, elected representatives in Congress and state legislatures can then focus on whether such collaborations are wise or effective policy for their respective constituents.

Jeffrey Polet, conversely, is suspicious of the Supreme Court's ability to handle such issues with the requisite intelligence and sensitivity, nor does he believe that wanting to avoid "debilitating political pressures" is sufficient warrant for bypassing the legislative process with its own evidentiary hearings and constitutional reasonings. He believes that a quick look at the broad historical sweep of church-state jurisprudence should undermine anyone's confidence in the Court's competency to handle such issues. His specific objections run along three lines. First, leaving such issues in the hands of unelected officials creates serious issues of accountability. Indeed, the inability of the legislature to come up with a workable plan is a proper reflection of public division on a contentious issue. Democracy is, after all, a representative mechanism for resolving public disputes. It ought to be contentious, messy, and even gridlocked. The desire for clean decisionmaking is a utopian fantasy. Second, current and past members of the Court have yet to display much understanding of the significance of religion—whether for individual believers or corporate traditions, or in respecting its role in the health of the Republic. Finally, the members of the Court, though competent legalists, are almost invariably weak theorists. The problems of constitutional order, especially in this case, are not simply legal problems. The Court is but one voice, albeit an important one, in a fragmented system that ultimately places legitimacy in the hands of the governed. Resting the power of legitimacy in the highly complex machinations of legal reasoning can only serve to further alienate the populace from their government. Finally, Polet believes that the image of the judiciary as a group of wise, reasoned, dispassionate analysts is more caricature than reality.

In either case, the constitutionality of faith-based programs is much more than a purely technical or legal determination. It obviously implicates a host of broader considerations about public expressions and manifestations of faith, the proper place of religion in public policy, and the competency and wisdom of the state to intentionally solicit faith-based actors' involvement in government business.[1] It is crucial that the burgeoning legal proceedings involving faith-based programs be informed by these issues, particularly as these debates over the constitutional status of religious programs intensify.

The debate pits "separationists" on the one side against various strands of "neutrality" advocates on the other. Separationist motives vary. For some it is a distrust of religion, a sense that it is an undesirable presence in public life.

From this perspective, religion is a primary cause of division and narrow-mindedness, and should receive no material assistance whatsoever. Others worry more about the religious entities themselves, and what might happen if they avail themselves of public dollars. They fear government money would inevitably pervert a religious organization by altering its primary mission or focus. Funding pervasively religious groups means the intrusion of government into those groups' activities, a sure entanglement that would interfere with the work of the church. But regardless of motive, they agree upon one thing: public aid cannot flow to religious institutions for religious activities, but must be limited to secular purposes alone.

In contrast, promoters of a neutrality standard approve of government aid for religious activities and organizations, provided it is applied evenhandedly and without favoring a particular faith or denomination. Any standard that would bar intensely religious groups from public contracting offends basic notions of evenhandedness and fairness. As long as a clear secular purpose is advanced, the extent of a group's religiosity is immaterial to its qualifications to address a problem and receive public funds. Neutrality permits incidental benefits to the religious side of the funded organizations as long as the secular ends are met. Unsurprisingly, those in this camp argue in the wake of *Mitchell v. Helms* (2000) that the "doctrine [of pervasive sectarianism] has now lost all relevance" (Institute for Public Affairs Public Policy Library 2001). Of particular importance for those of the "neutralist" persuasion was the use of vouchers, upheld by the Supreme Court in its *Zelman v. Simmons-Harris* (2002) decision.

As the battle over faith-based initiatives moves further into the judicial realm, state-subsidized religious social service programs face a variety of legal and constitutional challenges in lower courts across the country (Black, Koopman, and Ryden 2004, 253–259). The subjects of the lawsuits range from the relatively inconsequential to major issues. In some instances, the principle at stake is far more important than the monetary amount. For example, in a Texas court case, two public interest law firms questioned the use of $8,000 of state funds that helped pay for the purchase of Bibles for a job training and placement program (*American Jewish Congress and Texas Civil Rights Project v. Bost* [2000]).

Other cases confront the issue of whether public funds are in fact furthering what are inherently transformative religious activities. In a case filed in federal court in Louisiana, the American Civil Liberties Union challenged a state abstinence program that took federal welfare funds but that included "Christ-centered" skits, religious youth revivals, biblical instruction, and other overtly religious methods (*ACLU of Louisiana v. Foster* [2002]). Perhaps the most significant cases in this category are a pair of lawsuits filed in February 2003 in federal court in Iowa, challenging the InnerChange Freedom Initiative (*Ashburn v. Maples; Americans United for Separation of Church and State v. Prison Fellowship Ministries*). The goal of InnerChange, which was trumpeted by President Bush as a model faith-based partnership, is to help prepare prison inmates for their return to society and to reduce the likelihood that they will return to crime once back on the streets. While voluntary, the program is openly and intensely Christ-centered and Bible-based. It emphasizes the "spiritual and moral transformation" of participants through a rigorous course of Bible study, worship and prayer, and Christian counseling. Complicating matters are studies that indicate the program has had remarkable success in lowering the percentage of recidivism among released inmates. Unlike faith based programs typically funded under charitable choice in the welfare context, InnerChange is religious at its core. It seeks the secular benefit—rehabilitation and reduced recidivism—through religious and spiritual conversion. The two lawsuits confront head-on the propriety of a pervasively religious program that pursues a secular aim through religious means and does so with the benefit of public dollars.

Several lawsuits involve the sensitive issue of hiring and personnel rights of publicly funded religious organizations (*Pedreira v. Kentucky Baptist Homes for Children* [2000]; *Bellmore v. United Methodist Children's Home* [2003]). In the *Pedreira* case, the plaintiff, a lesbian, was dismissed from her job on grounds that her personal lifestyle was inconsistent with the mission and purpose of the Baptist Home.[2] In *Bellmore,* a Jewish therapist and a lesbian counselor were terminated on similar grounds.[3] More recently, a group of current and former Salvation Army employees filed suit against the Army in federal court in New York, alleging that they were pressured by the organization to evangelize and to reveal their denominational affiliations. These cases could be instrumental in clarifying the hiring and personnel rights of publicly subsidized religious providers.

The factual contexts of these legal disputes are necessary to resolving the questions surrounding the constitutionality of faith-based collaborations. These cases arguably will provide the framework necessary to allow a more meaningful and substantive constitutional debate. First, these cases shift the framework from the abstract level to the actual context of real faith-based programs and services. In the past, the discussion of the constitutionality of church-state partnerships has generally taken place on too abstract a level. The particulars of actual programs, rather than speculation or theorizing, should determine what is an unacceptable establishment of religion. Litigation bubbling up from the trial and lower appellate courts is essential to putting factual flesh on the establishment clause bones. Only through such decisions can we shape the proper boundaries of what constitutes acceptable interaction between religious groups and the government in real-world settings.

State Constitutions and Blaine Amendments: The Last Church-State Frontier

One potentially significant legal barrier remains before faith-based voucher programs receive widespread use: the constitutional status of the so-called

Blaine amendments that are contained in many state constitutions. Blaine provisions of state constitutions represent an uncharted legal frontier in church-state law. Though they received little attention amid the furor surrounding the Bush faith-based initiative, they now are thought by many to represent the final constitutional firewall against greater church-state interaction. The extent to which government actors pursue voucher-based religious social services delivery will depend on the interplay between the federal establishment clause and correlative state constitutional provisions.

Thirty-seven state constitutions contain explicit prohibitions on the use of public money for religious institutions or instruction. The language and text of these Blaine amendments vary widely from state to state. A few of these provisions merely replicate the federal establishment clause. The focus of many is to explicitly preclude funding of religious schools or education.[4] For example, California's constitution bars using public money for "the support of any sectarian or denominational school."[5] The Michigan constitution bars "tuition vouchers" from going to "nonpublic schools" where religious instruction takes place.[6] Others contain language that on its face would undoubtedly apply to religious social agencies and nonprofits. Several bar public funds to "the institutions of any religious sect or denomination."[7] Some disallow public funds for "any charitable or benevolent purposes" to "any denominational or sectarian institution or association."[8] The Indiana constitution flatly states that "no money shall be drawn from the treasury for the benefit of any religious . . . institution."[9] Whatever the variation in the language of the provisions, they are all much stricter and more precise than the First Amendment of the U.S. Constitution in banning the dissemination of state funds to religious organizations or for religious purposes.

Only in the wake of the *Zelman* school voucher decision have more sophisticated church-state scholars (and lawyers) turned their attention to these state constitutions. Indeed, advocates on both sides have trained their sights on the question of the federal constitutionality of these state provisions as a crucial establishment clause battleground (Brieve 2004, 246). Prior to *Zelman,* there had been little motivation on either side to test the viability of church-state provisions in state constitutions. But with the Supreme Court growing more sympathetic to government funding of religious institutions, the obvious strategic choice for faith-based opponents is to challenge such actions as running afoul of applicable state constitutions. Rather than concede defeat following *Zelman,* opponents of school vouchers looked to Blaine amendments that went further in explicitly prohibiting public funding of religious institutions. If taken literally, these amendments would almost certainly preclude public money from going to private religious institutions, whether for education or social services. If upheld, Blaine amendments would likely stop the voucher movement (or any state-funded faith-based social service program for that matter) in its tracks.

Even though the language of Blaine amendments is straightforward and seemingly hostile to their cause, those sympathetic to vouchers and collaboration between government and the religious sector in other contexts are also intent on legally attacking the state constitutions. The Institute for Justice, a provoucher legal advocacy group, has brought lawsuits in a handful of states to test their constitutions, either to resolve them in a manner consistent with *Zelman* or to create sufficient conflicts in the law that the Supreme Court's intervention will be required. Despite the clarity of the language barring aid to sectarian groups, faith-based proponents are eager to litigate what they see as vulnerable provisions, focusing specifically on their purported anti-Catholic bias.

So what weight should be given state constitutions that go much further than the U.S. Constitution in banning aid to religious institutions? Given the wide degree of divergence in their language, it is impossible to generalize on likely legal outcomes of legal challenges to these provisions. Even the most expert church-state analysts are wary of predicting how these constitutional battles will be resolved. Of most interest will be the extent to which the Supreme Court will consider the historical motives behind the state funding limitations. It is possible, but by no means certain, that lower courts might find the anti-Catholic impetus for the enactment of the Blaine amendments to be a discriminatory and hence unconstitutional barrier to funding of religious organizations.

The Faith-Based Initiative and Free-Exercise Issues

While establishment clause issues create significant interpretive difficulties, an equally important set of considerations center on free exercise and associational rights. Efforts by the state to guard against impermissible establishment or promotion of religion raise the specter that its actions impinge on the prerogatives and rights to which religious organizations are entitled. One set of issues relates to the impact that contracting with government may have organizationally on the agency. A key aim of charitable choice and the faith-based initiatives that followed was to remove the expectation that faith-based partners with government form a separate and independent corporate entity to receive and administer grants. This requirement was a disincentive for some religious groups to pursue government funding. Either they lacked the wherewithal in resources to create and maintain a parallel organization, or they believed they had to sterilize their services to remove any traces of the faith component. The practical effect was to bar many churches and other faith-based providers from the government contracting field. Public funds often flow directly to religious entities, including churches, mosques, and temples, and this practice is generally accepted as constitutional. In other words, it is no longer the nature of the religious organization receiving funds that matters constitutionally, but rather the nature of the activities being supported (see generally Lupu and Tuttle 2002).

Of course, feeding at the public trough does not necessarily mean it is the advisable thing for religious organizations to do. A more permissive legal/constitutional environment does not eliminate dangers that potentially accompany public funds. Scholars have warned of a host of perils that religious organizations must consider when they step into a formal relationship with the government (Smith and Lipsky 1993). While some faith-based organizations have suggested that government funds should come free of any strings or conditions attached ("Focus on the Family to Bush" 2004), it is generally conceded that with public funds come a variety of regulatory and oversight burdens. Reliance on government funds may ultimately translate into subtle pressure to alter one's mission, strategy, or staffing practices. It may mean diminishment of the organization's distinct identity, greater professionalism but at the expense of its volunteerism, and even less responsiveness to the real needs of its community. It almost certainly requires changes in the scale and administration of the organization. As a practical rather than constitutional matter, churches and other religious agencies should give serious thought to the ways in which the acceptance of and reliance on government funds will affect them.

But these are largely pragmatic considerations for churches and organizations to weigh prior to entering a relationship with a public agency, and should not affect the legality of such partnerships. Moreover, preliminary evidence from the studies in this volume suggests such concerns may be overblown. Once a grant is awarded, faith-based providers should expect to be confronted with standard monitoring and regulatory oversight practices. These requirements are necessary to guarantee compliance, both with the terms of the contract or grant and with constitutional parameters as well. As a general matter, the featured case studies suggest that publicly funded FBOs should face, and be expected to satisfy, the same expectations and rules that any other group must meet and abide by. Several of the faith-based programs discussed in this book involved direct funding of congregations. The analysis of Cookman United Methodist in Philadelphia by Heidi Unruh and Jill Sinha is instructive in cataloguing the potential practical complications for recipient FBOs. They may face real administrative challenges in meeting governmental standards on paperwork, facilities, performance evaluation, and other oversight demands. However, the Cookman example suggests that a healthy dose of flexibility and common sense on both sides of the contract goes a long way to ensuring that governmental demands for accountability and transparency are met without sacrificing program effectiveness.

Both the study of Cookman United Methodist and Joyce Williams's analysis of "A Tranquil Place" in Oakland painted quite a positive picture overall of the working relationship between the church and its public partners.

In both instances, the First Amendment tension did not play out in practice. There were no complaints of undue pressure by the churches on program participants. At the same time, the churches felt free to live out their mission in service without being pressured to mute or dampen their religious identity or core.

But this also is where the tensions arise between establishment constraints and free exercise and associational protections. As David Ryden notes in his study, it is precisely the hands-off approach resulting from the closer relationship between grantor and grantee that also creates an environment in which religious activities are more likely to creep into the services. The degree of autonomy may also depend on the level of government involved. The greater freedom that flows from a past working relationship with a city, county, or even state official may be much more difficult to realize when the public partner is the larger and more distant bureaucracy that is the federal government. This is precisely part of the reasoning behind federalism, which allows for twin protections against tyranny—by splitting authority in such a way as to avoid a monopoly and to give people the freedom to move to where things are done differently—and provides greater citizen control and accountability.

■ An Alternate Reading

Based on the distinction between "structural" and "substantive" concerns outlined in the Ryden chapter, a competing view is based upon a more positive and permissive understanding of neutrality. It combines the structural and substantive elements of church-state relations in a test for determining when religious activities can be part of a publicly funded program. In this view, the religiosity of the program matters not, *provided* the requisite structural criteria are met. In other words, it is not an unconstitutional advancement of religion to permit public funds to be applied to explicitly religious programs, as long as there are practical details in place that guarantee choice and religious liberty, and that protect against endorsement or coercion. As long as the funded activities further legitimate public goals or objectives and are genuinely voluntary in nature, their religious character is not objectionable. Stephen Monsma (1995) has contended that publicly funded programs are constitutionally permissible even if they advance religion, as long as the religious benefits are incidental to the secular ones and beneficiaries can choose from a range of alternatives to that program. Some might argue over what it means for the benefit to religion to be "incidental." But it at least allows for a stronger argument that a Bible-based prison ministry run with government funding is constitutional, as long as participation is voluntary and functionally equivalent secular programs are available.

What essentially divides these two views is a crucial question that must be answered. Can the government constitutionally utilize religion to its own secular ends even if it advances religion in the process? Can a direct aid program, which is both religious at its core and successful in serving larger societal goals, be supported by the government? Provided that the structural First Amendment criteria are met—the program is genuinely voluntary, it offers true choice for recipients, it respects the religious exercise rights of participants—can a state-subsidized program use an intensely religious provider to realize public aims even as it clearly advances religion along the way?

Those such as Sheila Kennedy (2003) and Ira Lupu and Robert Tuttle (Lupu and Tuttle 2002) would say the answer is straightforward. While a voucher-based program is permissible, the government cannot directly fund religious activities. The existing case law clearly supports this position. And yet the answer may not be quite that simple; while it probably accurately captures the law as it exists today, it may not reflect what the Supreme Court could decide tomorrow. It simply is not clear what the Court would do if faced with a direct aid case as described above. The doctrinal gap between the *Mitchell* and *Zelman* opinions leaves adequate room for competing positions. Justice Sandra Day O'Connor's artful *Zelman* decision leaves open the possibility that it could have application in a nonvoucher context. Her language stressed the importance of independent, genuine choices in insulating the government from religious endorsement. Does this mean direct public funds could support the religious activities of a program, provided a menu of choices includes both secular and religious providers, and the client opts for the religious? If the religious agency were only to be paid for those clients who voluntarily and freely choose its services, it is difficult to see how it would differ functionally from a voucher program. Ultimately, there is no conclusive or authoritative answer to how the Court would resolve a constitutional challenge to a publicly funded program that simultaneously advances a secular purpose and religious activities.[10]

For all of the intensity of the debate over the Bush faith-based initiatives, this central difference was never really addressed. Faith-based social services imply that there is public utility, not only in religious institutions, but also in religion itself. A long-cherished tenet of liberalism is the idea that religious disputes are best managed by privatizing belief. But the premise implicit in charitable choice and the subsequent Bush faith-based effort diverged from that model. Charitable choice and ventures between government and the religious sector are usually cast as efforts to level the playing field in pursuit of government funds. But among pioneers of the faith-based movement, something more profound was at work.[11] They desired to facilitate government's partnering with religious service providers so that the religious *content* of a program would itself play an instrumental role in confronting whatever social problem was at issue. As a result, they saw the "pervasively sectarian" prohibition on funding of more intensely religious organizations as deeply problematic; it barred that which they saw as essential to realizing genuinely effective treatment of dysfunctional behavior. Indeed, money should be able to go to overtly religious institutions precisely *because of* their religious character. That very religious dimension to treatment was central to healing and helping people. For the true believers in faith-based programs, religious conviction was an unparalleled means of addressing social problems.

This competing view gained a high-profile booster when President Bush took office. Bush frequently drew upon personal experience in preaching faith-based initiatives. He often cited the impact his religious conversion had on his behavior, particularly in helping him overcome his battle with alcohol. It was unsurprising then that Bush, as governor of Texas, stood fully behind drug treatment and correctional programs for convicted felons that made explicit use of Bible study, prayer, and worship. For the president, it was only natural to tap into the spiritual dimension of faith-based organizations, since this was precisely what made them so effective.

Yet this justification was largely muted during the debates over charitable choice and the Bush plan. As a result, the fundamental issue—whether the government could utilize religion itself to realize secular objectives—was never joined. Could the government, by funding more overtly religious providers, make use of religion to achieve nonreligious goals? Charitable choice backers skirted the issue, pretending that the law only reinforced existing Supreme Court precedent, often without adequately engaging the endorsement issue.

While charitable choice supporters downplayed any change in the church-state rules, the intensity of the opposition to the Bush plan was motivated by a distinct sense that it marked a qualitative shift in the role of faith-based providers. Earlier arguments had largely centered on the wisdom and efficacy of tapping into religious social service agents who might bring greater motivation to serve because of their religious convictions. The perceived benefits in increased efficiency and effectiveness were seen as flowing from faith-motivated social service workers driven by religious *conviction*. But opponents of the Bush initiative saw something more invidious in it. The benefits that President Bush wanted the government to fund stemmed from the religious *content* of the service itself and, usually, in clearly religious *circumstances*. Sharing of religious convictions *by* openly religious persons *in* openly religious settings was at the core of effective treatment and rehabilitation. This struck an ominous note, both with secularists and with civil libertarians who saw genuine threats to the religious freedom of program recipients.

Yet this is perhaps the crux of the debate over faith-based services, raising fundamental and deep-seated philosophical differences regarding religion as a source of public authority. For some, religion is predominantly a negative influence, at its core intolerant and oppressive, authoritarian and coercive. In a moment of unguarded honesty, Annie Laurie Gaylor of the Freedom from Religion Foundation commented that "all these state-faith partnerships will do more harm than good. . . . They promote religion as the 'cure-all' to our social problems and divert attention away from the *real* actions needed to achieve social and economic justice" (Gaylor 2001, emphasis added). The distrust of Bush and his faith-based initiative stems in large part from the belief that it ultimately would mean public dollars for religious transformation and conversion, which in turn would only further divide society.

Meanwhile, those of faith point to religion's power at both ends of the social service equation. In service provision, faith motivates those in service to go further in their efforts to help persons in need, at less cost. On the receiving end, religious conviction means program success. Faith's transformative dimension empowers beneficiaries to kick the addiction, live more productive lives. To cut religion out of the picture is to eviscerate the treatment. Whether public funds advance religion is beside the point. If a conversion-centered treatment "works," fund it for the effectiveness, not the faith.

The funding of more aggressively religious service providers implicates alternative foundational understandings of religion, its place in the public realm, and its standing relative to the government. There arise a host of auxiliary questions that are part of the challenge of constitutional handling of religion. Is the state able to identify those religious actors who ought to qualify for public funding? Does government have the competency to judge the authenticity of the ever-expanding universe of religious groups and faiths for purposes of grant making? Or, as the only pragmatic path to reasonably follow, should the government simply bar all religious groups from the public arena? Should the government adopt a stance of formal neutrality that makes no distinctions between religious actors or between religious and secular ones, but whereby all have equal admittance to policy involvement contingent on a record of programmatic effectiveness? If so, what criteria of success must religious actors meet to qualify for admission to the public arena? What demonstrable level of effectiveness on their part is necessary? Must they show a solid empirical track record supported by established social science principles? Does the privileging of "social science principles" itself constitute an establishment of a particular worldview, to the exclusion of others?

The Meaning of Neutrality

The host of demands that government imposes upon its private partners have implications for applying the concept of neutrality. Proponents of faith-based collaborations usually invoke neutrality in the establishment context. They favor a constitutional standard of neutrality because they believe it entitles religious groups to a level playing field and equal opportunity to access governmental social service funding. Too often, they ignore what neutrality might mean in terms of compliance with governmental requirements and expectations for contracting or grantee nonprofits—that is, on the free exercise side of the equation. A more rigorous application of neutrality requires that religious providers be prepared to yield to the array of demands that the government typically makes on its nonprofit partners.

Perhaps the more controversial questions relate to the standards by which faith-based agencies are considered in applying for public funds. Sheila Kennedy, in her chapter in this volume, gives voice to this view, as she argues that FBOs should not be awarded grants merely because of the religious dimension of their programs. Rather, they should be required to show evidence that they employ commonly accepted professional standards in service provision, and that they rely upon "science-based best practices" in their programs. The same holds true in measuring program outcomes. Hence Kennedy contends that public funding should only support faith-based providers who are able to demonstrate that their programs achieve "clinical competency" according to the usual means of gauging successful outcomes.

The insistence upon science-based standards and other professionally imposed practices, however, raises serious objections among proponents of faith-based services, who suggest it constitutes an implicit bias against religion itself. Faith-based leaders argue that such demands do not allow for the possibility that religiously driven services are effective for much different reasons than do other social services entities. It may be due to the motivation of employees and volunteers or a different emphasis on relational services. Or it may be because religion itself has the power to help, heal, and rehabilitate those who are the recipients of the services. Many claim it is the spiritual dimension to the program that is the most valuable component in achieving the desired outcomes. For backers of charitable choice, cooperation between government and the religious sector is desirable because religious conviction is a central answer to solving social problems for which government is responsible.

Yet religion, by its very nature, is not easily subjected to clinical testing or scientific validation. The rigid imposition of scientific standards and professional practices on religious providers may be facially neutral, but in practice it arguably skews access to the public social services domain against religious providers. For those who believe in religious conviction as a force for addressing behavioral dysfunction, these standards result in cutting out the core of effective programs. It means stripping faith-based providers of the distinctive character that is responsible for their success. Hence faith-based proponents have argued that neutrality should be geared around an alternative system of outcome-based evaluation. That would still require FBOs to demonstrate effectiveness on a par with their secular counterparts in meeting program objectives, but would allow them the latitude to pursue those outcomes in ways consistent with their mission.[12]

The Third Rail of the Faith-Based Initiative: Religion-Based Hiring

The most controversial issue on the free exercise rights side of the equation of faith-based programs is the extent to which funded groups maintain or sacrifice their right to hire based upon religious compatibility. No other aspect of the debate over the Bush plan generated such acrimony and emotion. For organizations intent on preserving their religious character, the right to hire individuals whose beliefs align with the organization's religious mission is a central imperative. Their ability to maintain their unique religious core is compromised unless they can hire people who identify with that. The Bush initiative recognized this, echoing those hiring protections contained in the original 1996 charitable choice law. The initiative specified that religious nonprofits would not forfeit their prerogative of making personnel decisions based on the religious commitments of applicants.

Yet the objections to the hiring autonomy of publicly supported religious nonprofits were instrumental in derailing the forward movement of the faith-based legislation. Those looking to sink the faith-based initiative stumbled on an issue with far greater appeal than abstractions about church-state separation. They proved adept at portraying the proposed protections as a guise for overly zealous religious organizations to practice intolerance through discriminatory hiring practices (Lazarus 2002). This became the public perception of the bill; the uproar that ensued over the hiring issue caught the public's attention as had no other aspect of the faith-based proposal (Goodstein 2001).[13] In the end, it proved fatal to the political popularity of faith-based initiatives.

The hiring issue also typified the disconnect between the public rhetoric surrounding faith-based proposals and the actual constitutional merits. The crude public exchanges over whether publicly funded religious providers could constitutionally exercise hiring preferences on the basis of religion failed to capture the actual complexities of the law. Congressmen who opposed the plan characterized religiously based hiring rights as "government funded religious discrimination" and "federally funded religious bigotry" (Milbank and Edsall 2001, A01). One charged that "if Bob Jones University qualifies for charitable choice dollars, they can put up a sign that says 'no Catholics need apply here'" (Rothstein 2000, 16). Senate majority leader Tom Daschle conjectured that it would "be a guise for intolerance, because it permits faith-based organizations to hire only those job applicants who can agree with the religious basis of their programs" (Lazarus 2001, 1). Interest groups chimed in. The Coalition Against Religious Discrimination decried the hiring provision as "turn[ing] back the clock on civil rights."[14] Nancy Zirkin of the American Association of University Women claimed it "would open women to all kinds of employment discrimination that is currently prohibited by federal law" (2001). Barry Lynn of Americans United for Separation of Church and State warned that it was "intended to permit some fundamentalist organization to put a sign on the door saying, 'no Jews need apply'" (cited in Hoover 2001).

An eclectic array of voices weighed in on the other side. Jeffrey Rosen (2001), writing in the *New Republic*, favored the right to hire based on religious beliefs, arguing that the same protection exists for any group, secular or religious. He offered the analogy of Planned Parenthood, which avails itself of public funds while retaining its freedom to hire based on its values and mission. Carl Esbeck, a primary drafter of the original charitable choice language, asserted that religious organizations can "hardly be expected to sustain their religious vision without the ability to employ individuals who share the tenets of the faith" (2001, 1). The Center for Public Justice's Stephen Lazarus similarly contended that "all should be free to hire staff that reflect their principled convictions, religious or secular" (2002, 1). For those of the neutralist persuasion, religious discrimination in hiring simply meant giving religious groups the same rights as their secular counterparts to hire based on commitment to their mission or philosophy.

A closer examination of the constitutional arguments reveals a more complicated and multifaceted issue. Even on this level, however, it is an issue where deep and arguably insoluble differences divide the opposing camps. At the heart of the conflict is the viability of the exempt status that churches and religious groups have enjoyed under the Civil Rights Act. That exception permits them to take religious affiliation or conviction into account in their hiring and personnel decisions, and was validated in a unanimous Supreme Court decision in *Corporation of the Presiding Bishop v. Amos* (1987).

If only the analysis were so simple. The exemption contained in Title VII of the Civil Rights Act did not specifically include *publicly funded* faith-based service providers. Some have argued, therefore, that *Amos* was inapplicable, and that the receipt of public funding disqualifies religious groups from exempt status under the civil rights laws. They contend that the extension of the religion-specific hiring exemption to situations involving federal contracts or grants is tantamount to governmental endorsement of discriminatory hiring. Indeed, initiative opponents turn the neutrality argument back on its supporters; it is incongruous, they say, to treat a religious provider as a neutral dispenser of secular services for funding purposes, while simultaneously giving it special allowance to hire religiously compatible workers and employees on grounds that they are essential to carrying out its institutional mission.

Not surprisingly, faith-based backers apply the neutrality standard differently. They point to publicly funded secular organizations that never would be compelled to hire applicants at odds with their ideological or policy aims.

Were publicly funded religious charities to lose their right to hire as they choose, it would represent a constraint on religious groups that is not required of secular organizations. This would send an unequivocal message of government bias against religious providers. Instead, neutrality merits that religious organizations' associational and free exercise rights outweigh any discrimination claims of individuals.

Melissa Rogers's nuanced piece captures the complexity of the issue that was absent from earlier and more public exchanges. After a careful reading of the relevant case law, Rogers concedes that religious organizations do not forfeit their Title VII exemption from federal civil rights hiring restrictions when they take public funds. She concludes that it is an open question under the pertinent case law whether these religious groups are free *under the U.S. Constitution* to make religiously based hiring decisions, since the Supreme Court has yet to face the question. Rogers marshals an argument based on policy considerations, historical and legal precedent, and broader constitutional values to reach the conclusion that the courts should find that the hiring right for religious groups receiving public funds violates the establishment clause.

By the same token, John Orr's case study demonstrates the classic dilemma faced by religious organizations in the competition for government funds. The California Supreme Court determined that Catholic Charities was obligated to obey a state law compelling all employer health care providers of a certain size to include contraceptive coverage in their plan, even though the law directly conflicted with Catholic teaching. The Catholic Church has always taken great care in its delivery of social services to maintain a clear division between the spiritual and the social services. Consequently, its approach to charity has served as the model for those of a separationist bent, who argue that a faith-affiliated group's social service programs should be scrubbed clean of any and all religiosity. Indeed, opponents of charitable choice and the Bush legislative plan have held up Catholic social services as evidence of why faith-based legislation is not needed. Why vary from the success of the long-standing interaction between government and major religious charities such as Lutheran Social Services, Catholic Charities, and Salvation Army? These partnerships have, from all appearances, thrived without compromising either the rights of program participants or the well-being of the religious nonprofits themselves.

And yet it was the purging of the religious trappings and programmatic dimension that led to Catholic Charities' downfall in California. To avoid entanglement and establishment problems, Catholic Charities' decision to remove the religious content from its social services led to the conclusion that its work was not religious, and as such did not deserve the religious exemption from the state statute. In sum, Catholic Charities found itself in the classic catch-22. In guarding against the pitfalls of the establishment clause, it lost its religious free exercise rights in the process. The decision undermines the notion that a religious entity can shape its public actions in accord with its theological creed in the face of contrary state or federal law. According to the California Supreme Court, the religious identity and organizational autonomy of a church are worth little when embodied in its social service branch.

■ Some Thoughts on the Public Role of Religion

We make no pretense that we are capable of providing a definitive conception of religion that would convincingly settle the complicated constitutional issues. From the beginning of the liberal experiment, religion has bedeviled thinkers who have recognized its tremendous power for good as well as its capacity for harm. They saw religion, in George Washington's words (2002), as an indispensable support for morality and the maintenance of social order. Even John Locke realized that the liberal experiment could not be maintained without some sort of minimal public theology: "The taking away of God, though but even in thought, dissolves all" (1990, 64).

The great question was how to formulate this public theology in the face of religious diversity. The worm in the apple of liberalism is the privatization of religion. When Alfred North Whitehead described religion as "what you do with your solitude," he conceptualized it in a way that would ensure a closeted existence among its adherents: they could believe in private but had to check those beliefs at the door when they entered the public square.[15]

One need not argue that all concerns are ultimately religious, that all decisions are made *cor deum*. We would advocate, however, that additional impositions ought not to be placed upon those who overtly believe, that they not bear a burden of alienation that those who choose not to believe are not asked to bear. We need not decide whether all forms of social organization and service delivery presume some "ultimate reality" that animates their actions, or whether these ideas are somehow theologically derived, in order to develop a constitutional doctrine more hospitable to and reflective of our own cherished beliefs and traditions. Government should neither prescribe the public expression of religion, nor proscribe it.

The religion clauses should pass no judgment on religious organizations qua organizations, since such judgments are almost surely beyond the competency of the state. But they should clear a space that would allow for the healthy competition among both religious and nonreligious organizations. James Madison saw the proliferation of religious sects as the greatest guarantor of religious liberty, and he also considered such competition to be constitutive of the public good. To be sure, irreligion needed additional protections afforded by the Constitution, given its comparative rarity and the public opprobrium it provoked. That equation has changed. It is religion that now is on the defensive and arguably in need of the same protections and opportunities previously afforded nonreligious organizations. State funding would never be denied an organization because it was nonsectarian; it is unclear that the sectarian nature of an organization likewise should be in any sense determinative. As long as the opportunities are equal and no religion or sect is preferred over any other, the public attempt to demonstrate its truthfulness and efficacy should not be held against any organization. If the Salvation Army wants to hire people committed to its mission, so be it. If Planned Parenthood wants to do the same, more power to them. A liberal society is strengthened by a highly pluralized social situation with distinctive institutions committed to their unique missions, providing multiple options.

In a society where religious groups and organizations feel increasingly alienated from the processes of government and society, confusion among the members of the Supreme Court can only fuel the general sense of unease. With respect to the social function of the church in democratic society, there is no such thing as government neutrality. An emphatically indifferent stand toward religion sends a message of the public irrelevance of religion, if not a preference for nonbelief. Inevitably what is publicly irrelevant becomes privately irrelevant too. If a person's religion is to mean anything, he or she must possess the right to expression with the potential to make a difference.

How then are we to conceive the relationship between church and state? More precisely, by what standard ought the Court to decide establishment clause issues? There is no easy solution to this problem. The Framers were primarily concerned with ratification of the Constitution. This meant above all that the amendments of the Constitution were meant as limitations upon the state, and not upon the church. At the same time, the Framers clearly did not want a federally established church. As a result they sought a delicate balance that would construct a limited government, allowing for religious freedom within a framework of diversity.

Unfortunately, in the debate over establishment the churches often overlook their own limits. With the resurgence of religious activism, there appears to be an increased eagerness on the part of the churches to co-opt the state for their own purposes. This can only work to the detriment of both church and state. A church that seeks common purposes with the state all too often becomes confused about its own mission, and consequently ends up restructuring its content to coincide with civil dogma. As this process increases, the church becomes increasingly irrelevant. The confusion of the ends of the church with the means of the state is bad for both.

Likewise, the state has a vital interest in the church's preservation of its status as a separate agency within society. It ought to be kept in mind that the Constitution accomplishes two things: it creates government, but also limits it. Government is limited in that it cannot interfere unduly in the religious lives of its citizens; but at the same time the Constitution encourages religion because the testimony of religion to a transcendent order of reality is a severe limitation and critical judgment on the otherwise expansive state. Furthermore, there is a large-scale debate among philosophers about the degree to which ethical reasoning can stand without an appeal to a transcendent order. If those advocating for a more traditional view are right, then the political goods described in the Preamble to the Constitution (justice, peace, general welfare, etc.) cannot be taken to be self-evidently good, but are demonstrated to be good when taken as part of a larger accounting of human life and reality itself.

The constitutional doctrine of church and state depends functionally in large part on how the legal decisionmakers think about religion. What does it encompass for purposes of determining establishment limitations and free exercise protections? More specifically, do the notions of religion entertained by judges correlate to spiritual realities for different religious traditions and their adherents and practitioners? Unfortunately, the short answer is no. The constitutional treatment of religion is undermined by two particular weaknesses in judicial understandings of religion: what it is, and what it includes. One of those weaknesses is a tendency to think of religion as an essentially private affair, and to minimize its public scope. The second shortcoming is the propensity to treat religion as a fundamentally personal, individualistic exercise, at the expense of its collective, associational, corporal aspects. Both of these tendencies fail to capture the authenticity of religious exercise for many people and religious traditions.

An example is the California Supreme Court's rejection of Catholic Charities' request for an exemption from the state's Women's Contraceptive Equity Act on the grounds that what Catholic Charities did was not religious work. The organization did not primarily serve Catholics; it hired non-Catholics; there were no elements of the social service programs that entailed mass or worship or involved the promulgation of Catholic doctrine or belief. In short, what Catholic Charities did was not Catholic religious exercise, or so the court said. But in reaching such a conclusion, the members of the court dismissed the idea that the Catholic Church might have theological tenets that as a matter of right flow down through its entire institutional structure, including its social service arm. In so doing, the court fell back on an assumption that runs through the constitutional body on free exercise rights, that religion is practiced privately. This tendency by the court implicates the very nature of religious conviction and the ways in which it is manifested.

But religious conviction is not merely contemplative in orientation. It includes outward acts of social service as well. This is why the Catholic Church could in good conscience still provide social services that were not outwardly or overtly "religious," but that were still a tangible exercise of its corporate religious practice. Loving the poor through service to their needs was in fact religious exercise. Religious conviction was at the heart of social service, whether or not it was accompanied by a sermon or attempts to evangelize. Indeed, one cannot understand the abolitionist movement, the civil rights movement, or the New Deal without reference to the religious motives of their advocates.

For many who are devoutly religious, the social conscience and commitment to service are every bit as much an imperative of their faith as prayer, meditation, or other aspects of their personal spiritual life. To portray religion for legal purposes strictly as a private phenomenon is an emaciated approach that diminishes the rich and multifaceted nature of religious exercise in the United States. It neglects a central aspect of religious motivation, that of service and commitment to one's community.

One must be careful not to paint too broadly with this generalization. We do not mean to suggest that corporate rights ought to be superior to or come before individual ones. Individual rights are prior to, not derived from, corporate rights. That is the fundamental basis of social contract thinking. To do otherwise would be to fall victim to what Whitehead called "the fallacy of misplaced concreteness"—to see abstract entities as more real than concrete ones. Hence it is appropriate when balancing individual rights against corporate rights to do what the Supreme Court typically does, which is to defer to the interests of the individual.

Yet this does not change the fact that there is a discernible bias in judicial understandings of church, one that is laid bare by the battle over the legal status of faith-based services. Recognizing social service as a legitimate form of religious exercise born of genuine spiritual conviction challenges the biased constitutional view of religion noted above. The constitutional approval of the administration of social services through religious providers contemplates a more expansive view of religion and how it is practiced publicly and collectively. It is premised upon an acknowledgment that religious commitment for many inspires outward action directed at others and conducted corporately.

We concede, however, that this understanding of religion does not comport with a highly individualistic American approach to things spiritual. That individualism is evident in the ever-expanding number of identifiable religious denominations, sects, and groups in the United States. It likewise is reflected in the infinite variety of personal approaches to faith and practice, and in the consumer-oriented, church-shopping approach to religious participation. Moreover, this version of religion is—for many secularists—an important reining in of what they see as the negative repercussions of religious conviction. If the predominant impact of religion is as an intolerant, narrow, divisive force in society, then its deleterious consequences can best be managed by confining religion to the private, personal sphere and erecting clear constitutional boundaries around it.

One must be careful, however, not simply to attribute this problem to the attempts of secularists to weaken religion. Religious groups have demonstrated a remarkable capacity to be their own gravediggers. Ever since Peter Berger in *The Sacred Canopy* (1967) demonstrated how religious organizations were susceptible to the corrupting influences of market economics and democratic majoritarianism, sociologists who study religion have examined carefully how these phenomena affect the behavior of religious groups, often to their own detriment. The phenomenon of the megachurch in many ways embodies the highly individualized consumer approach to religion that Berger believed (wrongly) would ensure the secularization of American life. Similarly, this is why Alan Wolfe (2003), in his review of contemporary American religion, is secure in telling his fellow secularists not to worry, that the churches have been too thoroughly co-opted by the culture to be a real threat.

But for others, the individualistic focus is a caricatured picture of religious faith and practice. It is too shallow and one-dimensional to capture the full picture of religious life in the United States. For many people of faith, religious devotion is not something that exists in isolation. One does not merely adopt religious belief and engage in religious practice by oneself. Rather there is a collective and communal dimension. Faith is a shared experience, not only in worship, but in a variety of other means as well. This corporate fact is reflected in the language of faith; we speak of "the church" and people belong to "the body of believers."

This reality runs counter to the current of the overwhelmingly individualistic cast of the Constitution and American constitutional jurisprudence. Constitutional doctrine generally lacks a nuanced and well-articulated understanding of rights and liberties as applied to and held by groups and associations, and not only in the context of religious practice. For example, while political parties have associational rights, those rights are viewed as residing in the members of the party, not the organization itself. As in many facets of constitutional jurisprudence, the Supreme Court has authenticated religious freedoms primarily in their individual or personal manifestations, to the exclusion of the corporate or communal.

As a result, individual rights invariably trump group ones. An individual's right to the job of his or her choice prevails over a religious group's right to hire those in sync with its theological beliefs. A woman's right to health care that includes contraceptive coverage wins out over the right of a church to provide services on a basis consistent with its theological beliefs. Admittedly, these are difficult issues, and in general faith-based initiatives have been careful in aiming to protect the rule of noncoercion against the proselytizing impulses of religious organizations. Still, a more pluralized constitutional approach to these issues would grant religious organizations the same sorts of freedoms more secular organizations enjoy in their processes of socializing employees and delivering their services to clients. Just as religious nonprofits have a particular identity that affects their approach to social service, so too do Planned Parenthood and Head Start have an identifiable mission, ideology, or philosophy that frames and drives their social service.

The problem is attributable in part to a hyperreliance on the language of rights. Mary Ann Glendon (1991) has aptly demonstrated the ways in which American "rights talk" fragments and calcifies political discourse. Rights by definition are nonnegotiable, and dressing preferences in the language of rights limits the democratic imperative to negotiate differences. As rights proliferate in our society, citizens become less civic minded, more atomistic, and less willing to seek or accept balance in the name of maintaining political order. Without minimizing the importance of rights, the constant appeal to them, together with the ceaseless creation of new ones, only serves to trivialize all of them.

In short, these skewed religious understandings toward the personal and private sides of religion undermine and weaken the constitutional standing of faith-based social service. The question of the religious rights of churches, religious organizations, and other religious collectives directly impact the legal issues surrounding the faith-based initiative. What are the free exercise rights of a church as a church? Does a religious nonprofit engaged in social service provision out of a sense of calling have constitutionally recognizable rights that might translate into its participation in publicly funded programs on the same footing as its secular counterpart? At the very least, the constitutional debate needs to acknowledge these religious realities, and the doctrine should in some way be reflective of them.

The constitutional understandings that stem from these superficial understandings of religion need to be addressed. This requires a restatement, and perhaps a reordering, of the balance between the establishment prohibition and the free exercise assurance. The First Amendment right to free exercise must acknowledge the corporate and collective dimensions to the expression of faith. Validation of the group right to free exercise of religion may encompass the living out of faith in a commitment to people on welfare on a basis equal to that enjoyed by other groups (i.e., through the receipt of government funds and contracts) (Gedicks 1989). Associational rights are what empower individuals to translate belief into meaningful action. This is no less true in advancing the social ends of religious conviction than it is in advancing a political agenda.

The constitutional and policy implications that would flow from this group-enhanced perspective are not self-evident. It need not give religious groups free rein in obtaining government funds for whatever use. It could sanction equal access and opportunity for religious groups to take part in those government-sponsored programs that fit within the definition of their faith. Or the courts might still ultimately conclude that the task of determining what constitutes the core of an individual's or group's faith is simply beyond the competence of our legal and judicial institutions. If so, this might compel an approach of strict neutrality and evenhandedness that makes no distinction between religious and secular providers. Or it could lead the courts to conclude that the only sensible approach is to err on the side of caution, and take a strict stance against any and all interaction between the state and the religious. But regardless of the particular policy ramifications, a more enlightened debate than is currently the case would do greater justice to belief systems that are central to millions of people in the United States.

The constitutional questions surrounding faith-based programs converge with a larger debate that has raged for the past decade over the health and vitality of civil society. Tocquevillian social concerns about an overly private and individualistic America parallel contemporary fears of a hyperindividualism that has enervated civic and associational life in the country. This has implications for the philosophical underpinnings of the free exercise clause.

The specific policy design of the faith-based social services movement is connected theoretically and explicitly to a broader goal of strengthening and energizing civil society. The name given the office by the Bush administration—the White House Office of Faith-Based and *Community* Initiatives—makes the point. Including "community" in the title admittedly was an attempt to enhance the political appeal of the proposal. But it was not solely politics. Rather, the name reflected important theoretical and intellectual roots from which the proposal grew.

Including faith-based and community providers in publicly subsidized social services is an important piece of a program launched by a communitarian critique of liberal social policy. That critique objects to social programs that treat recipients as atomistic, isolated, self-contained units, as government programs arguably do. Communitarians emphasize a person's need for social connectedness and call for greater attention to the cultivation of civil society and those intermediate organizations and associations that provide a needed sense of belonging. They criticize government social policy for having depleted civil society by displacing the small, local, social institutions that served this purpose with government itself. They contend that the government must now compensate by taking conscious and intentional efforts to renew civil society. One way to accomplish this is to encourage participation in publicly subsidized programs by small neighborhood-level organizations, many of which are faith-based. Churches and other religious nonprofits are well positioned to elicit social volunteerism and service from their members in efforts to care for those in need.

The explicit linking of "faith" and "community" in the WHOFBCI acknowledged this fact. The initiative made a special effort to highlight those faith groups that had served as grassroots community building blocks but that had been neglected in government-funded programs, especially in African American communities. In the past, government collaboration with religious entities had been limited mostly to larger agencies such as Catholic Charities and Lutheran Social Services, organizations with the institutional infrastructure to secure and administer government grants and contracts. Those agencies were not the model for grassroots service delivery, however. On the spectrum of social service agencies, they were closer to government agencies than were the grassroots providers whose work the government hoped to foster. Thus the faith-based initiative targeted smaller, autonomous, neighborhood-based groups that might lack the expertise or networks to partner with the government.

There are several other interpretive influences that push us in the direction of permissive or positive neutrality as the guiding principle of establishment clause doctrine. One of those is the acknowledgment of social development in the United States. Modern-era establishment clause jurisprudence suffers from an ahistorical blind spot. Church-state relations have been distorted by a failure to update establishment clause doctrine to better fit key developments in social evolution in the country.[16] The issues underlying contemporary debates fundamentally differ from those concerns that occasioned the inclusion of the establishment clause in the Bill of Rights in the late eighteenth century. Indeed, they differ significantly from those that triggered the modern era of establishment clause jurisprudence in the mid–twentieth century. We would likely have a far more productive exploration of the philosophical differences on church-state interaction, and ultimately a more sensible outcome, if the combatants were to acknowledge this.

The primary focus of the establishment clause at the outset was to preclude a dominant, government-sanctioned religion at the national level, while leaving states free to establish, or disestablish, particular faiths as they saw fit. Well into the separationist jurisprudence of the 1960s and 1970s, the focal point was the same (even as the First Amendment was expanded to apply to state governments as well); the fear remained that the governments of a highly religious nation would bestow special favor upon a particular faith or denomination. Typically this meant the need constitutionally to guard against governmental preference for the socially dominant religion.

In the face of the explosion of religious pluralism in America during the past half century, these concerns strike one as antiquated. The rich diversity and diffusion of religious affiliation and identity in the United States today undermines the fear that a dominant religion might materialize with the support of the state. The country, while still majority Christian, is home to increasing numbers of non-Christian faiths, with millions of individual followers. Moreover, the range of belief even within Christianity is broad and varied—including not only Catholic and Protestant, but also an extraordinarily diverse array of denominations within Protestantism. In the wake of this ever-expanding universe of faiths, that the government will throw its weight or support behind one is highly unlikely. Yet the rhetoric of a state-sponsored religion subjugating all others continues to dominate the public debate of church-state issues.[17]

This too ignores critically important aspects of progress in the United States, and what those developments mean for the relationship between government and religion. In short, the debate too often fails to take into account the practical consequences of the rise and expansion of the modern welfare state. The growth of the government during the twentieth century raises a number of questions for the church-state dialogue. One of those is the practical cultural impact of strict separation when the government reaches the size it has in the United States. Once upon a time, separationist interpretation of the establishment clause doctrine did not ensure a secularist state, because there was plenty of space within which religious organizations and nonprofits could operate, and even flourish. This may not be the case with a modern state whose reach extends to all corners of culture and society. If strict separation is constitutionally required of a government with this pervasive influence and power, the practical upshot may well be state-ordained secularism.

In sum, a governmental policy of neutral treatment of things religious best fits a modern United States characterized by a vast secular central state and a richly diverse religious makeup. That standard of neutrality would render no favor toward any particular faith or toward faith generally, but neither would it discriminate against faith by barring religious nonprofits from participation in the governmental enterprise alongside their secular counterparts. This simply seems most appropriate in light of the scope and reach of the state.

■ Federalism and Regional Diversity

This constitutional approach of *permissive neutrality* makes similar sense within the framework of American federalism. One of the manifest strengths of faith-based policy is its adaptability to the particular character of various regions and localities across the country—especially since so much social service delivery has a state and/or local governmental hand in it. Government can make as much or little use of religious nonprofits as is appropriate given the character of that particular place. In some heavily religious communities, the religious sector is a rich vein to be tapped by the state as it figures out how best to administer social programs. In other, more secular areas, churches may be much less of a potential resource. Demographic patterns, however, strongly support the conclusion that in general the poor live in areas with more localized and vibrant religious communities. Indeed, the churches are about the only institution not to have fled those neighborhoods. To discriminate against religious groups is to de facto discriminate against the poor. Nowhere has this dilemma been more keenly sensed than in the controversy over school vouchers.

The most recent church-state pronouncement by the U.S. Supreme Court, in *Locke v. Davey* (2004), reveals a willingness by the Court to favor a constitutional approach attuned to the federalist arrangement. *Locke* involved a Washington state scholarship program for higher education, and a challenge to the state's withdrawal of the scholarship from a student who planned to apply the scholarship to a pastoral ministries program. The student argued that the federal free exercise clause compelled the state to fund his religious studies major, an argument the Court rejected. Instead, it deferred to the state and its authority to deny state funds to someone who wanted to use them for religious purposes.

Locke suggests a willingness to defer to individual states and their laws and constitutions in navigating the church-state divide (Lupu and Tuttle 2004c). So while the U.S. Constitution may set thresholds on establishment and free exercise demands, the constitutional analysis could vary from state to state, depending on the specifics of state statutes and constitutions. Obviously, litigation pertaining to the validity of state constitutional Blaine amendments will directly impact this as well. It is unclear what direction this litigation will take, and this lack of certainty may have dire consequences for the ability of faith-based organizations to deliver services. Hopefully, this book can serve to allay fears at the same time it generates caution.

■ Conclusion

The 2000 presidential election was one of the most tightly contested in history, and certainly was the most visibly contested one. Studies of electoral maps lead many commentators to conclude that the United States was increasingly divided between red states and blue ones. These divisions are not only geographic but topographic as well. More and more there is a deepening sense that we are separating into "two Americas." In *One Nation, Two Cultures,* Gertrude Himmelfarb (2001) argued that America is polarized along moral lines. On one side are those steeped in traditional religion and morality—orthodox, traditional, conservative, and committed to older forms of social organization and virtue. The other America is populated by post-1960s dissidents who are countercultural, libertarian in sexual and private ethics, enamored of postmodernism, and committed to a peculiar idea of toleration. Likewise, Michael Barone (2004) has argued that the two Americas are characterized respectively by moralism and relativism, tradition and change, religious observance and nonobservance, or in short, religionists and secularists. The field is ripe with works that claim that the culture wars have divided the American spirit, as well as works that seek to debunk such claims, such as Alan Wolfe's *One Nation After All* (1999).

Whatever the scientific merits of such claims, a cursory observation of the social landscape in the United States indicates that something is afoot. Patrick Henry College in Purcellville, Virginia, an unabashedly Christian school, has been established specifically for the purpose of providing home-schooled children a college education. Indeed, the home-schooling movement, which in large part originated out of conservative Christian parents' fears of secular indoctrination in public schools, has increased tremendously over the past twenty years. Not content merely to withdraw from culture, however, the leaders of Patrick Henry have indicated they wish to prepare their charges to reclaim the culture that is rightfully theirs. They are seeking students "who will lead our nation and shape our culture with timeless biblical values." The president of Patrick Henry, Michael Farris, has said, "We are not home-schooling our kids just so they can read. The most common thing I hear is parents telling me they want their kids to be on the Supreme Court. And if we put enough kids in the farm system, some may get to the major leagues." Nancy Keenan, the education policy director for People for the American Way, has stated that the prospect "scares me to death" (Kirkpatrick 2004).

The Pledge of Allegiance, abortion, homosexuality and gay marriage, values and morality in the schools—these are wedge issues that produced the cleavages of the culture wars. More and more, these divisive issues have fallen into the province of the Supreme Court, which has attempted to mitigate the battles. The recent nondecision on the constitutionality of the pledge in *Elk Grove Unified School District v. Newdow* (2004) is yet another attempt by the Court to resolve an issue by refusing to engage it. On the occasions it does engage the issue, it usually does so with inconclusive and sometimes contradictory results.

In the traditional understandings of politics, society has a deep need for religion. Literally meaning "to bind together," religion has long been thought of as indispensable not only for the maintenance of public order, but also for the cultivation of the virtues necessary for good citizenship. In an age when the most sacred of our common promises—the marriage vow—has been reduced to a quaint relic, the absence of religious infusion into our social life can be keenly felt. The American experiment in ordered liberty, because it feared so deeply the peculiar form of religious strife that tore Europe asunder, sought from its inception to minimize the effects and influence of religion in the public sphere. To accomplish this, the Framers did two things: they elevated liberty to the pinnacle of the greatest political value, with all its destabilizing consequences; and they sought to stabilize the political system through maintaining Christian morality without establishing Christian faith.

This is, of course, the situation about which Friedrich Nietzsche prophesied with such vigor. To believe that Christian morality could be sustained without Christian faith, Nietzsche believed, was the most pernicious and consequential of all illusions. At some point, he predicted, the thunder would catch up to the lightning and the civilization would collapse. Once people became aware of the hollowness of their most cherished beliefs, they would be left with two options. They could become either the "last men" or the "over-men." The former were those who spent their lives concerned with petty pleasures, avoiding the abyss by anaesthetizing themselves against the pain of nihilism. The description sounds too much like television-watching contemporary Americans, who withdraw into themselves and their immediate circle, concerned primarily with physical comfort and petty pleasures. The latter were those who cared enough to stare steadfastly into the abyss and learn to be new creators, "beyond good and evil," restoring strength and dignity to the species.

But did the Framers, and Americans by extension, fear too much the disruptive possibilities of religion? What if the European model of religiously driven destruction was idiosyncratic rather than paradigmatic? Have religious groupings in the United States behaved in such a way as to legitimate the Framers' fears? The record is certainly mixed. Both religion and secular rationalism were used to justify slavery (as argued by Benjamin Franklin and Thomas Jefferson, for example). But religion was particularly instrumental in the abolition of slavery. Religion may be used to justify violence, but it also has been the single greatest factor in promoting peace. Religion may have been used to protect certain privileges, but it has also been influential in breaking down barriers. The two greatest speeches in U.S. history—Abraham Lincoln's second inaugural address and Martin Luther King Jr.'s "I Have a Dream"—were both unabashedly religious in tone and substance. Religion, at its best, cultivates the habits of humility, trust, service, and selflessness, which are essential to the formation of a good society.

Of course, public policy doesn't silence religion, but neither does it privilege, let alone encourage, it. More often than not, it is caricatured, trivialized, or otherwise misunderstood, though perhaps no one has been more responsible for the trivialization of religion than religious believers themselves. Still, religion seems to have been excluded from the full benefits of public life. Most people in the United States may well concede that, if a particular person "prefers" religion, that preference may produce positive personal consequences. The extension of those preferences into the public realm, however, partakes of the very crisis that besets the country: the absence of any commonly shared public philosophy. Whether a nation so conceived can long endure is, at best, an open question. If there is indeed a culture war under way, there will be victors and victims, the triumphant and the vanquished. There will indeed be two Americas.

The fear is that persons who are motivated by a religious commitment that permeates all their other commitments are living life at a significant disadvantage. The primary agents of socialization in this culture—the media, the schools, social service agencies—are willfully secular in orientation. The last haven, the family, is a battleground. Many religious believers find themselves experiencing great dissonance in their lives, wondering about the degree to which the United States is their country, and frustrated in their attempts to live fully integrated lives of service. These reflections ask us to reevaluate the basic assumption about religious life that have long animated the American experiment: that religious expression leads to religious disagreement, and that religious disagreement eventually leads to religious wars. In short, any encouragement of religion somehow sets us on the road to apocalypse. But perhaps we ought to be reminded that religion, in the end, can encourage the "better angels of our natures." We certainly desire nothing that even hints of a theocratic state, or that there be a comfortable union of church and state. But between a theocracy and a completely secular state, however, is a middle way, one that seeks a fuller harmony of a person's best and noblest impulses with his or her life in a community. To this end, we believe, a more complete understanding of the actual operations of religious organizations, as well as a thorough reexamination of constitutional doctrine, can serve to rectify a situation where religion in the United States, to paraphrase Louis Hartz (1983), remains an amiable sheepdog kept forever on a lion's leash.

■ Notes

1. Although, as we have indicated, it is contestable the degree to which poverty relief and other social services might be thought of as "the government's business"—or at least exclusively so.

2. The *Pedreira* case helped to stoke the furor over hiring issues when it aired about the same time as a much-publicized *Washington Post* story that revealed that the Salvation Army had lobbied the White House for an exemption from local antidiscrimination laws. The two stories, side by side, provided ammunition for those who charged that the faith-based initiative would lead to widespread discrimination against employees by religious service providers (Black, Koopman, and Ryden 2004, 258).

3. The parties to that suit eventually settled out of court on terms favorable to the plaintiff.

4. For illustrations, see N.M. Const. Art. 12, Sec. 3; Ohio Const. Art. 6, Sec. 2; S.C. Const. Art. 11, Sec. 4; Utah Const. Art. 10, Sec. 9.

5. Cal. Const. Art. 9, Sec. 8.

6. Mich. Const. Art. 8, Sec. 2.

7. N.H. Const. Art. 83; Oreg. Const. Art. 1, Sec.5.

8. Colo. Const. Art. 5, Sec. 34; Pa. Const. Art. 3, Sec. 29.

9. Ind. Const. Art. 1, Sec. 6.

10. This is reflected in the academic debate, which is phrased essentially in terms of the neutrality–pervasive sectarianism dichotomy. For illustrative works, see Monsma 1996; 2002; Laycock, 1997.

11. These pioneers included such people as Stanley Carlson-Thies, Marvin Olasky, and Carl Esbeck.

12. This also increases the importance of objective social science research on the effectiveness of faith-based social services relative to similar secular services. For an overview of that research and a thorough bibliography of the research to date, see Montiel 2003.

13. A survey conducted in March 2001 by the Pew Forum found heavy resistance to hiring rights of religious groups. Seventy-eight percent of those surveyed said they opposed funded religious groups being able to hire those of the same religious faith or beliefs (Goodstein 2001).

14. The quote is from Nathan J. Diament's testimony before the U.S. Senate Committee for the Judiciary, June 6, 2001. Institute for Public Affairs, Orthodox Union, http://www.ou.org/public/statements/2001/nate25.htm, accessed April 11, 2005.

15. No such limitation is imposed upon those who hold to no religious conviction at all. The great shift in American life is that, at one time, unbelief had to defer to belief. Now it is arguably just the opposite.

16. We recognize that such a claim is a potential red herring. Issues of originalism and dynamism in interpretation cannot be fully treated in this context. Despite some difference, we share a commitment to the unworkability of a *pure* originalism. *How* the "relevance" of the Constitution can best be maintained is open to debate; *that* it must be maintained is not. That the Constitution, as interpreted by the Supreme Court, seems out of step with both "the times" and the sentiments of many Americans is certainly an issue of major consequence.

17. We obviously do not have this fear. To be fair, we recognize that there are persons in minority religions who do have this fear; and we also recognize that on occasion religious groups, particularly Christian ones, talk in such a way to give succor to such fears.

Bibliography

American Civil Liberties Union. 2001. Amicus Brief of the ACLU filed in *Catholic Charities of Sacramento v. Superior Court of Sacramento*, January 18. http://aclunc.org/reproductive-rights/041004-css_amicus.pdf, accessed February 8, 2005.

American Jewish Committee. 1990. *Report of the Task Force on Sectarian Social Services and Public Funding.* New York: American Jewish Committee.

Ashcroft, John, and Stanley W. Carlson-Thies. 1996. *A Guide to Charitable Choice.* December. http://www.clsnet.com/ccqanda.html#qanda, accessed June 9, 1998.

Baptist Joint Committee on Public Affairs. 1996. "Our Stances: Resolution on the Charitable Choice Provision in the New Welfare Act." http://users.erols.com/bjcpa/timely/churches.html, accessed December 1, 2000.

Barone, Michael. 2004. *Hard America, Soft America: Competition vs. Coddling and the Battle for the Nation's Future.* New York: Crown Forum.

Berger, Peter. 1967. *The Sacred Canopy: Elements of a Sociological Theory of Religion.* New York: Doubleday.

Berger, Peter, and Richard John Neuhaus. 1996. *To Empower People: From State to Civil Society.* Washington, D.C.: American Enterprise Institute.

Berman, Harold. 2000. *Faith and Order: The Reconciliation of Law and Religion.* Grand Rapids, Mich.: W. B. Eerdmans.

Black, Amy E., Douglas L. Koopman, and David K. Ryden. 2004. *Of Little Faith: The Politics of George W. Bush's Faith-Based Initiatives.* Washington, D.C.: Georgetown University Press.

Boston Globe. 2002. "U.S. Courts Applications by Church Schools for Education Grants." July 21.

Breger, Marshall, et al. 2001. *In Good Faith: A Dialogue on Government Funding of Faith-Based Social Services.* Philadelphia: Feinstien Center for American Jewish History, Temple University, May.

Brieve, Jeremy. 2004. "Blaine Amendments in State Constitutions." In *Of Little Faith: The Politics of George W. Bush's Faith-Based Initiatives,* ed. Amy E. Black, Douglas L. Koopman, and David K. Ryden. Washington, D.C.: Georgetown University Press.

Brookings Institution. 2000. "God Fearing Voters, God Fearing Candidates: How Important Will Religion Be in the 2000 Election?" http://www.brookings .edu/comm/transcripts/20000920.htm, accessed January 26, 2005.

Brown, Dorothy M., and Elizabeth McKeown. 1997. *The Poor Belong to Us: Catholic Charities and American Welfare.* Cambridge: Harvard University Press.

Brownstein, Alan. 1999. "Constitutional Questions About Charitable Choice." In *Welfare Reform and Faith-Based Organizations*, ed. Derek Davis and Barry Hankins. Waco, Tex.: J. M Dawson Institute of Church-State Studies, Baylor University.

Bulluck, Clarence. 2002. Executive director of Faith Fellowship Community Development Corporation. Interview by author. Sayreville, N.J., December 3.

Burnbauer, Laura D., and Debra L. Dodson. 1990. *Election 1989: The Abortion Issue in New Jersey and Virginia.* New Brunswick, N.J.: Eagleton Institute of Politics, Rutgers University.

Bush, George W. 2001. Commencement address at the University of Notre Dame, South Bend, Ind., May 20, 2001. Reprinted in *Origins* 31, no. 3 (May 31, 2001): 46–48.

———. 2003. "State of the Union Address." http://www.cnn.com/2003/ allpolitics/01/28/sotu.transcript/, accessed January 26, 2005.

California State Department of Finance. 2001. "California's Annual Growth Exceeds Half a Million for Third Year." Press release.

Carlson-Thies, Stanley W., and James W. Skillen, eds. 1996. *Welfare in America: Christian Perspectives on a Policy in Crisis.* Grand Rapids, Mich.: Eerdmans.

Carter, Stephen. 1993. *The Culture of Disbelief: How American Law and Politics Trivialize Religious Devotion.* New York: Anchor Doubleday.

Castelli, Jim, and John McCarthy. 1998. *Religion-Sponsored Social Services: The Not So Independent Sector.* Working Paper Series. Washington, D.C.: Aspen Institute.

Census 2000 Brief: The Black Population. 2001. Washington, D.C.: U.S. Census Bureau, August.

Chang, Patricia M. Y., David R. Williams, Ezra E. H. Griffith, and John L. Young. 1994. "Church-Agency Relationships in the Black Community." *Nonprofit and Voluntary Sector Quarterly* 23 (Summer): 107–118.

Charitable Choice Compliance: A National Report Card. 2000. Annapolis: Center for Public Justice. http://www.cpjustice.org/stories/storyreader$296, accessed August 1, 2001.

Chaves, Mark. 1999. "Congregations' Social Service Activities." In *Charting Civil Society* series. Washington, D.C.: Urban Institute, December.

———. 2001. Interview by author. Chicago, April 15.

Chaves, Mark, and Lynn M. Higgins. 1992. "Comparing the Community Involvement of Black and White Congregations." *Journal for the Scientific Study of Religion* 31, no. 4: 425–440.

Christian Legal Society. 1997. "A Guide to Charitable Choice." http://www .clsnet.org/clrfPages/Pubs/pubs_charity1.php, accessed January 24, 2005.

Cnaan, Ram, Robert Weinburg, and Stephanie C. Boddie. 1999. *The Newer Deal: Social Work and Religion in Partnership.* New York: Columbia University Press.

"Conference Report on Economic Opportunity Amendments of 1972." 1972a. Report 92-987 (July 26).

"Conference Report on Economic Opportunity Amendments of 1972." 1972b. Report 92-1086 (September 5).

Cooperman, Alan. 2004. "Grants to Religious Groups Top $1.1 Billion: Administration Lauds Initiative." *Washington Post,* March 10.

Coughlin, Bernard J. 1965. *Church and State in Social Welfare.* New York: Columbia University Press.

Crew, Robert E., Jr. 2003. "Faith-Based Organizations and the Delivery of Social Services in Florida: A Case Study." *Roundtable on Religion and Social Welfare Policy,* October.

Davis, Belinda Creel. 2004. "Faith-Based Organizations and the Delivery of Social Services in Michigan: A Case Study." *Roundtable on Religion and Social Welfare Policy,* May.

De Tocqueville, Alexis. 1969. *Democracy in America.* Trans. George Lawrence, ed. J. P. Mayer. New York: Harper and Row.

de Vita, Carol J. 1999. "Nonprofits and Devolution: What Do We Know?" In *Nonprofits and Government: Collaboration and Conflict,* ed. E. Boris and C. Steuerle. Washington, D.C.: Urban Institute Press.

Demko, Paul. 1997. "Faith-Based Charities to the Rescue." *Chronicle of Philanthropy,* December 11.

DiIulio, John J., Jr. 1999. "Black Churches and the Inner City Poor." In *The African American Predicament,* ed. Christopher H. Foreman, Jr. Washington, D.C.: Brookings Institution.

———. 2001. "Know Us by Our Works." *Wall Street Journal,* February 14.

———. 2003. "Faith, Hope, and Government: A Former Bush Advisor Explains Why the Consensus Favoring Federal Support For Faith-Based Social Services Collapsed—And Why It Must Be Revived." *Boston Globe,* June 22.

Du Bois, W. E. B., Elijah Anderson, and Isabel Eaton. 1899. *Philadelphia Negro: A Social Study.* Philadelphia: University of Pennsylvania Press.

Earley, Mark. 2003. Interview by Cal Thomas. *O'Reilly Factor,* February 28. http://www.religionandsocialpolicy.org/news/article.cfm?id=423, accessed January 24, 2005.

Ebaugh, Helen Rose. 2003. "The Faith-Based Initiative in Texas: A Case Study." *Roundtable on Religion and Social Welfare Policy,* October.

Esbeck, Carl H. 1997. "A Constitutional Case for Government Cooperation with Faith-Based Social Service Providers." *Emory Law Journal* 46 (Winter): 1–83.

————. 2001. "Isn't Charitable Choice Government-Funded Discrimination?" Center for Public Justice. www.epjustice.org/stories/storyreader$375, accessed February 7, 2005.

"Faith-Based Executive Order." 2004. White House press release. June 1. http://www.whitehouse.gov/news/releases/2004/06/print/20040601-1.html, accessed January 24, 2005.

Farris, Anne. 2004. "Washington Conference Seeks to Advance Faith-Based Program." May 10. http://www.religionandsocialpolicy.org/news/article_print.cfm?id=1487, accessed May 11, 2004.

Flores, Liesl. 2003. "New Community Corporation Celebrates 35 Years." *Catholic Advocate* (Newark, N.J.), February 5.

"Focus on the Family to Bush: No Strings on Faith Grants." 2004. http://www.religionandsocialpolicy.org/news/article.cfm?id=1207, accessed January 29, 2004.

Fois, Robert A. 2002. "Putting Public Faith and Hope in Private Charity: A Closer Look at Faith-Based Initiatives." *Empire State Report,* June 2002, 28–33.

Formicola, Jo, and Mary Segers. 2002. "The Bush Faith-Based Initiative: The Catholic Response." *Journal of Church and State* 44, no. 4 (Autumn 2002): 693–715.

Formicola, Jo Renee, Mary C. Segers, and Paul Weber. 2003. *Faith-based Initiatives and the Bush Administration: The Good, the Bad, and the Ugly.* Lanham, Md.: Rowman and Littlefield.

Frazier, Franklin E. 1964. *The Negro in the American Church.* New York: Schocken Books.

From Promise to Policy: A Discussion of the White House Office of Faith-Based and Community Initiatives. 2001. January 30. http://www.pewforum.org/events/index.php?EventID=4, accessed January 24, 2005.

Gallup, George, Jr. 1995. "Religion in America: Will the Vitality of Churches Be the Surprise of the Next Century?" *Public Perspective,* October–November.

Gaylor, Annie Lawrence. 2001. "Bush's 'Faith-based' Plans Assault Constitution." *Freedom from Religion Foundation*, January 29. http://archive.aclu.org/congress/ffrRelease.pdf, accessed October 23, 2003.

Gedicks, Frederick Mark. 1989. "Toward a Constitutional Jurisprudence of Religious Group Rights." *Wisconsin Law Review* 99 (January/February): 99–169.

Glendon, Mary Ann. 1991. *Rights Talk: The Impoverishment of Political Discourse.* New York: Free Press.

Goggin, Malcolm L., and Deborah A. Orth. 2002. "How Faith-Based and Secular Organizations Tackle Housing for the Homeless." *Roundtable on Religion and Social Welfare Policy.* October.

Good Samaritan Ministries (GSM). 1997. *Organizing Churches for Welfare Reform.*

Goode, W. Wilson. 2002. Interview by author. July 23.

Goodstein, Laurie. 2001. "Church-Based Projects Lack Data on Results." *New York Times,* April 24. http://www.nytimes.com/2001/04/24/politics/24fait.html?searchpv=nyttoday, accessed August 21, 2001.

Green, John C., and Amy L. Sherman. 2002. *Fruitful Collaborations: A Survey of Government-Funded Faith-Based Programs in Fifteen States.* Washington, D.C.: Hudson Institute.

Green, Steven K. 2002. "Religious Discrimination, Public Funding, and Constitutional Values." *Hastings Constitutional Law Quarterly* 30 (Fall):1–37.

Gunther, John J. 1990. *Federal-City Relations in the United States: The Role of Mayors in Federal Aid to Cities.* Newark: University of Delaware Press.

Hamburger, Philip. 2002. "Beyond Separatism: Church and State." *Journal of Law and Politics* 18, no. 7: 7–64.

Harris, Frederick C. 2002. *Strategic Action Under Constraints or Narrow Self-Interest? The Civic Engagement of Black Ministers and Churches in Chicago.* Cambridge: Harvard University Press, December.

Hartz, Louis. 1983. *The Liberal Tradition in America: An Interpretation of American Political Thought Since the Revolution.* San Diego: Harcourt Brace.

Henderson, Wade. 2001. "Black Think Tank II: State of the Black Union," transcript. At conference convened by Tavis Smiley and Tom Joyner. Washington, D.C., February 3.

Himmelfarb, Gertrude. 2001. *One Nation, Two Cultures: A Searching Examination of American Society in the Aftermath of Our Cultural Revolution.* New York: Vintage Books.

Hoover, Dennis R. 2001. "Faith-Based Update: Bipartisan Breakdown." *Religion in the News.* http://caribou.cc.trincoll.edu/depts_csrpl/RINVol4No2/faith based.htm, accessed January 26, 2005.

Houston, Jim. 2003. "Bill Would Ease Access to Funds in Georgia." *Columbus Ledger-Enquirer,* January 19. http://www.religionandsocialpolicy.org/news/ article.cfm?id=336, accessed January 24, 2005.

Hunter, James Davison. 1991. *Culture Wars: The Struggle to Define America.* New York: Basic Books.

Institute for Public Affairs Public Policy Library. 2001. "The Constitutionality of 'Charitable Choice.'" *Union of Orthodox Jewish Congregations of America.* http://www.ou.org/public/publib/constit.htm, accessed January 15, 2005.

Jaime, Pastor Beverly. 2001. "Pray the Bay." *Lighthouse of Prayer Newsletter,* June (San Jose).

Jeavons, Thomas H. 1994. *When the Bottom Line Is Faithfulness: Management of Christian Service Organizations.* Bloomington: Indiana University Press.

Jensen, Laura. 2001. Interview by author. Indianapolis, May.

John-Hall, Annette. 1999. "Taking Advantage of Charitable Choice." *Philadelphia Inquirer,* August.

Joyner, Tom, and Tavis Smiley (convened). 2001. "Black Think Tank II: State of the Black Union," transcript. Washington, D.C., February 3.

Kennedy, Sheila S. 2003. "Privatization and Prayer: The Challenge of Charitable Choice." *American Review of Public Administration* 33, no. 1: 5–19.

Kenny, Jane. 2001. "Acting Governor Announces $2.5 Million for Faith-Based Groups." New Jersey State Department of Consumer Affairs, October 30.

Kirkpatrick, David. 2004. "College for the Home-Schooled is Shaping Leaders for the Right." *New York Times,* March 8, A1.

Kramnick, Issac, and R. Laurence Moore. 1997. "Can the Churches Save the Cities? Faith-Based Services and the Constitution." *American Prospect,* November–December.

Laycock, Douglas. 1997. "The Underlying Unity of Separation and Neutrality." *Emory Law Journal* 46 (Winter): 43–74.

Lazarus, Stephen. 2001. "An Uphill Climb to True Tolerance." *Capital Commentary*, August 13. http://www.cpjustice.org/stories/storyReader$564, accessed January 15, 2005.

———. 2002. "Re-Igniting the Faith Based Initiative." *Capital Commentary*, May 20. http://www.cpjustice.org/stories/storyReader$735, accessed January 15, 2005.

League of Women Voters of New Jersey. 1969. *New Jersey: Spotlight on Government.* Montclair, N.J.

Lehrer News Hour. 1999. "Faith-Based Welfare." November 11.

Leland, John. 2004. "Offering Ministry, and Early Release, to Prisoners." *New York Times,* June 10.

Lenkowsky, Leslie. 2001. "Funding the Faithful: Why Bush Is Right." *Commentary* 111, no. 6: 19–24.

Leonard, Mary. 2001. "Bush Targets Support of Blacks." *Boston Globe,* March 11.

———. 2002. "Proponents of Vouchers See Opening, Planning Suits in Six States." *Boston Globe,* November 18. http://www.religionandsocialpolicy.org/news/article.cfm?id=228, accessed May 26, 2004.

Lincoln, C. Eric, and Lawrence H. Mamiya. 1990. *The Black Church in the African American Experience.* Durham: Duke University Press.

Locke, John. 1990. *A Letter Concerning Toleration.* Buffalo, N.Y.: Prometheus Books.

"Loophole in Bill Would Give Wiggle Room on Benefits for Faith-Based Organizations." 2004. *New York Sun,* April 16. http://www.religionandsocialpolicy.org/news/article.cfm?id=1399, accessed January 25, 2005.

Luchenitser, Alex J. 2002. "Casting Aside the Constitution: The Trend Toward Government Funding of Religious Social Service Providers." http://au.org/site/DocServer/Luchenitser.pdf?docID=185, accessed February 8, 2005.

Lupu, Ira C. 2001. "Government Messages and Government Money." *Pew Forum on Religion and Public Life.* http://pewforum.org/issues/display.php?issueid=3, accessed March 4, 2003.

Lupu, Ira C., and Robert W. Tuttle. 2002. "Government Partnerships with Faith-Based Service Providers: The State of the Law." *Roundtable on Religion and Social Welfare Policy,* December.

———. 2003. "*Zelman*'s Future: Vouchers, Sectarian Providers, and the Next Round of Constitutional Battles." *Notre Dame Law Review* 78, 4 (May): 917–994.

———. 2004a. "Legal Developments Involving the Faith-Based and Community Initiative." June 8. http://www.religionandsocialpolicy.org/legal/legal_update_print.cfm?id=24, accessed June 8, 2004.

————. 2004b. "Settlement of the Bellmore Litigation." http://religionand socialpolicy.org/docs/legal/cases/1-5-2004_bellmore_settlement_analysis .pdf, accessed May 28, 2004.

————. 2004c. "State of the Law 2004: Partnerships Between Government and Faith-Based Organizations." http://www.religionandsocialpolicy.org/ publications/publication.cfm?id=51, accessed February 7, 2005.

Marsden, George. 1990. "Afterword: Religion, Politics, and the Search for an American Consensus." In *Religion and American Politics: From the Colonial Period to the 1980s*, ed. Mark Noll. New York: Oxford University Press.

McConnell, Michael. 1992. "Religious Participation in Public Programs: Religious Freedom at a Crossroads." *University of Chicago Law Review* 59 (Winter): 115–194.

Merrow, Katherine B. 2003. "Faith-Based Organizations and Social Service Delivery in New Hampshire." *Roundtable on Religion and Social Welfare Policy,* October.

"Michigan's Block Grant Proposals." 1996. http://www.mfia.state.mi.us.tsmfprop .htm#al, accessed April 28, 1998.

Milbank, Dana. 2000. "Bush to Host Black Ministers." *Washington Post*, December 19.

Milbank, Dana, and Thomas B. Edsall. 2001. "Faith Initiative May Be Revised; Criticism Surprises Administration." *Washington Post*, March 12.

Miller, Paul. 2003. "The Challenges of Implementing Faith-Based and Community Initiatives in Montana." *Roundtable on Religion and Social Welfare Policy,* October.

Minow, Martha. 1999. "Choice or Commonality: Welfare and Schooling After the End of Welfare As We Knew It." *Duke Law Journal* 49 (November): 493.

Monsma, Stephen. 1995. *Positive Neutrality: Letting Religious Freedom Ring.* Grand Rapids, Mich.: Baker Book House.

————. 1996. *When Sacred and Secular Mix: Religious Nonprofit Organizations and Public Money.* Lanham, Md.: Rowman and Littlefield.

————. 2002. *Church-State Relations in Crisis: Debating Neutrality.* Lanham, Md.: Rowman and Littlefield.

Montiel, Lisa M. 2003. "The Use of Public Funds for Delivery of Faith-Based Human Services." *Roundtable on Religion and Social Welfare Policy,* June.

————. 2004. "Government Partnerships with Faith-Based Organizations in New York State: A Case Study." *Roundtable on Religion and Social Welfare Policy,* April.

Morgan, Richard E. 1972. *The Supreme Court and Religion.* New York: Free Press.

Murray, Charles. 1994. *Losing Ground: American Social Policy, 1950-1980.* New York: Basic Books.

Nathan, Richard P., and Thomas L. Gais. 1999. *Implementing the Personal Responsibility Act of 1996: A First Look.* Albany, N.Y.: Nelson A. Rockefeller Institute of Government.

"Nation's First Faith-Based Prisons Seek to Reduce Recidivism." 2004. http://www.religionandsocialpolicy.org/news/article_print.cfm?id=1498, accessed May 18, 2004.

Netting, F. Ellen. 1982. "Secular and Religious Funding of Church-Related Agencies." *Social Service Review* 56, no. 4: 586–604.

Neufeldt, Victoria, and David B. Guralnik, eds. 1998. *Webster's New World Dictionary*. 3rd ed. New York: Simon and Schuster.

New Jersey Department of Consumer Affairs. 1999. *Annual Report 1998*. http://www.state.nj.us/dca/98annual/aisle2.pdf, accessed January 25, 2005.

New Jersey Statutes Annotated Constitution of the State of New Jersey. 1997. St. Paul, Minn.: West Group.

Nolan, Bruce. 2004. "Bill Pits Religious, Health Care Agendas." *Times-Picayune*, May 1. http://religionandsocialpolicy.org/news/article_print.cfm?id=1443, accessed May 4, 2004.

O'Keefe, Mark. 2002. "Federal, State Agencies Quietly Foster Faith-based Initiatives." *Newhouse News Service*, March 8.

Olasky, Marvin. 1992. *The Tragedy of American Compassion*. Washington, D.C.: Regnery Gateway.

Oshinsky, Dan. 2003. "New Head Start Plan Passes by One Vote." *States News Service*, July 25.

Owens, Michael Leo. 2000. *Sectarian Institutions in State Welfare Reforms: An Analysis of Charitable Choice*. New York: Rockefeller Institute of Government.

Page, Clarence. 2004. "It's Time to Level the Faith-Based Playing Field." *Chicago Tribune*, May 2. http://www.religionandsocialpolicy.org/news/article_print.cfm?id=1462, accessed May 4, 2004.

Peterson, Barrie A. 2001. "Working with the New Jersey Office of Faith-Based and Community Development Initiatives: A Case Study." Paper presented at the annual meeting of the Northeastern Political Science Association, Philadelphia, November.

Pew Forum on Religion and Public Life. 2001. "Post 9-11 Attitudes: Religion More Prominent, Muslim-Americans More Accepted." *Pew Research Center for the People and the Press*, December 6. Washington, D.C.

Protecting the Civil Rights and Religious Liberty of Faith-Based Organizations: Why Religious Hiring Rights Must Be Preserved. 2003. Washington, D.C.: White House Office of Faith-Based and Community Initiatives.

Pyeatt, Matt. 2001. "Inmates Get Religion in Prison Release Program." *CNSNews.com*, September 7.

Ragan, Mark, Lisa M. Montiel, and David J. Wright. 2003. "Scanning the Policy Environment for Faith-Based Social Services in the U.S.: Results of a 50-State Study." *Roundtable on Religion and Social Welfare Policy*, October.

Raibley, Matt. 2001. Interview by author. Indianapolis, July.

Raymond, Bill. 1998. Interview by author. June 3.

Reed, Adolph, Jr. 1999. *Stirrings in the Jug: Black Politics in the Post-Segregation Era*. Minneapolis: University of Minnesota Press.

Robbins, John Charles. 2004. "Grant Will Help Students Through Mentoring." *Holland Sentinel,* June 5.

Rorty, Richard. 2003. "Religion in the Public Square: A Reconsideration." *Journal of Religious Ethics* 31, no. 1 (Spring): 141–152.

Rosen, Jeffrey. 2001. "Religious Rights: Why the Catholic Church Shouldn't Have to Hire Gays." *The New Republic* 48, 224 (February 26): 16–18.

Rothstein, Betsy. 2000. "GOP 'Charitable Choice' Unnerves Dems." *The Hill,* June 28.

Ryden, David K. 2003. "Faith-Based Initiatives and the Constitution: Black Churches, Government, and Social Services Delivery." In *New Day Begun: African American Churches and Civic Culture in Post-Civil Rights America,* ed. R. Drew Smith. Durham, N.C.: Duke University Press.

Salamon, Lester M. 1995. *Partners in Public Service: Government-Nonprofit Relations in the Modern Welfare State.* Baltimore: Johns Hopkins University Press.

Saperstein, David. 2003. "Public Accountability and Faith-based Organizations: A Problem Best Avoided." *Harvard Law Review* 116, (March): 1353-1396.

Schemo, Diana J. 2003. "House G.O.P. Drafts Bill to Overhaul Head Start." *New York Times,* June 13.

Scott, Jason. 2004. "Mayors See Role for Faith-based Groups in Assisting Ex-Offenders."http://www.religionandsocialpolicy.org/news/article_print.cfm?id=1460, accessed May 4, 2004.

Sharpton, Reverend Al. 2001. "Black Think Tank II: The State of the Black Union," transcript. At conference convened by Tavis Smiley and Tom Joyner, February 3. Washington, D.C.

Sherman, Amy L. 1997. *Restorers of Hope: Reaching the Poor in Your Community with Church-Based Ministries That Work.* Wheaton, Ill.: Crossway Books.

———. 2000. *The Growing Impact of Charitable Choice: A Catalog of New Collaborations Between Government and Faith-Based Organizations in Nine States.* 2000. http://www.cpjustice.org/stories/storyreader$315, accessed February 14, 2003.

Sider, Ronald J., and Heidi Rolland. 1996. "Correcting the Welfare Tragedy: Toward New Model for Church/State Partnership." In *Welfare in America: Christian Perspectives on a Policy in Crisis,* eds. Stanley W. Carlson-Thies and James W. Skillen. Grand Rapids, Mich.: Eerdmans.

Sinha, Jill Witmer. 2000. *Cookman United Methodist Church and Transitional Journey: A Case Study in Charitable Choice.* Washington, D.C.: Center for Public Justice, August.

Smith, Stephen Rathgeb, and Michael Lipsky. 1993. *Nonprofits for Hire: The Welfare State in the Age of Contracting.* Cambridge: Harvard University Press.

Solomon, Lewis, and Matthew J. Vlissides Jr. 2001. "In God We Trust: Assessing the Potential of Faith Based Social Services." Policy report. Washington, D.C.: Policy Progressive Institute.

Stackhouse, Max L. 1996. "Beneath and Beyond the State: Social, Global, and Religious Changes That Shape Welfare Reform." In *Welfare in America: Christian Perspectives on a Policy in Crisis,* eds. Stanley W. Carlson-Thies and James W. Skillen. Grand Rapids, Mich.: Eerdmans.

Stammer, Larry B. 2003. "College Barred From Running Program Because of Christians-Only Hiring Policy." *Los Angeles Times,* November 1. http:/www .religionandsocialpolicy.org/news/article_print.cfm?id=1014, accessed November 5, 2003.

Stone, Melissa, Mark A. Hager, and Jennifer Griffin. 2001. "Organizational Characteristics and Funding Environments: A Study of a Population of United Way–Affiliated Nonprofits." *Public Administration Review* 61, no. 3: 274–287.

Stronks, Julia K. 1996. "Social Service Agencies and Religious Freedom: Regulation, Funding, and the First Amendment." In *Welfare in America: Christian Perspectives on a Policy in Crisis,* ed. Stanley W. Carlson-Thies and James W. Skillen. Grand Rapids, Mich.: Eerdmans.

Sullivan, Kathleen. 1992. "Religion and Liberal Democracy." *University of Chicago Law Review* 59 (Winter): 195–224.

Tenpas, Kathryn Dunn. 2002. "Can an Office Change a Country? The White House Office of Faith-Based and Community Initiatives: A Year in Review." Preliminary report prepared for the Pew Forum on Religion and Public Life, February.

Transitional Journey Ministry. 1998. "Annual Report."

Trattner, Walter I. 1994. *From Poor Law to Welfare State: A History of Social Welfare in America.* 5th ed. New York: Free Press.

Trulear, Harold Dean. 2000. *Faith Based Institutions and High Risk Youth.* Public/Private Ventures. http://www.ppv.org/ppv/publications/assets/24 _publication.pdf, accessed January 26, 2005.

U.S. Census Bureau. 2001. *Statistical Abstract of United States: 2001.* 121st ed. Washington, D.C.

U.S. Congress. 1996. *Personal Responsibility and Work Opportunity Reconciliation Act of 1996.* 104th Congress, 1st sess. P.L. 104-193. August 22.

U.S. Department of Heath and Human Services. 2004. "What Is Charitable Choice?" Center for Faith-Based and Community Initiatives. http://www .hhs.gov/faith/choice/html, accessed January 25, 2005.

U.S. House. 2003. *School Readiness Act of 2003.* 108th Congress, 1st sess. H.R. 2210. July 24.

U.S. House Committee on Education and the Workforce. 2003. *Testimony of Carl H. Esbeck, Isabelle Wade and Paul C. Lyda.* Hearing before the Subcommittee on Select Education. 108th Congress, 1st sess. April 1.

U.S. House Committee on Government Reform. 2001. *Effective Faith-Based Treatment Programs.* Hearing before the Subcommittee on Criminal Justice, Drug Policy, and Human Resources. 107th Congress, 1st sess. May 23.

U.S. House Committee on the Judiciary. 2001. *Testimony of David Saperstein.* Hearing before the Subcommittee on the Constitution. 107th Congress, 1st sess. June 7.

U.S. Senate Judiciary Committee. 2001. *Faith-Based Solutions: What Are the Legal Issues?* Hearing. 107th Congress, 1st sess. June 6.

USA Today. 1997. "Law Lets States Increase Churches' Welfare Role." October 1.

Wall Street Journal. 1997. "In God's Name." March 17.

Washington, George. 2002. "Farewell Address." In *The American Republic: Primary Sources,* ed. Bruce Frohnen. Indianapolis: Liberty Fund Press.

Washington Post. 1997. "Michigan County Finds Jobs for All Welfare Recipients; Community Is First to Reach Goal Since Reform." September 16.

Webster's Collegiate Dictionary. 1996. 10th ed. Springfield, Mass.: Merriam-Webster.

White House. 2001. "Rallying the Armies of Compassion." January. http://www.whitehouse.gov/news/reports/faithbased.pdf, accessed January 15, 2005.

White House Office of Faith-Based and Community Initiatives (WHOFBCI). 2003. "Partnering with the Federal Government: Some Do's and Don'ts for Faith-Based Organizations." http://www.whitehouse.gov/government/fbci/guidence/partnering.html, accessed July 19, 2003.

Williams-Alston, El-Rhonda. 2002. Director, New Jersey Office of Faith-Based Initiatives. Presentation to Rutgers University class on ethical issues in public policy and administration. March 12.

Wilson, James Q. 1974. *Political Organizations.* New York: Basic Books.

Wineburg, Robert J. 2001. *A Limited Partnership: The Politics of Religion, Welfare, and Social Service.* New York: Columbia University Press.

Wolfe, Alan. 1999. *One Nation After All.* New York: Penguin Books.

———. 2003. *The Transformation of American Religion: How We Actually Live Our Faith.* New York: Free Press.

Wood, Richard. 1997. "Social Capital and Political Culture: God Meets Politics in the Inner City." *American Behavioral Scientist,* 40 no. 5: 595–605.

World Vision. 2002. "Annual Review.: http://www.worldvision.org/worldvision/comms.nsf/stable/ar2002.2, accessed January 25, 2005.

Wuthnow, Robert. 1988. *The Restructuring of American Religion.* Princeton, N.J.: Princeton University Press.

Zirkin, Nancy. 2001. "Statement on the Community Solutions Act (H.R. 7)." July 17.

■ Cases Cited

Abington School District v. Schempp, 374 U.S. 203 (1963)

ACLU of Louisiana v. Foster, ED Louis. (2002)

Agostini v. Felton, 521 U.S. 203 (1997)

Aguilar v. Fenton, 473 U.S. 402 (1985)

American Jewish Congress and Texas Civil Rights Project v. Bost, SD Tex. (2000)

Americans United for Separation of Church and State v. Prison Fellowship Ministries (filed February 13, 2003 S Iowa)

Arriaga v. Loma Linda University, 10 Cal. App. 4th 1556 (1992)

Ashburn v. Maples (filed February 13, 2003, south district, Iowa)

Bellmore v. United Methodist Children's Home (filed August 1, 2002, Superior Court, Georgia; settled November 11, 2003)

Board of Education v. Allen, 392 U.S. 236 (1968)

Bowen v. Kendrick, 487 U.S. 589 (1988)

Capitol Square Review and Advisory Board v. Pinette, 515 U.S. 753 (1995)

Catholic Charities of Sacramento v. Superior Court of Sacramento County, SO99822 (2004)

City of Boerne v. P. F. Flores (Archbishop of San Antonio), 521 U.S. 507 (1997)

Corporation for the Presiding Bishop v. Amos, 483 U.S. 327 (1987)

Dodge v. Salvation Army, U.S. Dist. LEXIS 4797 (SD Miss. 1989)

EEOC v. Townley Engineering and Manufacturing Co. 859 F.2d 610 (9th Cir. 1988)

Elk Grove Unified School District v. Newdow, 02-1624 (2004)

Employment Division v. Smith, 494 U.S. 872 (1990)

Engel v. Vitale, 370 U.S. 421 (1962)

Epperson v. Arkansas, 393 U.S. 97 (1968)

Espinosa v. Rusk, 10th Cir. (1980)

Everson v. Board of Education, 330 U.S. 1 (1947)

Garcia v. United States, 469 U.S. 70 (1984)

Grand Rapids School District v. Ball, 473 U.S. 373 (1985)

Grove City College v. Bell, 465 U.S. 555 (1984)

Hall v. Baptist Memorial Health Corporation, 215 F.3d 618 (6th Cir. 2000)

Lemon v. Kurtzman, 403 U.S. 602 (1971)

Little v. Wuerl, 929 F.2d 944 (3d Cir. 1991)

Locke v. Davey, 124 U.S. 1307 (2004)

Lynch v. Donnelly, 465 U.S. 668 (1984)

Meek v. Pettinger, 421 U.S. 349 (1975)

Mitchell v. Helms, 530 U.S. 793 (2000)

Mueller v. Allen, 463 U.S. 388 (1983)

Pedreira v. Kentucky Baptist Homes for Children, WD Ky. (2000)

Roe v. Wade, 410 U.S. 113 (1973)

Rosenberger v. Rector and Visitors of University of Virginia, 515 U.S. 819 (1995)

Saucier v. Employment Security Department, 954 P.2d 285 (Wash. App. 1998)

Sherbert v. Verner, 374 U.S. 398 (1963)

Siegel v. Truett-McConnell College, 13 F. Supp. 2d 1335 (ND Ga. 1994)

Tilton v. Richardson, 403 U.S. 672 (1971)

Walz v. Tax Commission, 397 U.S. 664 (1970)

Witters v. Washington Department of Services for the Blind, 474 U.S. 481 (1986)

Wolman v. Walter, 433 U.S. 229 (1977)

Young v. Shawnee Mission Medical Center, 1988 U.S. Dist. LEXIS 12248 (D Kan. 1988)

Zelman v. Simmons-Harris, 536 U.S. 00-1751 (2002)

Zorach v. Clausen, 343 U.S. 306 (1952)

■ Executive Orders

Executive Order no. 8802, 6 Fed. Reg. 3109 (June 25, 1941).
Executive Order no. 10925, 26 Fed. Reg. 1977 (March 6, 1961).
Executive Order no. 11246, 30 Fed. Reg. 12319 (September 25, 1965).
Executive Order no. 11375, 32 Fed. Reg. 14303 (October 17, 1967).
Executive Order no. 13279 (December 12, 2002).

■ Statutes

42 U.S.C. Sec. 9849(a) (2005).
42 U.S.C. Sec. 20003(b) (2005).
42 U.S.C. Sec. 2000e-1(a) (2005).
42 U.S.C. Sec. 2000e-2 (2005).
42 U.S.C. Sec. 2000e-2(e)(1) (2005).
42 U.S.C. Sec. 2000e-2(e)(2) (2005).
42 U.S.C. Sec. 604a (2005).
42 U.S.C. Sec. 604a(f) (2005).
42 U.S.C. 2000bb *et seq.* (2005).
42 U.S.C. Sec. 12635 (2005).
42 U.S.C. Sec. 5057 (2005).
42 U.S.C. Sec. 291 *et seq.* (2005).
42 U.S.C. Sec. 300a-7 (2005).

The Contributors

Sheila Kennedy is associate professor of law and public policy at the School of Public and Environmental Affairs at Indiana University, where she is a member of the Philanthropic Studies faculty and an adjunct to the political science department. Her recent publications include "Government Shekels Without Government Shackles: The Administrative Challenges of Charitable Choice" (*Public Administration Review,* 2002), "Privatization and Prayer: The Challenge of Charitable Choice" (*American Review of Public Administration,* 2003), and "Social Responsibility, Accountability, and U.S. Welfare Reform: The Context of America's Faith-Based Initiative" (in *Transatlantic Perspectives on Liberalization and Democratic Governance*, 2004).

Joyce Keyes-Williams is senior research associate for the Roundtable on Religion and Social Welfare Policy at the Rockefeller Institute of Government. Her research examines faith-based organizations and government partnerships in the implementation of welfare reform. She is currently a doctoral candidate in the Public Administration and Policy Department at the Rockefeller College of Public Affairs and Policy at the University at Albany, State University of New York.

John Orr is director of special projects for the Center for Religion and Civic Culture at the University of Southern California. His recent publications include *Church-State Relations in Los Angeles' Religiously Based Community Development Programs* (1996) as well as articles in *Social Progress, Encounter, Church and Society, Current*, and *Mission Journal*.

Jeffrey Polet is associate professor of political science at Hope College in Holland, Mich. His research interests include contemporary continental political thought, liberal and democratic theory, constitutional law, and legal hermeneutics. He has had articles published on the Supreme Court's decisions in *Term Limits v. Thornton* and *Bush v. Gore*, as well as articles dealing with issues in political theory.

Frank A. Pryor III is a member of the political science department at Villanova University. His disciplinary focus is on black politics, and he has done extensive research on charitable choice and faith-based social services as they relate to African American communities and churches.

Melissa Rogers is an attorney who currently serves as visiting professor of religion and public policy at Wake Forest University Divinity School. She previously served as the founding executive director of the Pew Forum on Religion and Public Life and as general counsel to the Baptist Joint Committee on Public Affairs. She is coediting a book on religion and law.

David K. Ryden is chair of the political science department at Hope College in Holland, Mich. His publications include *Representation in Crisis: The Constitution, Interest Groups, and Political Parties* (1996), *The U.S. Supreme Court and the Electoral Process* (2001), and (as coauthor) *Of Little Faith: The Politics of George W. Bush's Faith-Based Initiative* (2004).

Mary C. Segers is chair of the political science department at Rutgers University. She has written and published widely on religion and ethical values underlying public policy. She has authored or edited half a dozen books, including *A Wall of Separation? Debating the Role of Religion in American Public Life* (1998), *Piety, Politics, and Pluralism: Religion, the Courts, and the 2000 Election* (2002), and, with Jo Renee Formicola and Paul J. Weber, *Faith-based Initiatives and the Bush Administration: The Good, the Bad, and the Ugly* (2003).

Jill Witmer Sinha is a doctoral student at the School of Social Work at the University of Pennsylvania. Her publications include *Cookman United Methodist Church and the Transitional Journey Program: A Case Study on Charitable Choice* (2000) and "Churches and Public Funds: Risks or Rewards?" in *PRISM* (2001) (coauthored with Heidi Unruh).

Heidi Rolland Unruh is associate director of the Congregations, Community Outreach, and Leadership Development Project and is a policy analyst and church consultant with Evangelicals for Social Action. She is the co-author of *Churches That Make a Difference: Reaching Your Community with Good News and Good Works* with Ronald J. Sider and Phil Olson (2003) and *Saving Souls, Serving Society: The Faith Factor in Church-Based Social Programs* with Ronald J. Sider (2005). She has authored numerous articles and book chapters on social welfare and faith-based initiatives.

Index

177–206; defined, 44; First
Amendment rights, 5, 7–8, 20, 24,
31, 82–83, 85–124, 127, 141, 146,
173, 179, 184, 187, 191–193, 196,
198–199; funding of secular
activities, 2, 18, 20, 22, 23, 33,
45–46, 49, 51, 55, 63, 65, 67, 68,
73–74, 80–81, 91, 113, 117–118,
121–123, 130, 147, 181, 186–187,
192, 199; government oversight, 37,
45, 60–61, 66, 121, 163, 185;
litigation, 5–6, 32, 49, 86–87,
90–91, 112, 179, 184, 203;
monitoring of, 45, 47, 66, 73–74,
77, 151, 185; private funding of
religious components, 36–37, 70,
73, 81, 110, 115, 117, 123, 137,
145; professional credentials and
norms, 36–37, 43–44, 72, 95, 155,
190; religious rights, 79, 86, 91,
199; secular alternatives, 2, 46, 51,
62–65, 74, 147, 186. *See also* Faith-
based initiatives; Faith-based
programs; Faith-based social
services; Government/religious-
nonprofit collaboration; Hiring
rights
Faith-based programs: client choice, 2,
37, 46, 62, 70–74, 80–83, 147, 187;
client perceptions of religious
dimension, 78–79; opt-out
provisions, 64–65, 70, 78, 74. *See
also* Faith-based initiatives; Faith-
based organizations; Faith-based
social services;
Government/religious-nonprofit
collaboration; *specific programs*
Faith-based social services:
constitutional issues, 1–2, 6–8,
17–19, 21–23, 31–32, 35–36, 38,
40, 47–49, 68, 83, 87, 97, 127, 135,
142, 158, 164, 181, 183, 189, 197,
199, 202; drug treatment, 22,
32–33, 36–37, 40–41, 43–44,
47–50, 53, 122–123, 136–138, 150,
188–190; motivation, 26, 40, 58,

66, 71, 76, 79, 189–190, 197, 205;
payment options, 72, 75; prisoner
rehabilitation, 7, 35–37, 40, 44,
47–48, 50–51, 130, 155, 170, 181,
186, 188, 190; professional
standards, 36–37, 43–44, 72, 95,
155, 190; religious transformation,
20, 36, 40, 48, 53, 55, 59, 61, 65,
68, 76–77, 80, 137, 157, 182, 189;
staff, 51, 56, 71–82, 91, 93, 99,
107–108, 110, 118, 121, 137,
152–153, 170–171, 192; voucher
based, 22–23, 33, 36–37, 49–50,
182–183, 187. *See also* Faith-based
programs
Faith Fellowship Community
Development Corporation
(FFCDC), 154–155
Faith-infused organizations, 18–19,
41, 47–48, 50–51, 86; compared to
faith-based organizations, 47;
constitutional issues, 47, 48;
examples of, 47, 48; funding of,
48
FaithWorks, 42, 89
Falwell, Jerry, 162
Fauntroy, Reverend Walter, 140
Federal departments: Education, 3, 53,
138; Health and Human Services, 3,
53, 106, 138, 151; Housing and
Urban Development, 3, 53, 138,
152; Justice, 3, 53, 138; Labor, 3,
53–54, 67, 138
Federalism, 29, 126–127, 186,
202–203
Fee-for-service payment. *See* Faith-
based social services
FFCDC. *See* Faith Fellowship
Community Development
Corporation
First Amendment, 1, 7–8, 20, 22, 26,
35, 37, 45, 48, 55, 60, 80, 83, 85,
87, 100, 102–103, 114–115,
123–124, 127, 135, 145, 158, 172,
183, 186–187, 201; associational
rights, 87, 186, 193, 198–200. *See*

67; Good Samaritan Ministries, 54, 64
Isaiah House, 150, 152–153, 156

Jackson, Jesse L. Sr., 139–140
Jackson, Justice Robert, 15–16. *See also* U.S. Supreme Court
Jacksonian democracy, 12
Jakes, Bishop T. D., 139–141
Jefferson, Thomas, 11, 205
Jewish Board of Family and Children's Services, 37, 40
Johnson, Lyndon B., 106, 116, 120
Judaism, 42, 62–63, 67, 148, 150, 152, 156, 182, 192. *See also* American Jewish Committee; Jewish Board of Family and Children's Services; Religion
Judicial minimalism, 128. *See also* O'Connor, Justice Sandra Day

Keenan, Nancy, 204
Kennedy, John, 25, 106, 116
King, Martin Luther, Jr., 131, 205

Lautenberg, Frank, 148
Lawsuits. *See* Litigation
Lazarus, Stephen, 191–192
Legislation. *See individual acts;* U.S. Congress
Lemon test, 16–18, 60–61, 63; excessive entanglement, 16–17, 26, 46, 60, 68, 113. *See also* Establishment clause; *Lemon v. Kurtzman;* Neutrality; U.S. Supreme Court
Lemon v. Kurtzman (1971), 16–18, 26, 60–61, 63, 68, 112–114, 122. *See also Lemon* test
Lincoln, Abraham, 205
Lincoln, Eric, 131–132
Linder, Reverend William J., 153–154, 159
Litigation, 5–6, 16–18, 22, 32, 36, 50, 86, 88, 115; discrimination, 91, 110–112, 182; establishment clause,

93, 182; funding, 15, 181–182; schools, 49; and state constitutions, 8, 90, 93, 103, 181, 184, 203. *See also individual cases;* Pervasive sectarianism; Salvation Army; U.S. Supreme Court
Little v. Wuerl (1991), 110
Locke, John, 194
Locke v. Davey (2004), 202–203
Lupu, Ira, 164, 187
Lutheran Church, 109
Lutheran Social Services, 1, 130, 145, 158, 163, 193, 200
Lynch v. Donnelly (1984), 25
Lynn, Barry. *See* Americans United for Separation of Church and State

Madison, James, 12, 194
Mamiya, Lawrence, 131
Mann, Horace, 14
McConnell, Michael, 26
McGreevey, James E., 145–146
Megachurches. *See* Church
Mercy Ministries, 166
Mfume, Kweisi, 139
Mitchell v. Helms (2000), 20–22, 114, 181, 187
Monsma, Stephen, 186
Moriel, Marc, 139
Mormon Church, 112–113
Mueller v. Allen (1983), 17
Murray, Charles, 29, 162

NAACP. *See* National Association for the Advancement of Colored People
Nathan, Richard, 161, 162
National Association for the Advancement of Colored People (NAACP), 133; Mfume, Kweisi, 139
National Black Church Family Project, 132
National Congregational Study, 132
National Urban League, 137; Moriel, Marc, 139

About the Book

Does federal funding of a church's welfare-to-work program constitute government endorsement of a particular religion? Do religious organizations that accept public funds lose the legal autonomy needed to preserve their religious identity and mission? Wading into the constitutional battle over whether government can and should enlist the help of religious organizations in delivering social services, *Sanctioning Religion?* investigates the potential—as well as the perils—of mixing religion and politics in the United States.

David K. Ryden is associate professor of political science at Hope College. **Jeffrey Polet** is associate professor of political science at Hope College.